Elizabeth I: A New Hope?, see page 152

THE BIG BOOK OF BRITAIN

THE
BIG
BOOK
OF
BRITAIN

Cheers to the Crown, Churchill, Shakespeare,
The Beatles, and All Things British!

Tim Rayborn
Illustrations by Jo Parry

CIDER MILL
PRESS

BOOK
PUBLISHERS

CONTENTS

CHAPTER 1:

PREHISTORY, THE BRONZE AGE, AND THE CELTS
(UP TO THE FIRST CENTURY CE)

CHAPTER 2:

THE ROMANS
(FIRST TO FIFTH CENTURY)

CHAPTER 3:

THE ANGLO-SAXONS AND VIKINGS
(FIFTH CENTURY TO 1066)

CHAPTER 4:
THE MIDDLE AGES
(1066 TO 1485)

CHAPTER 5:
THE TUDORS
(1485-1603)

CHAPTER 6:
THE STUART AND HANOVER CENTURIES
(1603-1837)

CHAPTER 7:
THE VICTORIANS AND EDWARDIANS
(1837–1914)

CHAPTER 8:
TWO WORLD WARS AND MORE
(1914-1945)

CHAPTER 9:
MODERN BRITAIN
(1945-PRESENT)

Introduction

Britain is a fascinating country (or rather, a collection of countries) with a history that stretches back thousands of years. During that time, this small island at the northwest corner of Europe has had a remarkable influence on the world, for both good and bad. This book will look at some of the most important people and moments in that history, as well as lesser-known facts and unusual anecdotes. After all, history should be much more than just names and dates!

Speaking of names, the word "Britain" comes from the Latin word, *Britannia*, which itself comes the Greek words, *Brettania* and *Prettanikē*, both of which were used by the Greek historian Pytheas in about 320 BCE to identify the island.

If you've ever been confused about what the nation is called and why it seems to have more than one name, here is a quick guide: "Great Britain" now refers to the main island itself, and the three nations that are a part of it—England, Scotland, and Wales. The "Great" came into common use in English in the early eighteenth century (when England and Scotland unified under a single government), mostly to identify the main island, as opposed to the smaller islands around it, such as the Isle of Wight and the Isle of Man. The "Great" also helps to distinguish the island from the region of Brittany, which sits across the English Channel in northwest France.

On the other hand, "The United Kingdom" or "UK" is the name for the combined nations of Great Britain and Northern Ireland. From the Middle Ages to the early twentieth century, all of Ireland was under British rule, but the Irish had a thing or two to say about that, and most of Ireland gained its independence in 1922. Northern Ireland is still a part of the UK, a reality that remains a problem for many residents of the Emerald Isle, in both in the north and south. The famed British Union Jack flag (which technically shouldn't be called that unless it's flown on a ship), is a blend of the flags of England, Scotland,

and Northern Ireland—poor Wales got left out, and one wonders why, since Wales has an awesome dragon on its flag, and who wouldn't want a dragon on their flag?

If this is all too confusing, "Great Britain" is a perfectly good name to stick with. But calling this work *The Big Book of Britain* might make you wonder just what's inside. To be fair, it's weighted heavily toward England, but also includes important facts and stories about Scotland, Ireland, and Wales. In any case, *The Big Book of England* doesn't sound as good! So "Britain" and "British" are the words most commonly used in this book.

Here is an introduction to the fascinating history and people of this small group of nations. There are more than 200 stories about everything from social history to political plots, from music to weird foods, from inventions to plagues, and from wars to rock and roll. At the end of every entry, you'll find an interesting extra (and often strange) fact that might help you win a few trivia quizzes or bets!

Britain in all of its identities is a remarkable land, with countless tales of the times and the many different people that have called this island home over the centuries. No one book can do it justice (well, maybe if the book were *very* big!). Here is just a small sample of that ongoing story.

CHAPTER 1

PREHISTORY, THE BRONZE AGE, AND THE CELTS

(UP TO THE FIRST CENTURY CE)

STRANGE PREHISTORIC
ANIMALS ABOUND

When we think of Britain's animals today, we think of pretty common creatures, like sheep and cows. If we imagine wild animals, we'll probably think about the badger, the fox, the hedgehog, the ravens and crows, none of which honestly seem very "wild." But if we journey back through the centuries and millennia, we find that an incredible collection of fabulous beasts once roamed the land, especially when Britain wasn't an island and was connected to continental Europe. Here is a sample of some of the amazing and mostly extinct animals that used to call Britain and Ireland home:

Woolly Mammoths: As amazing at it might seem, these huge and majestic creatures once roamed prehistoric Britain. Evidence shows they were stomping around the Thames River as recently as 14,000 years ago, near the very land where London would come to stand. It must have been an incredible sight to see them grazing along the banks of the river!

Megaloceros: Also known as the "Irish Elk," this amazing animal's range stretched from Ireland to Siberia. While they resembled a deer that had moose-like antlers, these beauties could measure almost seven feet tall at the shoulder! Even more impressive, the antlers on either side of its head could be as much as twelve feet from tip to tip! Imagine seeing this incredible creature charging over a hill toward you...

Woolly Rhinoceros: Rhinos in Britain? Yes, it's true! The woolly rhino, as you likely guessed, was not like the modern African rhino, but more like the mammoths, covered in thick fur that helped keep it warm during the Ice Age.

Hippos: Wait, seriously? Yes! A type of hippo once swam in the lakes and rivers of prehistoric Britain. Remains of one that lived 120,000

years ago have been found under the street of a modern neighborhood. Imagine a herd of hippos walking past your flat!

Giant Beavers: Though they were more common in North America, these big beavers (also known as Castoroides) seem to have lived in ancient Britain as well, up to 700,000 years ago. And unlike the little beavers of today, these animals could grow up to eight feet long! They don't seem to have chewed on trees or made dams, which is probably just as well; can you imagine how big those dams would have been?

Cave Bears: Long before Paddington, there were other bears in Britain. The cave bear roamed Albion until about 24,000 years ago. Its cousin, the brown bear, lived in Britain into the time that written histories began to appear. Some think that they died out about 3,000 years ago, but there is also evidence that they may have hung around in some particularly wild regions as late as the sixth century. But it's also possible that these later bears had been brought to Britain by the Romans, or that they were the descendants of these imports.

> **Wild world fact:** Many other amazing animals, including crocodiles, lived on this island in prehistoric times, and archaeologists are continually uncovering new remains of incredible animals as they dig deeper.

THE FIRST PEOPLE

B ritain wasn't always an island—for thousands of years it was connected to the European continent. The land has been attracting various species of humans for as long as 900,000 years (including Homo heidelbergensis and Neanderthals), but the first peoples to make a continual habitation (i.e., they didn't just stay for a while and then leave) were Homo sapiens (modern humans) about 13,000 years ago. These people were hunter-gatherers and were more adaptable than some of those who came before them. Another factor: the ice age was ending, which made Britain warmer, more liveable, and more desirable.

But as the ice melted in the warmer climate, the sea levels began to rise, and over a few millennia, water came to cover the low-lying areas surrounding Britain to the south and east. By about 6500 BCE, the region east of Britain, known as Doggerland (perhaps it was populated with wolves who were especially good boys?), had filled in with water and become what is now known as the North Sea. All that melt also cut Britain off from mainland Europe, creating the English Channel, as well as the island we know and love today. In the grand scheme of things, Britain hasn't been an island all that long.

Farming seems to have become a big thing by about 4000 BCE, a development that allowed for larger and more settled communities to take root. From there, cultures and civilizations eventually sprang up. So, who were these people? What did they believe? What languages did they speak? They must have had religions, myths, stories, and cultures all their own. As with any look back to a time with no written records, it's frustratingly difficult to get good answers. Archaeological discoveries, cave paintings, and other physical remains allow us to tease out a few answers, but much of the information about who these people were will forever be hidden from us.

One of the most fascinating fellows from these long-ago times is Cheddar Man, the name given to a 10,000-year-old skeleton and skull excavated back in 1903 at Cheddar Gorge in Somerset. After studying the bones and obtaining a precious DNA sample, scientists were able to find out a lot about the people inhabiting Britain at this time. First of all, Cheddar had the genetic markers for darker skin, similar to those held by people in sub-Saharan Africa, giving him about a 76% chance of being dark skinned. Second, his eyes were either blue or green. Previously, scientists had thought that pale eyes came to Europe with pale skin, but lighter skin color seems to have been something that came along later, maybe with the arrival of peoples from the Middle East. Dutch artists Alfons and Adrie Kennis have created an amazingly lifelike reconstruction of Cheddar Man's head and face, and even given him a little bit of a smirk, as if he's pleased to be seen again after so many thousands of years.

> **DNA fact:** About 10 percent of the British and Europeans still share the same DNA type of Cheddar Man and his people, showing just how far back we can now trace our ancestry.

STONE CIRCLES ABOUND

J ust about everyone has seen Stonehenge (or at least photos of it), the majestic collection of stones on the Salisbury Plain. But Stonehenge is only one of many such circles ranging from north of Scotland all the way down to Spain. Not far from Stonehenge is Avebury, a much bigger set of stone circles that actually contains a whole village. Go up north to the Lake District and you'll find Castlerigg, a ring surrounded by the hills and mountains of the region. And then there are the pointy and mysterious Callanish Stones on the Isle of Lewis in the Outer Hebrides, off the west coast of Scotland. Stone circles abound in Brittany in northern France, as well as farther south in Spain. They began appearing around 5,000 years ago, and they range in size from almost tiny to absolutely huge. The fact that there are so many still surviving today—Britain and Ireland alone have over 1,300—hints at their importance to the people who built them.

As you can imagine, people have been wondering who built them and why for hundreds, if not thousands, of years. Everyone from aliens to Atlanteans have been proposed, and some have suggested that the practice of putting up big blocks of stone might have developed independently in different places. But these days, more and more researchers think that the first stone circles were built in northwest France and that the concept spread from there. It might be significant that stone circle–making is mostly found in the areas that border the Atlantic Ocean. That suggests the idea of circle-making was taken to new lands by people sailing in boats. Stone circles would later appear in Germany and Scandinavia and as far away as Bulgaria; there are even circles in east Africa.

Was there a common culture among the Atlantic civilizations that made those people want to put in huge amounts of effort to lift up these massive stones? And most importantly, why were they built? What did they mean? Were they all built for the same purpose, or did they have different uses? Certainly, some of them were calendars that marked important dates, like the summer or winter solstices. Stonehenge itself is aligned with the rising of the winter sun, and it was part of a much larger complex of structures that would have been awe-inspiring to those seeing them from across the plains. Were they used for religious rituals, too? Very possibly, though it's one of the standard archaeological jokes that, when you don't know what an item or a location was used for, you automatically must assume it was for "ritual purposes," whatever those might have been ...

> **Stone cold fact:** Stonehenge's smaller stones, called bluestones, came from Wales, but research shows that other, bigger stones were first carved at a place called Waun Mawn, near the Pembrokeshire Coast in western Wales, and then taken all the way to Wiltshire in England. The amount of work required to do this would have been enormous, and suggests that these stones were revered all by themselves, not just when they were placed and arranged together.

THE CELTS

"**C** elt" is a much more complex word than you might think. These days, most people associate it with the people from Ireland, Scotland, Wales, and Brittany. We talk of Celtic languages, Celtic music, and so on. But historically, it's a more difficult word to pin down. People who have been called "Celtic" lived in not only Britain and Ireland, but also Gaul (France), northern Spain, and Switzerland. But they were not necessarily the same people, and didn't share the same language (though they were similar), or the same beliefs and culture.

What we often think of as "Celtic art" originated with the La Tène culture in Central Europe, and then spread throughout the continent, reaching as far as Britain and Ireland. But this art wasn't just unique to the so-called Celts; other cultures either copied it or traded for objects featuring its ornate designs.

As for languages, those in the know have pointed out that the language of the Gauls actually has less in common with Old Irish than it does with Latin, and the two groups of speakers might have had a hard time understanding each other!

Culturally, there seem to have been many different kinds of Celtic societies, ranging from monarchies to something like republics.

Taking all of this into account, can we confidently say that "Celtic" actually means anything? Modern scholars often like to use the word only to describe the languages, with many archaeologists convinced that there wasn't one common culture. More likely the "Celts" were a diverse group of people with similar languages and possibly similar religious beliefs, though these also vary as one moves from region to region. The Celts were a collection of tribes that lived in different areas and had different customs. Sometimes they were allies, but they were just as likely to despise each other and go to war.

The Celtic people of the British Isles are often called the Britons, which is a good way of identifying them with one place. Like their continental counterparts, they were fierce and warlike, but also skilled artisans with a complex spirituality overseen by the Druids (see the next entry). They tended to believe in reincarnation, and so were fearless in battle, as many unlucky Romans found out! They also liked to decapitate their opponents and take the heads as trophies; in other words, they were head-hunters. They probably moved into the British Isles in small waves, so there wasn't one mass migration. Estimates place these moves between 1000 BCE and 600 BCE, but they could have started a bit earlier. Whenever they began to arrive, the Celts were the dominant culture in Britain until the arrival of the Romans in the first century CE.

> **Mistaken identity fact:** The great stone circles of Britain, such as Stonehenge and Avebury, are often associated with the Celts. Today, neopagan and Celtic groups often use them in rituals and celebrations, but the Celtic Britons had nothing to do with making them. These megalithic marvels had already been built thousands of years earlier by other peoples. Maybe the Britons used them for something, but they definitely didn't build them!

THE DRUIDS

There are a lot of different takes on the Druids, and, let's be honest: a lot of them are not great. They've been portrayed as everything from bloodthirsty, murdering cult leaders to enlightened wizards from Atlantis. The reason for this wide net is that not much is known about them, despite their notoriety. They didn't commit their own teachings to writing; everything had to be memorized, which of course, took years. So, when the Druids were weakened by the

Romans (in Gaul and Britain) and then finished off by the Christians (in Ireland), whatever secrets and history they had went with them to the grave.

There are hints here and there about what they believed and how they went about their business, and there are writings by Romans and Greeks who encountered them, especially Julius Caesar. But it's important to remember that Caesar had conquered Gaul, so it was in his best interest to make sure the Druids didn't look too good. If he'd said that they were wonderful, thoughtful philosophers, many might have questioned why he was determined to eliminate them. But if he could paint them as dangerous, murderous, and barbaric, then he had a good defense for taking them out. History is written by the winners, after all. The Druids were likely the heart and soul of western Celtic society and spirituality, so weakening them or removing them would have made it much easier to subjugate the Gauls, and later, the Britons.

The Druidic system seems to have been divided into three roles: Bards, Vates or Ovates, and Druids. Each group took a long time to master the skills particular to it. Bards were singers and storytellers, the keepers of lore and history in a culture without much literacy. Ovates conducted divinations, and yes, performed sacrifices, often watching nature and natural signs, while Druids were judges, political and legal advisors, and even medical doctors.

They were crucial to the societies of Gaul, Britain, Ireland, and elsewhere, and were highly esteemed. Most kings and chiefs had Druids as advisors, and at least one bard in their entourage. It was said that bards were so important that no one would dare kill one, even if they served a hated enemy, for it would bring terrible luck on the killer. So, it seems the Druids gave order to Celtic society; they communicated with the gods and set down laws.

What about the thorny issue of human sacrifice? The answer is yes, the Druids probably did sacrifice humans from time to time, since archaeologists have found the well-preserved remains of human sacrifices in bogs in Ireland and Denmark. These victims were probably most often prisoners of war or criminals (such as murderers), and occasionally, even volunteers. So, while no amount of wishful thinking can say otherwise, it probably wasn't something that was common.

> **Fiery sacrifice fact:** Caesar claimed that the Gauls would load people into giant, hollow wicker statues and burn them alive, but there isn't much evidence for this. Wicker is weak and collapses quickly when burned, so such statues would likely have fallen over and broken apart before the flames could kill anyone. He was possibly just exaggerating to make himself, and his decision to take them out, look good.

CHAPTER 2

THE ROMANS
(FIRST TO FIFTH CENTURY)

THE ROMANS
WANT BRITAIN

The island of Britain had appealed to the Romans for a long time, and they were eager to add it to their growing list of nations (collect them all!). But it wasn't just a matter of sending a bunch of troops across the channel and taking over. There was a lot of planning required to move the necessary soldiers such a great distance, and the native population wasn't too thrilled about the whole invasion thing. So, the "British" conquest took a lot longer than the Romans had hoped it would, since they encountered several bumps in the road along the way.

Julius Caesar failed to invade. After conquering Gaul (and a lot of other places), it would seem obvious that Julius Caesar was the right man to invade Britain. He was definitely up for it, and he'd received word that at least some of the British chiefs wanted to have him as an ally against their enemies, always a good excuse for Romans to go sticking their noses (and swords) into another country's business. But when Caesar launched his ships and sailed there in 55 BCE, he was met with extremely hostile resistance from the British tribes, and was pummelled by the good old British rain and bad weather. Caesar tried again the following year, but the weather was equally unwelcoming, so he gave up.

Caligula and the seashells. Emperor Caligula was, without a doubt, completely mad. According to some ancient historians, he marched an army up to northern Gaul and the English Channel in 40 CE. Did he intend to invade Britain? Probably, but according to the Roman historian Suetonius, he actually stopped and ordered his soldiers to collect seashells instead. Some say this was proof of his insanity, others that he was punishing the soldiers for threatening to mutiny. Some say this bizarre order never happened at all. Whatever the truth, Britain was once again not invaded.

Roman soldiers chickened out. Emperor Claudius decided on another invasion attempt in 43 CE. But by that time, many of his soldiers had heard all sorts of tales about Celtic/Briton "barbarians" on the island, who cut off enemy heads and performed human sacrifices. Britain was a wild, unknown, and scary place! Once the army reached the shores of northern Gaul, fear got the better of many of these soldiers, as they refused to set foot on British soil. So Claudius sent an ex-slave to humiliate them and shame them into going. Amazingly, it worked, and the invasion began.

Claudius finally succeeded (and he brought an elephant). Claudius, who had a stutter and a limp, succeeded where others before him had failed. His 40,000 soldiers did the job and established a Roman presence on Britain that would not go away for over three centuries, despite fierce resistance from the locals. The Romans established a capital at what is now the English town of Colchester, and Claudius brought an elephant with him to show off Rome's unimaginable might. Just think what this amazing animal must have looked like to the Britons who'd never seen one ... talk about using psychological warfare against your enemies!

> **Stable fact:** It's often said that Caligula appointed his horse, Incitatus, to the Roman senate. While he was crazy enough to make it happen, he didn't actually do it. It seems this rumor sprung from one of Caligula's criticisms of the government, when he claimed that his horse could do a better job than many of the senators!

ROMANS VERSUS DRUIDS, ROMAN GODS AND THEIR HYBRIDS

As we've seen with Julius Caesar, it was in the best interest of Rome to claim that the Druids were barbaric murderers that needed to be wiped out. So when the Romans finally invaded Britain, they set about trying to eliminate them, just as they had in Gaul. The Roman general Gaius Suetonius Paulinus decided that the only way to bring Britain firmly under Roman control was to destroy the heartland of Druidic ritual and belief. This place was on the Isle of Anglesey, off the northwest coast of what is now Wales. At the time it was called Mona, and it was where the Druids had their sacred oaks and temples. It also served as a refuge for those fleeing from Roman occupation. Had it been left alone, it would have become a powerful center of the resistance, as the island was only a short distance from the mainland of Wales, across a narrow strait.

Around the year 57 CE, Paulinus marched his army through enemy territory, fending off guerrilla attacks from natives, but not encountering any serious resistance. Secretly though, many soldiers feared the Druids and the Britons, thinking that they worked magic that could cause the invader great harm. By the time the Romans reached the shore of northwest Wales and were facing Mona, they could see their enemies on the other side, waiting: Druids waving their hands in the air, warriors shouting and waving their weapons, and, most unnerving of all, a group of women with wild hair shouting curses and screeching, moving between the others with torches held high. A terrifying sight, to say the least!

But Paulinus would not be intimidated, and he urged his soldiers on. Fortunately for Rome, they were brave enough to follow him across the strait. And, once they met their Celtic enemies, their courage came back in full. The Britons were no match for the highly disciplined, well-trained Roman army, which overwhelmed the hearty

natives. Wanting to send a message, the Romans killed virtually everyone on the island, and took the survivors as slaves. They also burned the sacred oak groves and other temples. Druidry as a force in Britain was wiped out. Some still practiced in secret in the lands to the west, and Druids continued to play an important role in Ireland for several more centuries, but their grip on Britain had ended.

After the Romans settled down into occupying Britain and made permanent homes there, many of these new residents did what Romans frequently did in new lands: they adopted some of the local gods. This practice might have been common for any number of reasons. Perhaps the Romans sought to appease those gods they might have angered when killing their followers. Or they wanted to make their new subjects comfortable. Or maybe they simply found some of these strange new gods appealing. Whatever the reason, the Romans were extremely open to novel gods, even blending some with Roman ones. At Bath, the Roman goddess Minerva was seen as the same as the Celtic goddess Sul, for example, and Mars was later blended with British war gods, becoming known as Mars Belatucadros or Mars Cocidius. People had public and private spiritual lives, so they might go to the big festivals on certain days to honor the Roman gods, while at home they might honor a mixture of Roman gods, British gods, local spirits, and more.

> Far-flung fact: The Romans brought gods from very faraway lands with them to Britain, such as Mithras (from Persia), Isis (from Egypt), and importantly for Britain's future, Christ.

THE FOUNDING
OF LONDON

London is rightly seen as one of the world's greatest cities, a place with more history and culture packed into it than any city should have a right to. Eighteenth-century writer Samuel Johnson was famous for noting that when one is tired of London, one is tired of life, and there are probably many people who still believe this. This city of cities has a long, nearly 2,000-year history, but of course, it had much more humble beginnings, starting as a Roman settlement sometime after 43 CE. It's possible that there were permanent settlements there long before; Romans often built in areas that were already in use by the locals, after all, but most historians now think that by the time the Romans arrived, London was mainly rolling hills and river, and that they chose the spot because it was useful to them.

Strangely, historians are not certain of the origin of the name "London." It might have come from a Celtic word or the name of a famed chieftain that was Latinized, but since no one bothered to write down where it came from, we'll probably never know for sure. But soon "Londinium" was on the map, and it would grow to be an important settlement in Roman Britain. As we will see in the next entry, it also had the dubious distinction of being burned to the ground by the Celtic queen Boudicca less than twenty years after its founding. But this destruction actually paved the way for it to be rebuilt as a properly planned settlement, rather than just a collection of buildings. Parts of the city would burn again before the year 120, though this fire seems to have been an accident, just like the dreadful 1666 fire so many centuries later.

While earlier records barely mention Londinium at all, by the second century, it probably had a population of as many as 60,000 people, and had all the features that we've come to associate with Roman cities: temples, bath houses, an amphitheater, docks, vibrant trade,

Roman-style architecture, and much more, including an impressive wall on the north side of the city that would last in one form or another until after the Renaissance, defining the boundaries of London as a city separate from other areas that we now associate with the city (such as Westminster). Londinium was another imposing monument to Roman colonialism, and must have been impressive and bewildering to many of the native Brits.

The city was at its height in the second century, but began a slow decline afterward that would eventually lead to ruin when the Romans departed Britain in the late fourth century.

> **Pirate fact:** Maybe as a foreshadowing of what was to come, Londinium suffered from raids by Saxon pirates beginning in the mid-third century. These attacks got so bad that the Romans had to build a wall on the River Thames side of the city to keep them out! By the time the Saxons came to Britain in large numbers by the fifth century, they had been eyeing the island for a long time.

BOUDICCA'S REBELLION

With the Romans firmly in charge of Britain and occupying ever more of it, they seemed unbeatable. The might of Rome had once again marched to a distant nation and subdued it. But the Romans were about to get a painful and brutal lesson that occupying this island wasn't going to be quite as easy as they'd hoped, as the terror of Queen Boudicca was to be unleashed upon them!

Boudicca was queen of a tribe of Britons known as the Iceni, who lived in lands north of London, in what is now Norfolk. Her husband King Prasutagus died in 60 CE. They had two daughters, but no male heir. So, Prasutagus left his wealth to his family and to the Roman Emperor Nero, in the hopes of gaining Roman favor. He'd been on decent terms with the Romans and wanted that to continue after his death. Unfortunately, this isn't what happened. The Romans took possession of Prasutagus' lands, whipped Boudicca, violated her daughters, and laughed while they claimed all of his riches for Nero and themselves.

But there was one thing they didn't count on: Boudicca was not going to let these outrages stand. She discovered that quite a few other tribes were also fed up with the Romans, and were eager for a fight. She also learned that the general Paulinus was away on a military campaign in Wales, so she planned an attack while he was gone.

And what an attack it was.

Rallying thousands of Britons to her side, Boudicca and her forces met the Roman Ninth Legion and destroyed it; the Celts were known for their ferocity in battle, and this meeting only enhanced that reputation. Boudicca and her army then marched to the Roman settlement of Camulodunum (modern-day Colchester). Her forces destroyed it and massacred the civilians, both Roman and pro-Roman Britons. The army moved on to London and did the same, burning it to the ground. They then destroyed Verulamium (modern-day St. Albans) and various military posts along the way. In all, these rebel Britons probably killed 70,000 to 80,000 people.

By this time, the Romans were panicking, and Paulinus had to rush back from Wales to deal with the growing threat. The two armies met north of London for what would be the decisive battle, with the future of Britain at stake. Though the Romans had fewer numbers, they were more disciplined, and Boudicca's army could not inflict the same kind of damage on these well-trained soldiers. Her forces were defeated, and it's thought that Boudicca (and probably her daughters) took her own life with poison, rather than be captured by the Romans.

While Rome would go on to occupy Britain until the late fourth century, its leaders never forgot the incredible butt-kicking handed to them by Boudicca, and they learned to be better prepared in the future. Today, Boudicca represents the struggle for freedom and justice in Britain, and there are many monuments and remembrances to her.

> Female battle fact: Boudicca, like many Celtic and British women, was trained in fighting and the arts of war. She was able to step into the role of a military leader quickly and easily, and her people were more than willing to follow her.

THE ROMANS BROUGHT PUBS TO BRITAIN

There are probably not many things more British than the pub. This humble (and sometimes not-so-humble) establishment is a fixture of every city, town, and village up and down the length and breadth of the island. Pubs are traditionally gathering places for the locals to meet and socialize and share good times over a drink (or three). They are known for their creative signs, which hang outside and often indicate the pubs' names in pictures. They can have names like The Pig and Rooster or The Silver Swan, or literally thousands of other colorful titles. Quite a few serve food, from snacks to full-on meals. A lot of them are even child-friendly. Yes, Britain would not be Britain without its pubs, so it might surprise you that the idea of pubs was actually brought to Britain by the Romans!

Back on the continent, people in Rome and beyond had long enjoyed going to the taberna (from where we get the word tavern), which served food and wine, and often provided rooms for the night. Some places would hang plants or grape vines outside to show that they served wine. If someone couldn't read (and this was true for a lot of people back then), they would know the taberna by the greenery outside. This kind of early pub sign was carried over into Britain, and while the Romans did plant grapes and produce wine on the island, farther north, it was too cool to grow them properly, so taberna owners would improvise and put out other kinds of plants, such as evergreens that would look colorful throughout the year. They also began serving ale and/or beer, drinks more common to Britain.

The Romans built very long and straight roads to get them quickly from one settlement to the next, but it was still necessary to have rest stops for weary travelers and troops. So of course, tabernas started to spring up along the routes, every twenty miles or so. These places were roadside inns where people could spend the night in relative comfort and safety, and get something to eat, or at least to drink. While it's true that things got a bit more chaotic in the centuries after the Romans pulled their troops out of Britain (the Vikings probably didn't stop at the local ale house for a drink before heading back out raiding, for example), the idea of a comfortable place to enjoy food and drink never completely went away.

At first, these stops were isolated, but over time, settlements began to grow up around them, creating what would eventually become the classic village pub.

> Tavern equality fact: Women were most likely the traditional makers and brewers of ale at home, so when the Romans came and wanted to expand to serving ale at the taberna, it was women who usually did the job. In fact, it seems that some women opened their own tabernas to meet the local demand.

WEIRD ROMAN FOODS

As the Romans settled down to make permanent homes in Britain, they brought a lot of their foods and food culture with them. Of course, the working class ate pretty much the same foods throughout the ages: bread, vegetables, fruits, and, on rare occasions, meat. Wine was a big deal in Roman culture, and the Romans began planting vineyards in the south of the country to meet the demand.

But those rich folks who had lavish homes and villas built for themselves brought a selection of Roman delicacies with them, some of which were really weird, while others were just plain gross! People didn't necessarily eat these awful things every day, mind you, but they would serve them at parties and banquets, to show off their wealth. And their weird tastes.

A late Roman cookbook attributed to the Roman foodie Marcus Gavius Apicius (early first century CE) listed all kinds of strange foods, including:

Sea urchins: These spikey little creatures were served in many ways. One popular method was simmered in olive oil, wine, and seasonings such as mint and pepper.

Unusual and colorful birds: Flamingo with leeks, vinegar, dill, and coriander was a hit, as were flamingo and peacock tongues (?!).

Sow's womb: Apicius' book lists at least five ways to serve this dish, most often with vinegar and herbs. Not your typical pork chop!

Rose custard and pie with brains: Ah, custard and brains, that classic combo! This dish was made by taking rose petals, adding broth and calf brains along with wine and oil, and then simmering the mixture in a hot pan until the brains were fully cooked.

Other dishes with brains: Apicius loved brains, in fact. The book has recipes for: brain sausage, eggs and brains, boiled brains, brain pudding, stewed brains, brains and bacon, brain fritters, brains with peas, pig stomach stuffed with brains ... well, you get the idea.

Garum: This was one of the most popular sauces in Roman times, like Roman ketchup or mustard. Pliny the Elder (23–79 CE) tells us how to make the best version: "It is prepared from the intestines of fish and various parts which would otherwise be thrown away, macerated in salt; so that it is, in fact, the result of their putrefaction." So, fish blood and guts were salted and left to rot and ferment in the sun for several weeks. The upper bit was skimmed off and made into garum. It could be mixed with vinegar and/or honey, and was served with just about every food. Yum?

Of course, living far away in Britain, not all of this gross grub would have been readily available, but rich Romans often spared no expense in getting the latest fashionable food to their tables to impress their friends, and the wealthy people living in Britain were no different.

Foul food fact: Romans also ate jellyfish, weasel (which was thought to treat epilepsy), camel (which might have been good to protect you from disease ... or not), ostrich boiled in vinegar and wine with herbs, snails soaked in milk, and many other less-than-appetizing dishes that we can be glad no longer exist on menus!

HADRIAN'S WALL

The fact that Emperor Hadrian (CE 76-138) wanted a wall built across northern Britain only a few years after the disappearance of the Ninth Legion might well not be a coincidence. If that legion really was massacred, then he might have decided that enough was enough, and it was time to set a definitive boundary on the Empire's reach.

By far the most famous of the walls and barriers constructed by the Romans, this massive wall was begun under the direction of Hadrian beginning in the year of his visit to Britain 122, though it had probably been planned for at least a few years before then. It served as the final border between Rome and the "uncivilized" world to the north. It is an amazing architectural achievement, and significant portions of the wall can still be seen across northern England today, stretching over some seventy-three miles from coast to coast. Along the way, there are more than a dozen archaeological sites attached to it, including Roman forts and towns, occupied by the soldiers who were charged with keeping the border secure. At the time, there might have been a watch tower every third of a mile or so, and the wall itself was said to be twelve feet high and in places eight feet thick. It was a massive architectural project that took years to complete.

Though the wall is much diminished now (people over the centuries pilfered a lot of the stones for use in other buildings), lengthy portions of it still exist, along with the remains of those Roman forts and outposts. One can imagine how shocking it might have been for a soldier from warm, sunny Italy to be stationed at this outpost at the end of the Roman world, in cold and rainy northern England! But the wall served its purpose, and marked the frontier of Roman power in Britain. It was not just to keep people out, but to keep people in, and to regulate travel between the Empire and beyond. The "barbarians" who lived north of the wall could enter through it at specific locations to trade, for example. Like so many Roman monuments, it was a massive display of Roman power and dominance, created as a constant reminder to the locals of who their masters were.

> **Wall touristy fact:** Hadrian's Wall was quite famous in its own time, and the forts along it became populated with visitors. Nearby residents even created little souvenirs such as miniature pans that identified the fort travelers visited, and also showed a picture of the wall. They were like the refrigerator magnets of the time!

THE LOST LEGION IN SCOTLAND AND THE ANTONINE WALL

As we've seen with Boudicca's rebellion, the Romans weren't quite as unbeatable as they thought they were. And this was truer the farther north into Britain they tried to establish themselves. By the time the Roman armies reached Caledonia (what is now Scotland), the native Picts residing there were having none of it, and the Romans discovered that they had truly met their match.

According to legend and some very serious scholars, the Ninth Legion marched into Caledonia at some point in the early second century and vanished. They were probably massacred by the native Picts, a dreadful warning to any other Romans who might be considering an invasion. Some scholars think that the Ninth actually survived and was redeployed in the Netherlands, and possibly later in the Middle East, but the lack of records as to the fate of the legion suggests that something awful might well have happened to it. Maybe the army wanted to keep quiet about it?

Not content with just Hadrian's Wall (see the previous entry), the Romans decided twenty years after it was built that yet another wall should be built farther north. Emperor Antoninus Pius ordered the construction of a shorter wall, stretching from what is now Edinburgh to the west, between the Firth of Forth and the Firth of Clyde. Known as the Antonine Wall, it was mostly made of dirt on stone foundations, and so was not as long and as impressive as Hadrian's Wall. Why did the Romans build this second wall further north? Mostly as insurance against Pictish attacks and to protect the few roads they had in the area north of Hadrian's Wall. But this work in no way means that the Romans conquered Scotland—not even the area between the two walls. Indeed, by the year 162 CE, the Antonine Wall was no longer serving its purpose and the Romans withdrew permanently behind Hadrian's Wall, which ever after marked the final frontier of the Roman Empire.

No strength in numbers fact: Roman legions were large. The Ninth was made up of about 5,000 men, so the fact that this number of trained fighters could be wiped out by the people of northern Britain must have sent more than a few chills down the spines of the Romans remaining in northern Britain. Maybe that's why the legion's fate is so mysterious? No one wanted to admit that the Romans had suffered such a catastrophic defeat!

WHO WERE THE PICTS?

The Picts were clearly a ferocious people, enough that the Romans gave up on occupying Caledonia and built two walls to try to keep them at bay! But who were they? Well, that's the big question. Historians aren't quite sure, because they left no written records. It seems that they weren't one people (in spite of the Romans lumping them all together), but possibly separate groups who were descended from the Iron Age people that inhabited the far north of the isle. There are ancient legends of them coming from Central Asia (and they might have even believed this themselves), but this origin is unlikely to be true.

They might have fought among themselves forever if the Romans hadn't tried to invade. There was no doubt to the Romans that they were a pain in the backside, and as we've seen, eventually, they caused the Roman emperors to give up trying to expand the empire into the north of Britain, building walls to contain them instead. So the Picts—or the group of peoples called that—have the honor of being one of the only people to fend off the Romans and keep them out, which is quite an achievement! Eventually, after the Romans left, the Pictish tribes banded together and formed a unified kingdom that would last for hundreds of years. Migrations of people from Ireland

and the Viking invasions changed the makeup of their society, and Pictish culture probably fizzled out around the year 900. Later Pictish art is definitely Celtic in design.

The word *Pict* means "painted people" and probably refers to the Pictish practice of either painting or tattooing their bodies. This might have been done mostly by warriors, and Roman writers noted it. Seeing a band of these warriors, all painted and howling as they ran toward an unfortunate Roman legion must have been a terrifying sight!

The Picts left behind a large number of standing stones with patterns carved into them, often spirals and geometric designs, along with animal images, all of which give some clues about the designs they might have painted on their bodies. These designs might also have something to do with their language(s), but since nothing was ever written down, we just don't know. So, these amazing stones offer an intriguing mystery.

We will probably never know too much about Pictish culture, language, or religion, but we do know that they were farmers and hunters that extended their settlements as far north as the islands of Orkney and possibly Shetland, off the north coast of Scotland. And of course, we know they were more than willing to go to war against a common enemy when the time came. For the Romans, that spelled a lot of trouble!

> **Roman dad joke fact (warning!):** Hadrian's Wall – Picts or it didn't happen!

WHY DID THE ROMANS LEAVE BRITAIN?

By the early fifth century, the Romans had been in Britain for over 350 years, an occupation that forever changed the culture and landscape on the island (just consider all those roads, pubs, and villas, for starters). Archaeologists still regularly make new finds of Roman remains in Britain: buildings, coins, art, and much more. Many of the native British population had long since adopted Roman ways (though many had not), and it seemed that this hybrid culture would go on forever. Except it didn't.

Trouble was brewing back in Rome, and had been for a long time. Rome had been weakened by political in-fighting and many usurpers claiming the throne for themselves. Meanwhile, more and more Germanic peoples were entering the empire, often legally, and becoming citizens, or at least legal residents, but not all of them. There were an increasing number of attacks along the Roman frontiers, and Roman soldiers were needed to fight off the "barbarians," which meant that some of these troops were called away from wherever they were stationed to fight in Germany and in other areas. Between about 383 and 410, Roman troops departed from Britannia forever.

In 407 CE, Roman troops that didn't want to leave Britain declared support for their leader, Constantine. He tried to proclaim himself as the new emperor and took the title Constantine III. There was just one problem: Rome already had an emperor, Honorius, who had been recalling British-Roman troops! Constantine and his supporters marched to the continent to secure his power, establishing him as a ruler in Gaul and Hispania (Spain). But that claim wasn't going to last. Attacks from outside, fighting from within, and some of his troops switching sides all combined to undermine Constantine's authority, and by 411 he had lost everything. Some believe he was also assassinated.

The years 409 to 411 were also critical for Roman Britain. In taking his troops from Britannia, Constantine had basically left the island undefended. As word of this spread, groups of invaders from the Netherlands, Germany, and Denmark began launching raids. But instead of rushing back to defend Britain, Rome's attitude was basically, "Sorry, you're on your own now. We have too many other problems to deal with." Rome was abandoning its outpost at the edge of the known world.

This doesn't mean that Roman Britain collapsed overnight, of course, but society began to change pretty quickly over the next few decades, as Saxons, Angles, and Jutes arrived, sometimes peacefully, sometimes not. The use of Roman coins ceased pretty quickly, and new Roman villas and towns stopped being built. Did society "collapse?" Not exactly, but the rapid changes probably wouldn't have been very pleasant for those who lived in, for example, London and considered themselves to be fully Roman. The fifth century in Britain became a chaotic and, at times, lawless era, when the old way of doing things vanished, and northern Germanic cultures began to replace the Mediterranean one the Romans had established.

A dark age fact: Out west, some Celtic tribes actually tried to become more "Roman" when the Romans left, an effort that might be a source for some of the original Arthurian stories and legends, as we'll see in the next chapter.

CHAPTER 3

THE ANGLO-SAXONS AND VIKINGS

(FIFTH CENTURY TO 1066)

INVASION OR MIGRATION?
KING ARTHUR: MYTH OR TRUE STORY?

I n the popular imagination, King Arthur was a champion of Britain in a time when many enemies were closing in. The great tales of Arthur, his Knights of the Round Table, and Camelot fired the imagination of medieval listeners, and the adventures of Arthur, Merlin, Lancelot, Guinevere, Gawain, and many others have thrilled readers for centuries. But as historians began doing more research, it became obvious that these stories were mostly medieval inventions, and only a few came from earlier than the twelfth and thirteenth centuries.

Still, some people have thought that Arthur was a real person, a Celtic or Roman leader who helped hold back the invasion of Britain by Germanic peoples from the European continent. If that's the case, he probably lived in the fifth or sixth centuries, and was able to resist these invaders, at least for a while. But eventually, they were able to overrun Britain and push the Romano-Britons into Cornwall and Wales.

But in recent years, archaeologists and others have wondered if this story is true. Evidence for a personage named Arthur is thin, to say the least, and even if he had a different name, it now looks like the story of the people who would come to be known as the Anglo-Saxons is very different. They came to Britain from what are now the northern Netherlands, the west coast of Denmark, and northern Germany, and they were made up of several groups of people—the Angles, the Saxons, and the Jutes, among others—who spoke similar languages, and had similar beliefs and customs.

These groups might have been coming to Britain since Roman times, serving in the Roman army or as mercenary soldiers. So after the Romans left, many of them were already there. That's not to say that groups of Angles, Saxons, and Jutes didn't invade after Rome left; they absolutely did. But archaeologists have long wondered about the lack of evidence for large invasions. There aren't a lot of ruins of towns that were burned and destroyed, or mass graves full of Celtic and Roman victims all over the country, for example.

While there probably were many unpleasant meetings between those already living in Britain and these newcomers, including full-on battles, there's also evidence that some of these newcomers simply settled, more or less peacefully. Britain was not very populated at the time, so there was enough room for everyone. Certainly, the new groups might have looked down on the natives and encouraged them to go away, either by pointedly asking them to, or by pointing swords at them!

Were the Angles, Saxons, and Jutes bloodthirsty barbarians or peaceful settlers? The answer is probably both. But once they began arriving in bigger numbers by the fifth century, it was obvious they were in Britain to stay, and would soon set up new kingdoms of their own.

> Geographical fact: The very word "England" comes from "Angle-land." There weren't necessarily more Angles than any other group, but that was the name that stuck. In Germany there is a region called Saxony, and in Denmark, there is an area called Jutland. So everyone got a regional name of their own eventually!

BRITONS OR WELSH?

The people who had been living in the mainland of Britannia, the Britons, had been there for centuries. They spoke a Celtic language and shared some things in common culturally with other Celtic-speakers in the continent. But the idea that they were a unified group that got driven into what is now Wales by invaders is not entirely true.

The word Wales comes from the Anglo-Saxon word *wealas*, which was used to describe the people living on the island. Wealas itself probably comes from a proto-Germanic word, *Walhaz*, which came from the name of a group of Gauls that the Romans called the Volcae. Whew, that's quite an etymology! Over time, *wealas* also came to mean something like "foreigner," which, considering that the Saxons and their buddies were the actual invaders, just seems insulting! But you can see how it's not a big jump from *wealas* to Wales. The word also shows up in the second half of the name for the far west region of Britain: Cornwall. *Wealas* was used by the Anglo-Saxons to refer to any area associated with the Britons, not just Wales itself.

But what about the Briton-Welsh connection? Certainly, some Britons might have fled westward if they were pushed out by the Saxons (an event which might have spawned some of those Arthurian legends), but the Welsh of today are not one group of people, genetically speaking. While the modern Welsh have DNA dating back to the earliest Celtic settlers, they are by no means a single, unified population. In fact, the people of North and South Wales have less in common with each other genetically than the Scots and the English do!

But what did the early and medieval Welsh say about themselves? According to a book called the *Historia Brittonum*, which was a Welsh history written in northern Wales around the year 890, the Britons had originally come from the city of Troy. Yes, they were Trojans fleeing the Trojan War that escaped to Britain, becoming the first people to settle there. Now, of course, archaeology and science have long since proven this legend to be completely untrue, but the Troy-to-Britain connection was a belief that persisted well into the Middle Ages.

What about the Welsh language? The Brittonic language that became Welsh—which was spoken by the people of Britain who faced the Romans and then the Saxons—probably came to the island with Celtic settlers around 600 BCE. It certainly wasn't an ancient language going back thousands of years, or a Trojan language. Though, of course, there were Celtic peoples living as far away as modern Turkey (where Troy is located), so perhaps that's one source of these legends.

As you can see, the whole Briton-Welsh question is complicated and confusing. There were already people in Wales when the Romans and then the Saxons arrived, and it's entirely possible that other groups of people migrated there during these periods, as the modern Welsh are more united by a language than by a genetic ancestry.

> Celtic language fact: Welsh is related to Cornish and Breton, known as the Brythonic branch of the Celtic languages, but these are a different group than the Celtic languages of Ireland, the Isle of Man, and Scotland.

ANGLO-SAXON RELIGION AND THE DAYS OF THE WEEK

The Angles, Saxons, and Jutes who came to Britain brought their ancient Germanic religious beliefs with them, and kept them when they settled in these new lands. While they would become Christians starting in the seventh centuries, it took a long time for the new beliefs to wipe out the old, and many people probably continued worshipping their old gods in secret, even if they weren't supposed to! There's a funny story about an early Christian missionary who convinced an Anglo-Saxon king to erect an altar to Christ. When the missionary went to see it, he was horrified that the king had simply put up the altar next to those altars dedicated to his other gods. In the king's mind, this new god had yet to prove himself worthy. It would have never occurred to him to remove all the other altars. Why risk angering those gods when trying out a new one?

The Anglo-Saxon gods were related to the Norse gods, with similar names and duties. There was Woden, the one-eyed god who traveled the world in search of wisdom, Thunor, a god of elements and storms, Tiw, a god of justice, and Frigg, a goddess of the home, who was also Woden's wife. You might notice that these names seem familiar to those found in Norse mythology, and we'll look at the names of the Norse gods a little later on in the chapter and see how they compare to those in Britain.

But you might also be surprised to learn that, despite all the attempts to stamp out belief in these gods and in pagan customs, their names survive as the names of our days of the week in English!

- **Sunday (the sun)**

- **Monday (the moon)**

- **Tuesday (Tiw's day)**

- **Wednesday (Woden's day)**

- **Thursday (Thunor's day)**

- **Friday (Frigg's day)**

- **Saturday (Saturn, the Roman god ... well, all right, the Anglos didn't get every day!)**

The thing is, folk customs take a long time to disappear, and sometimes, they just get repackaged. Even though Christian missionaries from Rome visited the Anglo-Saxons before the year 600, and 100 years later, the kingdoms were Christian, at least in name, the common people took a lot longer to be convinced, frequently holding onto their traditional beliefs for centuries. Indeed, many early Anglo-Saxon kings only converted to Christianity because they saw advantages in being united with other Christian kingdoms in Europe, improving trade, forming alliances, and so on. Quite a few of these kings "converted" and then went right on behaving and believing just as they had before.

Anglo-Saxon religion was sometimes a curious mix of Christian and pagan beliefs. Priests would tell people what to believe on Sundays, but those same people, never thinking twice, did things the priests wouldn't like on other days of the week.

> **Charming fact:** Some Old English charms and prayers survive to this day that seem to address both the Christian and other gods. It never hurts to hedge your bets!

THE ENGLISH LANGUAGE

E nglish is one of the most-spoken languages on Earth. It's become so important around the world that countless people who speak other languages have learned it as a second language. But the English of, say, 1,200 years ago, called "Old English" or simply, Anglo-Saxon, was a very different beast, indeed. You probably wouldn't be able to recognize a lot of it—just imagine if someone came up to you and started speaking like this:

Widsið maðelode, wordhord onleac

What? Different letters, different pronunciations, different words ... this can't be English! But it *is* English. These words are the first line of the poem "Widsith" from the tenth century (it was probably composed long before that). The poem tells about the adventures of a traveler, and all he has seen. In modern English, the line reads:

"Widsith spoke, unlocked his word hoard"

The letter "ð" is called "eth" and was pronounced as a "th" sound. It eventually disappeared from regular use, but it looks cool, and is still used in the modern Icelandic language. Another Old English letter was "thorn," which was written as "þ" and also pronounced as "th." Confused yet?

The Anglo-Saxons (and Vikings) liked to use kennings, words and phrases that meant something else; a "word hoard" is a wonderful kenning for one's vocabulary. In a time when few people could read or write, the word hoard was an amazing idea: words are treasures, each one like a gold coin that is hoarded. People should guard their own hoard of words the way a dragon guards a hoard of coins. So, with each new word you learn, you are adding another treasure to your collection.

Another example of a kenning is the "whale road," which means the sea. Why? Because the sea is the "road" where whales swim. As you can tell, even then poets liked to play around with words. In the days before television and internet, listening to a vivid story told by a master poet and/or singer (called a scop, pronounced "shop") would have been an amazing experience. English was also used by kings and monasteries to record histories, philosophy, religious works, and many other things. The history known as the *Anglo-Saxon Chronicle* is written in Old English, and we have a good number of poems, like "Widsith" and "Beowulf," though sadly, not as many as we'd like.

This vibrant language would change over time, and after the Normans conquered England in 1066, they imported the French spoken at their courts. Hundreds (and then thousands) of French words eventually made their way into the English language. At first, French stayed strictly in the top levels of society, so the rulers and the people couldn't understand each other at all, (kind of like citizens and politicians these days)! But English didn't disappear; it absorbed and adopted those French words and grammar to become a new version of English, similar to the one we know today. Eventually, this Frenchified English came to the upper levels of society, so that even kings and queens and their nobles spoke it. And English continued to grow into the language we have today. Our word hoards are still growing!

> Language fact: A majority of the 100 most common English words used today are Anglo-Saxon in origin!

THE SUTTON HOO BURIAL

In May and June 1939, in a field northeast of Ipswich, one of the most amazing archaeological finds of the twentieth century was uncovered. The owner of the land, the splendidly named Edith Pretty, had allowed digs and investigations in burial mounds on the property since 1937. But in 1939, Basil Brown, a self-taught archaeologist connected with the nearby Ipswich Museum, was digging in what was known as Mound 4 with his assistants. Basil's team found a piece of iron that Brown recognized as a ship rivet. This was no mere small piece of debris; as they continued digging, they soon discovered that an entire ship was buried under Mound 4! But why?

Turns out, this wasn't a ship used to sail, but rather a ceremonial ship that had held the body of someone important, such as a king. And this king was buried in a chamber in the ship with many treasures. Over the summer, Brown, along with archaeologist Charles Phillips (a fellow at Selwyn College, Cambridge) and a whole team uncovered an astonishing collection of royal treasures dating back to sixth- or seventh-century England. These incredible finds proved once and for all that the Anglo-Saxons were not just barbarians, but possessed a sophisticated culture, art, advanced metal-working skills, and much more. The rich images described in the poem *Beowulf* were true after all! Among the items were:

- An amazing ceremonial helmet and mask, richly decorated with images of warriors and creatures. It was in poor shape, but preserved well enough that modern replicas of it have been made, showing its true wonder.

- Weapons, such as spears and a sword. The sword was positioned in a way that suggested the user had been left-handed.

- Buckles and clasps, which were used for fastening clothing. The "Great Buckle" in particular is a marvel of gold knot work, with intricate patterns requiring tremendous skill to make.

- The remains of a shield. The metal parts of the shield were found, even though the wood had long since rotted away.

- Drinking horns and other eating utensils, including objects from as far away as the Byzantine Empire. These items showed that the Anglo-Saxons were trading and engaged in business with cultures outside of the island at an early date.

But who was buried there? This question has been asked many times over the last eighty years. The most likely candidate seems to be Rædwald, a king of East Anglia who died around 624. He was initially a convert to Christianity, but seemed to have been talked out of it by his wife and others, so he kept alters to both Christ and the Saxon gods in his temple, much to the annoyance of the Christian missionaries. The monastic historian Bede was especially irritated by this! But where was Rædwald's body? The acidic soil in the area probably dissolved it over the centuries, but his incredible burial legacy remains.

Dig that fact: The Sutton Hoo treasures are now housed in the British Museum for all to see!

MONKS AND MONASTERIES

C hristianity spread across the British Isles in fits and starts for several hundred years. Even after the kingdoms of Anglo-Saxon England were "officially" Christian, a lot of folk practices and pagan beliefs held on, for centuries in some spots. The churchmen had to learn to live side-by-side with beliefs they frequently condemned. But one place Christians could go to immerse themselves in their religion was the monasteries, which began springing up all over England beginning in the seventh century. Given the chaos and uncertainty of the time, these houses must have been attractive to many for providing safety, a guarantee of food and shelter, and a chance to find inner peace.

Monks followed the Rule of St. Benedict, a very strict code of conduct that told them when and what to eat, when to pray, and how they should behave at all times. They were expected to live lives of prayer, to work and study, and to give up their old lives. They were supposed to eat humbly, not drink much, and refrain from indulging in worldly pleasures. But, as you might expect, that's not always how it worked out! There were many complaints about monks enjoying lavish feasts, lots of beer and wine, music, and the company of outsiders in their monasteries. In 734, the monk and scholar Bede (who wrote a very important early history of the time) even wrote a letter to the

Bishop of York, complaining that monks were living with their wives and children!

Perhaps the most famous and important monastery in those early days was Lindisfarne Priory, just off the coast of northeast Northumbria and not far from the border of modern Scotland. It sat on a tidal island, meaning that sometimes one can access it from the mainland, and sometimes the high tide makes it a true island. The monastery was founded in about 634 by the Irish monk Aidan (who later became a saint), and quickly became a refuge from the troubles of the time. It was also a hotspot for the spread Christianity in the north. The intricate and gorgeous manuscript known as the Lindisfarne Gospels was produced there, sometime after the year 700.

But Lindisfarne has a much darker claim to fame, for it was the site of an attack by Vikings in the year 793, the year that many consider to be the first of the so-called "Viking Age." The great work known as the *Anglo-Saxon Chronicle* (more on that later) recorded: "This year came dreadful fore-warnings over the land of the Northumbrians, terrifying the people most woefully: these were immense sheets of light rushing through the air, and whirlwinds, and fiery, dragons flying across the firmament. These tremendous tokens were soon followed by a great famine: and not long after, on the sixth day before the ides of January in the same year, the harrowing inroads of heathen men made lamentable havoc in the church of God in Holy-island by slaughter."

It must have felt like the end of the world! The Vikings sailed up to the island in their long ships, attacked, killed monks, took precious items of gold and silver, and burned buildings before storming off. They were basically pirates on a raid. Historians think that this attack actually happened in June, rather than January; an early medieval typo! June would have been a much better time for sailing than January, with its freezing cold and unpredictable weather. This attack changed everything for the Anglo-Saxons, ushering in fear and chaos that would afflict the area for the next two hundred years.

Monkish fact: Children were often sent to monasteries to be educated. Many became monks after that, whether they wanted to or not!

THE VIKING INVASIONS

The Anglo-Saxons certainly had their differences. They weren't united into a single kingdom and argued with each other all the time, going to war regularly. But at the end of the eighth century, something big happened, which forever changed the way the Anglo-Saxon kingdoms viewed the world and their place in it. That big event was the start of the Viking invasions, the most famous of which, as we've just seen, was the attack on the monastery at Lindisfarne in northeast England in the year 793.

"Viking" doesn't refer to a group of people, as it does with the English or the French. In fact, some very educated people still aren't quite sure where the word came from. For many at the time, it meant something like "pirate," which was a good enough description of what the early Viking raids resembled. Vikings would sail across the North Sea from Denmark or Norway and strike easy targets, like monasteries, taking their gold and other wealth, and sometimes people as hostages or slaves. You might imagine that they were tall, fearsome warriors, wearing helmets with horns, but that's not quite right. You see, the Vikings never wore horned helmets. As far as archaeologists can tell, that never happened, and seems to be a silly invention of the nineteenth century.

You might also be surprised to learn that most of the people from Scandinavia were not warriors and pirates. They were farmers, laborers, merchants, craftspeople—the kinds of folks that make up any ordinary society. And many, if not most, stayed right where they were

all of their lives. So what were the Viking attacks all about? There are several ideas, but some think it was because there were too many people and not enough farmable land in Scandinavia, which forced some to move away. The expansion might also have been influenced by rivalries within families. Since the oldest sons tended to inherit everything, the younger sons could have gone to sea, looking for new lands to claim and trying to make their own fortunes.

In any case, England was a great place for these raiders to visit, and, eventually, to settle. After a while, it wasn't just warriors, but whole families that came and settled on the eastern side of Britain. Of course, the English who lived there weren't too happy about this, and often fought the newcomers, but these northern settlers kept coming and eventually, showed that they were there to stay. So many of them lived in and controlled those areas that the east side of Britain eventually became known as the "Danelaw"—the place where the Danes made the laws, rather than the English.

Quite a few modern towns in Britain started as Viking settlements. Anywhere that ends in "by" or "thorpe" was once a place where Vikings settled and named (Rugby and Derby are two well-known examples). The city of York gets its modern name from Jorvik (pronounced "Yorvick"), which had been there since Roman times, and gone through a few name changes by the time the Vikings took over and changed the name. The Nordic people left a permanent mark on Britain and the English, in both good and bad ways.

> **Another language fact:** The English language borrowed a number of words from Old Norse, including: club, law, husband, sale, dirt, skate, bull, crawl, get, give, run, want, bag, skirt, skin, guest, and happy, to name a few.

VIKING RELIGION

What we know about Viking spiritual beliefs comes mostly from writings in twelfth- and thirteenth-century Iceland. A man with the wonderful name of Snorri Sturluson (who lived from 1179 to 1241), an Icelandic poet and historian, helped preserve many of the Norse myths by writing them down in the *Prose Edda*. Another (anonymous) work, the *Poetic Edda*, also contains some of these amazing stories. Although these works were written long after the last Viking ships sailed, they recorded myths and legends that had been popular for many centuries, and from them scholars have managed to get a pretty good understanding of the basic beliefs the Vikings held. These myths were vast, epic, and often violent tales for a strong and hardy people. While they're not as famous or influential as the Greek myths, you've probably heard of at least some of these gods:

Odin: The one-eyed god known as the Allfather, he was the leader of the Norse gods. Odin is god of poetry and wisdom, but also battle and death. Warriors who worshipped Odin hoped to die in battle and gain a seat at Odin's table in the hall known as Valhalla. Two ravens, Huginn and Muninn, fly all over the world and bring information back to him.

Thor: The son of Odin, known as the "God of Thunder," Thor wields a mighty war hammer known as *Mjölnir*, a weapon with which he fights giants, trolls, dragons, and other foes. Some legends say that he rides in a chariot pulled by two goats, which might look a bit funny, but who would dare tell him?

Loki: A trickster god, seen by some as evil and by others as simply mischievous, Loki is actually the son of a giant and a goddess, but he dwells amongst the gods in Asgard, even though he often annoys them or makes enemies of them. It is said that he will play a role in the end of the world.

Freya: A goddess of love, beauty, wealth, and war, Freya is also a master of magic, which she is said to have taught to Odin. Some say that she takes half of the warriors who die in battle to join her at her hall, *Sessrúmnir*, while Odin gets the other half. She rides in a chariot pulled by two cats (who else but a goddess could get cats to do this?), and has a cloak made of falcon feathers, which allows her to transform into a bird and fly.

Frigg: The wife of Odin, Frigg is a goddess of hearth and home, as well as marriage. She is the queen of Asgard, and renowned for her wisdom.

There are many other gods and goddesses, as well as giants and monsters in the Norse stories. These beliefs also told of an event, Ragnarok, the end of the world. During Ragnarok, most of the gods would die, but afterward a new world and new gods would be born.

Now, you might be thinking that some of these names sound familiar, and you would be right: Oden-Woden, Thor-Thunor, Frigg-Frigg. The reason for this is that the original religion of the Anglo-Saxons was related closely to that of the Scandinavians. While they eventually abandoned those ways to become Christian, folk beliefs about the old gods held on for centuries.

> **Religious contact fact:** English churchmen were always complaining about people continuing to perform pagan practices, well into the eleventh century! When the Vikings came to England, were they a constant and uncomfortable reminder to the Anglo-Saxons of their own pre-Christian past?

VIKING WOMEN

We usually assume that in ancient times, women had a pretty bad go of things, seen as nothing more than the possessions of men, and treated as little better than slaves. This was true a lot of the time, but interestingly, Viking women seem to have fared better than many women in cultures farther south. It might have been because they lived in the very cold climate of Scandinavia, so people had to hold each other in equal regard and work together in order to survive the harsh winters. Whatever the reason, women in Viking culture had rights that many females at the time could only dream about, a reality that remained after their migration to England.

Norse women were in charge of the home when their husbands left (whether on a merchant's journey, or to go raiding). A woman's word was basically law in his absence. A husband would leave all the keys in his wife's hand and everyone was expected to obey her. Upon getting married, the woman received money and gifts from her husband, which she got to keep, even if they later divorced. Speaking of divorces, women in the Viking world could divorce their husbands for any number of reasons, including if her husband hit her, lost all his money, settled in a new land, or if she was just unhappy with him!

Women could also claim land for themselves—in fact, it was easy: as much area as they could walk in a day while leading a cow behind them!

Women were depicted as strong, powerful figures in Norse myth and legend. The female Valkyries took the souls of warriors killed in battle, either to the god Odin, or to the goddess Freya. Freya herself was a goddess of war. It's been said of Frigg, Odin's wife, that while Odin ruled Asgard (the realm of the gods), she ran things day-to-day.

It was women who were expected to practice Norse magic: charms, spells, divination, and *seiðr*, a kind of trance that enabled a journey to other realms. It was considered strange if men practiced magic, and, in some places, it was even forbidden! The graves of some wise women, known as Völvas, have been found, and they were often buried with honor and some of their magic items and herbs.

Not everything was rosy and wonderful for women in Norse society, though. The Arab traveler, Aḥmad ibn Faḍlān, who journeyed from the Middle East up into northern Europe, described a horrific funeral ritual, where a young slave woman was sacrificed so that she could accompany her (male) master into the afterlife. Her body was placed on a ship with his and then the whole boat was burned. This story was only about one group of Norse people living in Russia, though, so perhaps it wasn't something forced on women throughout Scandinavia. From what we've seen, it's doubtful that a lot of Norse women would have put up with it!

> Fighter fact: Historians long thought that women were not warriors in Viking society, but recent discoveries might force that opinion to be revised. A skeleton in a grave in Birka in Sweden has recently been identified as being that of a woman who was buried with weapons (including a sword), exactly as a male warrior would have been. Was this woman a warrior? Or just someone important enough to receive an honorific burial?

KING ALFRED THE GREAT AND THE LAST KINGDOM

B y the early 870s, things were looking pretty bleak for the Saxon kingdoms. The Danish Great Army had spread across the island, taking land after land until only Wessex remained in Anglo-Saxon hands. This "Last Kingdom" was in danger of falling, too, and English history might have been very different if it had. As luck or fate would have it, the throne of this kingdom passed to a young man named Alfred. Alfred was the youngest of his father's sons, at least three of whom had been king before him: Æthelbald, Æthelberht, and Æthelred (pay attention, there will be a quiz on them later!). Not much is known about the first two, though Alfred fought alongside Æthelred against the Vikings, winning some battles and losing others. But Æthelred died in 871, and the throne fell at last to Alfred, who now had the monumental task of trying to fight off the Danes and save what was left of Anglo-Saxon England.

The fortunes of Alfred and his kingdom teetered for the next few years. He was never able to drive out the Danes entirely and had to settle for peace treaties that kept the invaders at bay for a time. Of course, these treaties were not always honored, and Alfred suffered more than a few defeats along the way. Things got so bad that he was forced to retreat to an island in the marshlands of Somerset in 878 and hide. This self-imposed exile was probably humiliating, but it also gave Alfred a chance to regroup and call for reinforcements. A famous legend says that when Alfred was on the run, he took refuge with a peasant woman who didn't know who he was (secrecy was very important, of course). She asked him to mind some wheat cakes since she had other work to do. He promised he would, but was so concerned about the fate of his kingdom that he let them burn. When she came back and saw the mess, she scolded the king for his carelessness. The whole tale might well just be made up, but it's been a popular story since the Middle Ages.

From the marshes, Alfred's forces were able to strike back, and over the next two years, won a series of victories that beat back the Danes and their leader, Guthrum. Trapping the Danes in their fort, Alfred was able to besiege them into submitting. Guthrum agreed to convert to Christianity. His army and people settled in the east, and promised not to return to attack Wessex again. This was not the end of the Danish attacks, of course; many other Danes would come to Britain

seeking riches and glory. But Alfred had saved his kingdom and established it as a force to be reckoned with. He strengthened Wessex and reformed its laws, taxes, and administration over the next twenty years, setting the stage for later kingdoms to follow its example.

Alfred was a devout Christian who valued learning and wanted to increase literacy. During his reign, a history was begun that would be added to by monks and historians for several centuries. Written in English (rather than Latin), it later came to be known as the *Anglo-Saxon Chronicle* and it provides a priceless look into the goings-on of the country during those centuries between the Roman departure and the Norman Conquest.

> Royal title fact: Because of his great victories and other achievements, Alfred is the only English king ever to be known as "the Great."

ÆTHELFLÆD,
LADY OF THE MERCIANS

Æthelflæd (c. 870-918) was the daughter of King Alfred the Great. In recent years, she has been popularized in the hit television show, *The Last Kingdom*, though actual details about her life are a bit scant. As we've seen, Alfred had been waging war against the Danes on several fronts, fighting to save the Kingdom of Wessex and prevent a total takeover by the Danish armies that swept across England in the ninth century. In the year 886, he managed to capture London and free it from Danish control. The thing is, London had always been a city at the southern tip of the Kingdom of Mercia, which bordered Wessex on the north. So, in a magnanimous gesture, Alfred offered the city back to Mercia and its king, Æthelred (not to be confused with the king, "Æthelred the Unready"), in order to cement their alliance and give the two nations a greater chance of fighting off those ravaging Vikings; strength in numbers, and all that.

Alfred had some conditions for this gift, however: the new alliance meant that Mercia had to acknowledge the superior position of Wessex, even if they were technically allies and equals. Alfred also included the condition that Æthelred was to marry Æthelflæd, a union that would allow Alfred to unite the two nations and keep a closer eye on what was going on north of him by having his daughter in that court. Æthelflæd, who was only 16 at the time, probably had no say whatsoever in her fate.

But if anyone thought Æthelflæd was going to be a wallflower that simply deferred to her new husband, they were very mistaken. She showed remarkable skill in strategy and tactics, and soon was helping her husband kick the Danes out of Mercian territory. In one instance, a group of Vikings were causing trouble outside of the city of Chester (near the border of modern north Wales). Æthelflæd rode with an army to meet the Danes, feigned a retreat to draw them inside the city, and then wiped them out. These kinds of clever tactics won her great acclaim throughout the country.

After a long illness, Æthelred died in 911 and so Æthelflæd became the sole ruler of Mercia, a queen in all but name. In actuality, he'd been sick since 902, so it's possible that she was Mercia's effective ruler for several years before his death. After 911, she continued to show her bravery and skill in resisting Danish aggression, often working with her brother Edward, Alfred's son (and now king of Wessex) toward the goal of a united England. Though she died in her early 40s, she left an amazing legacy and was one of the most remarkable women of the Anglo-Saxon age.

> **Right to rule fact:** In Anglo-Saxon England, women were allowed little, if any, political power. Even Alfred's widow, Ealhswith, didn't keep the title of queen after his death. So that fact that Æthelflæd was able to

hold onto power and had the strong support of her people was nothing short of astonishing. Perhaps being known as the "Lady of the Mercians" (at least as far as the English chronicles were concerned), rather than the "Queen of the Mercians" (though she is called queen in some Welsh and Irish manuscripts) and being willing to hold a role that was, in theory at least, subordinate to Edward, helped her to retain her leadership of her adopted home for years.

BEOWULF

One of the most popular works in all of English literature, *Beowulf* is a very long poem in three parts, and a masterpiece of the Old English language. It is by far the longest work in Old English that survives, but we almost lost it to the flames in October 1731. A collection of Anglo-Saxon manuscripts, including *Beowulf*, were being held with a lot of other books in a building called Ashburnham House in London, which caught fire. The fire damaged and destroyed a huge number of books, though thankfully, *Beowulf* was saved when it and other manuscripts were thrown out a window, though it was burned around the edges. Maybe that's fitting, since the last portion of the poem tells of Beowulf fighting a fire-breathing dragon! In any case, *Beowulf* survived to be printed and translated, and has thrilled readers and scholars ever since. J. R. R. Tolkien, author of *The Lord of the Rings*, was fascinated by the poem and gave a lecture in 1936 about it, "Beowulf: The Monsters and the Critics," which many still consider a masterful exploration of the work.

Though the poem is written in Old English, it tells a tale set in Denmark several centuries earlier. Most people know the basic story. Beowulf and his band of heroes arrive at a hall called Heorot, where Hrothgar, king of the Danes, is facing a terrible problem. The

monster Grendel comes to his hall at night and kills people, but always escapes. Beowulf fights Grendel and eventually kills him; he rips off Grendel's arm, and the creature, howling in pain, retreats to his lair, where he soon dies. Then in part two, Beowulf has to deal with Grendel's very angry mother! He also manages to dispatch her after swimming down to her lair. In the final part of the poem, set decades later, Beowulf has ruled peacefully for many years. Now an old man, he must fight one last battle against a fire-breathing dragon, an encounter he ultimately does not survive. He is given a hero's burial and honoured throughout the land.

Beowulf has fascinated and captivated readers for centuries, and its themes of heroism, sacrifice, and doing the right thing in the face of great danger still resonate today.

> Oral vs. written fact: Scholars are divided on what form *Beowulf* took when it was created. The poem might have been told for centuries in various versions by different poets and singers, in which case, it was written down later and Christian elements were added in. Or, it might have been written by Christian monks to begin with, and made to sound more pagan, in imitation of those older epic poems that no longer survive. No one is quite sure.

THE RIDDLES OF THE EXETER BOOK

Another priceless Anglo-Saxon manuscript is the *Exeter Book*, which was written by Benedictine monks in the later tenth century. It is a treasure trove of Old English poems (including *Widsith*), and also a large collection of riddles. These great little brain teasers must have been just as fun for the people of the time as they are now. Maybe the monks enjoyed trying to stump each other with them! They often are written in first person, and may describe themselves in cryptic ways, ending with the phrase, "say what I am called," or a similar request. Most scholars see this as proof that they were intended to be spoken aloud and were meant for entertainment.

The concept of the riddles being a party game is further suggested by the fact that they are written in Old English, the everyday language of the time, rather than Latin (though Latin riddles from the time also exist). In addition, these riddles do not have answers provided, meaning that they might have been commonly known, or they were deliberately intended to keep people puzzled. This has been a bit of a problem for modern scholar, to say the least, since they have had to tease out some of the answers by making educated guesses. There are some riddles that we still aren't quite sure what the answer is!

The subjects are often religious, but not always. Some are commonplace, some could even be read as dirty jokes if you know the correct answer. Some are very long, but here is a nice short example to give you an idea of how tricky they can be, first in Old English, and then in modern English.

Ic þa wiht geseah | on weg feran;

heo wæs wrætlice | wundrum gegierwed.

Wundor wearð on wege; | wæter wearð to bane.

I saw a creature wandering the way:

She was devastating – beautifully adorned.

On the wave a miracle: water turned to bone.

What's the answer?

Riddle-me-this fact: An iceberg! If you think about it, an iceberg is white and could indeed look like "water turned to bone." You can see how clever these riddles are!

ANGLO-SAXON AND VIKING FOOD AND DRINK

You might think that the foods of the Anglo-Saxons and Vikings must have been pretty boring, and while it's true that their meal-time options weren't as diverse as those peoples in the south, both groups whipped up some pretty interesting dishes. Piecing together exactly what people ate in this time is a little trickier, since there were no cookbooks, no manuscripts like *Ragnar's Recipes*, *Frigg's Fritters*, *Æthelstan's Apples*, or *Wulf's Waffles* (and no, Alfred's scorched wheat cakes—which probably never even happened—is not a recipe!). What we do know can be teased out by archaeology and written accounts of what people ate.

Bread: These loaves weren't the nice, soft kind that we get today. Since wheat was a luxury (or nonexistent), bread was usually made from barley, oats, and/or mashed peas, with wild yeast, and it tended to be thick and stodgy. Also, these loaves usually had grit in them thanks to the grains being ground down by stones. This grit tended to wear down people's teeth over time and settle in their stomachs, making the thought of these crude loaves even tougher for the modern epicure to swallow.

Legumes: Beans of various kinds and peas were common, as they grew well in England's unpredictable weather. Of course, these tended to make people gassy, a reality that was the subject of much humor, as well as condemnation by churchmen, who sometimes saw flatulence as a sign of the devil!

Vegetables: Leeks, onions, garlic, carrots, turnips, cabbage, and lettuces were all pretty common. Not the most exciting foods in the world, but they were filling for the poor, and provided necessary vitamins. Again, many of these veggies were known for their gas-producing tendencies, meaning the north of England was far from sweet smelling around dinnertime.

Fruits: Apples, pears, and berries were the most readily available, and really the only source (other than honey) of anything sweet.

Meats: Meat was something of a luxury, but cows, pigs, sheep, and chickens were all common enough animals in England. One's wealth could even be measured in terms of how many cattle one owned. Back in Scandinavia, the Norse would sometimes eat animals like moose, seal, whale, and even polar bear! Of course, they didn't have access to such delicacies when they moved to England.

Mead: Probably the most important drink in the Anglo-Saxon and Viking world was mead, an alcoholic drink made from honey. It could be sweet or dry, and was highly valued by kings and the gods themselves, though common people probably tasted it only rarely, if ever. Mead was so important that it even provided the name for the spaces where feasting and entertaining would occur: the mead hall.

> **Missing foods fact:** There were no tomatoes, potatoes, bell peppers, or pumpkins in England during this era. These were all from the New World, and wouldn't be brought back to Europe until the fifteenth and sixteenth centuries. Citrus fruits like oranges were known in the Middle East at the time, but they would have been fabulously expensive to import, and even the wealthiest kings and nobles probably never tasted them. The same was true of sugar. Also, sorry to say, there was no coffee, tea, or (worst of all) chocolate!

THE REAL MACBETH

"**B**ubble, bubble, toil, and trouble ..."

The three witches in Shakespeare's *Macbeth* immediately set the tone for the darkness of the play. The story of a Scottish nobleman tempted by power and egged on by his wife to commit murder and other foul deeds is well known and is a warning about becoming consumed by ambition. The play is filled with treachery, plotting, murder, counterplotting, violence, and intrigue ... you know, the good stuff! Shakespeare's audiences loved it, but it gained a reputation for being cursed fairly early on. One legend says that the young actor who played Lady Macbeth died during the first run (boys played the roles of women at the time), and his ghost has haunted every production after. Throughout the centuries, there have been stories of bad luck visiting performers in the play, many of whom have been injured on set. One is not even supposed to say the play's name in a theater (instead, one should refer to it as "the Scottish play") unless the play is being produced and/or rehearsed. Otherwise, the person uttering the offending word must complete some cleansing ritual, such as going outside, spinning around counterclockwise three times, and then knocking and asking to be allowed to re-enter the building.

All of this makes for great stories, but what does any of it have to do with the real Macbeth? Very little, sorry to say. Mac Bethad mac Findláich, as he was known, was born in central Scotland around 1005, making him a contemporary of the kings of England, Æthelred the Unready, and Cnut. He was the grandson of King Malcolm II of Scotland through his mother, Doada. His father, Findláich MacRuaridh, was the *mormaer* (earl) of Moray, a region in the north of Scotland. So Mac Bethad was positioned to become king himself, though others stood in his way and had no intention of letting him get that far. Indeed, when he was about fifteen, Mac Bethad's cousins

Malcolm and Gillecomgain killed his father, possibly as a harbinger of things to come.

But Mac Bethad didn't let that stop him. Malcom II died in November,1034, and his son Duncan was elected as king. Duncan ruled for six years, but wasn't all that good at it—he seemed to be most concerned with the awesomeness of being king. Eventually, Mac Bethad and others had enough, defeating Duncan's army and killing him in August 1040. Mac Bethad then proceeded to have himself crowned king of Scotland. No witches, no assassinations, no evil wife urging him on, just a typical medieval warrior doing warrior things.

Mac Bethad ruled for the next seventeen years, and was known as a fair and just king who made several reforms to help improve the status of women, among other important changes. He wasn't a tyrant, and seems to have been well liked. Things went well until the 1050s, when trouble reared its head in the form of Duncan's son, Malcolm MacDuncan, who obviously wanted revenge and felt that the throne belonged to him. Rallying his own supporters, he fought Mac Bethad for several years. The two sides battled evenly until August 1057, when Mac Bethad was finally killed near Aberdeen. His stepson, Lulach, succeeded him on the throne, but Lulach was a marked man, and his reign stood no chance. Only seven months later, Malcolm's forces killed him and Malcolm was finally able to take the throne. So there's the real intrigue and murder!

> Bad history fact: Shakespeare's *Macbeth* is based in part on information from a book called *Holinshed's Chronicles*, published in 1587. Obviously, it was a great story, but had nothing to do with real history!

LADY GODIVA: THE NAKED TRUTH

The name "Godgyfu" is probably not one that you would recognize right away, but of course, it's simply the Old English spelling of Godiva, which is itself a Latin Spelling. Godgyfu (pronounced "Godyeevuh") was a wealthy noblewoman who lived in the tenth and eleventh centuries. She was married to Leofric, Earl of Mercia, and they had nine (!) children. Both were said to be generous donors of wealth and property to the church.

Born in 990, Godgyfu lived for a long time, dying sometime between 1066 (the year of the Norman conquest of England) and 1086, which seems like quite a span, but it shows just how uncertain records of the time can be! Still, she is mentioned in William the Conqueror's Domesday Book as one of the few English nobles that still owned a significant amount of land after the conquest, and the only woman to do so. So clearly, Godgyfu was important in her time.

Of course, it's her famous horse ride that is remembered today. It is said that when Godgyfu was young and beautiful, Leofric was taxing the people of the village of Coventry unfairly. According to legend, Godgyfu asked him to lower their taxes, and he agreed, but only if she rode on a horse through town, naked except for her long hair. He obviously was trying to get her to change her mind, and perhaps teasing her a little for his own amusement. To his shock, of course, she did just as she was asked—after ordering all of the locals to stay inside. Leofric had no choice but to stand by his word.

This legend is almost certainly fiction, since it doesn't appear in any record before the thirteenth century. Godgyfu, who was said to be a very religious woman, likely wouldn't have resorted to such an extreme act of protest. Furthermore, while Coventry is often portrayed as a decent-sized town in art and versions of the stories, it was a small village at the time, not large enough for either Leofric or Godgyfu to get so worked up over. But the tale remains a popular one, and has been immortalized in countless paintings and sculptures.

Tom-foolery fact: Despite Godiva ordering the people of Coventry to remain indoors as she rode through the village, an eighteenth-century addition to the legend says that one man named Thomas couldn't resist a quick glance, and decided to peer out of his window as she rode by. Becoming known to history as "Peeping Tom," it was said in some versions of the story that he was struck blind for his insolence and rudeness, so let that be a lesson to all of you potential Peeping Toms!

HAROLD GODWINSON: LEGITIMATE KING OR NOT? HARALD HARDRADA: THE LAST VIKING?

By the notorious year 1066, England was once again a mess. The old king, Edward the Confessor, had died without any children. This wasn't always a problem, but in this case, there had been serious questions about who should rule after him. Two different men claimed that Edward had left them the crown: Harold Godwinson and William, Duke of Normandy. Historians have knocked the question of who Edward really chose back and forth many times, but it seems like he did indeed choose William, at least at first, and Harold was either lying, or somehow got the king to change his mind in his last days. Either way, there was bound to be a fight, since Harold had himself crowned king right after Edward's death, and naturally, William was furious about it.

It was pretty obvious that William wasn't going to just let it go, and rumors of his planned invasion began circulating in England. But summer came and went, the bad weather arrived, and there was no sign of a Norman fleet. Some people began to relax. That was until they heard about a Norse invasion in the north. King Harald Hardrada of Norway had chosen September 1066 to invade, so Godwinson had no choice but to march his English army north and try to put a stop to it.

Hardrada lived an amazing life, having served as a member of the Byzantine emperor's elite Varangian Guard in Constantinople, and fought battles throughout the eastern Mediterranean. He later returned home to become king of Norway. Though he is sometimes called the "last Viking," he really wasn't a Viking at all. Being a Viking was a job, not an ethnicity or nationality. Hardrada wasn't a pirate, and he had his eyes on England in order to rule it, not simply to plunder it and then sail away. So no, Hardrada wasn't the last Viking, but he was the last real threat to England from Scandinavia. Of course, the Normans were descended from the Vikings, but by the eleventh century, they had little in common culturally with their ancestors.

Hardrada allied himself with Tostig Godwinson, a brother of Harold's that he had banished. Tostig found his way to Hardrada's court in Norway, and persuaded him that he had a claim to the English throne. Hardrada's army sailed to England and then up the Humber River, meeting Harold's men at Stamford Bridge in Yorkshire. The Anglo-Saxon army destroyed the Norse forces, and both Hardrada and Tostig were killed on September 25, 1066. Harold celebrated the victory—until he got word that William was setting sailing for England just then!

Godwinson's army was exhausted, but they marched all the way down to southern England in a matter of days, and prepared to meet the Normans at the now-legendary site of Hastings on October 14. The amazing thing is, the Anglo-Saxons had the high ground on a hill, and the battle went badly for the Normans at first. It looked like Harold might just pull off a miraculous victory and remain king. But fate and William's determination won out. By the end of the day, the Normans had overpowered the English forces, and Harold was dead. Anglo-Saxon England had come to an end.

Excruciating fact: According to legend, Harold was killed when he was shot through the eye by an arrow, an event that seems to be recorded on the famous Bayeux Tapestry. However, more recent research suggests that this tapestry image might have been a Victorian "restoration" and was not there originally. Harold most definitely died, though!

CHAPTER 4

THE MIDDLE AGES

(1066 TO 1485)

WILLIAM THE CONQUEROR, HASTINGS, AND ALL THAT

The year 1066 is a date that everyone knows, even if they don't know much about it. In October of that year, William, Duke of Normandy, sailed across the English Channel with his Norman forces and met with the Anglo-Saxon forces of Harold Godwinson at Hastings. William's forces won and Harold was killed, bringing an end to Anglo-Saxon rule in England. William installed himself as King William I two months later in London, but he would ever after be known as "William the Conqueror."

As mentioned in the previous chapter, William himself was a descendant of Vikings who had settled in Normandy a few centuries before his birth, but there was nothing "Norse" about him or the Normans by that point. They had been completely "Francified," and brought a new, more continental form of governance and culture to England. William started handing out tracts of land to his most loyal nobles, taking them away from the Englishmen who held them. William also began replacing the English clergy with French churchmen, leaving no doubt that he intended to bring England into his cultural sphere. He brought the Norman practice of building castles to England, which were used to keep watch over lands and send a message about who was in control. At first, these fortresses were made of wood, but soon they were being constructed out of stone, eventually becoming the classic medieval castles that England is still so famous for.

French was the new language of the courts, and English was discarded. Some historians say that the English language survived rather than developed during those years, but it did begin to incorporate words that would change it into the diverse language that we use today.

Needless to say, a lot of the English weren't at all happy about this change in management, and rebellions broke out in various parts of the country. But William was able to suppress them all. In some cases, he took horrifying revenge, such as with the "Harrying of the North" in 1069-70. William's knights put down a rebellion in Yorkshire and the surrounding areas, and completely destroyed the region, burning villages and crops, killing people and farm animals, and ruining the land. Tens of thousands of people are believed to have died in the famine that followed. This scorched-earth policy was meant to send a powerful message about who was in control. It worked.

There were other rebellions over the next few years, but nothing as organized as the one that William had squelched so brutally in the north. His response told the people that the Normans weren't going anywhere. And they never did.

> New governing fact: While the Normans were brutal in forcing their new regime on the English people, William did bring about some surprising new reforms to English law. He abolished the death penalty (though it was later brought back by his son, Henry I), and also outlawed slavery, both of which were common in Anglo-Saxon times. But this was too little, too late for most of the English, and "living under the Norman yoke" became a common way to describe life in the country during the decades that followed.

WESTMINSTER ABBEY

Perhaps the most "British" of all of the nation's cathedrals (though Canterbury and York might have something to say about that!), Westminster Abbey has stood in various forms for centuries, being the place where every monarch since William the Conqueror (except Edward V and Edward VIII) has been crowned. Its burials include a veritable who's who of British history, with everyone from Henry VII and Elizabeth I to Geoffrey Chaucer, Isaac Newton, George Frederick Handel, Charles Dickens, and Charles Darwin being interred there.

The history of the building dates to about the 960s, when a group of Benedictine monks took up residence on the site of the abbey with royal support. By the 1040s, King Edward the Confessor wanted to rebuild this abbey to make it suitable as a royal burial site. The new abbey was consecrated on December 28, 1065, just one week before Edward died. He was buried there, the first of many monarchs to come. Edward was devoutly religious, and if you recall, the controversy over who he named as his heir led to the Norman invasion later that year, forever changing the nation.

In order to press the legitimacy of his claim for conquering England and to prove that Edward had named him as successor, William the Conqueror had himself crowned in the abbey on Christmas Day, 1066, and all monarchs (except for the two mentioned above) that came after him would also do so, right up to and including Elizabeth II. But curiously, no Norman or Plantagenet kings were buried in the abbey until Henry III in the thirteenth century. Henry III was deeply devoted to Edward the Confessor as a saint, and construction on the abbey as it stands today was begun during his reign, with additions being added in the fourteenth century.

Given that the abbey and the palace at Westminster sat right next to each other, they were inextricably linked over the centuries, though the monks there rarely received special treatment, even though the abbot was later allowed to take his place in the House of Lords. During the Dissolution of the Monasteries by Henry VIII (see page 146), the monks were dispersed, but Henry kept the building as a royal cathedral, saving it from ruin. Still, the abbey suffered some damage at the hands of the Puritans during the civil war of the seventeenth century.

The towers were actually built in the eighteenth century in gothic revival style, and somehow, the abbey suffered relatively minor damage during the Blitz in World War II. The abbey remains the setting for royal weddings, such as that of Prince Charles and Lady Diana, and most recently has been a part of Queen Elizabeth II's platinum jubilee celebration. With the love and care lavished on the building, it might just last another 1,000 years!

Portal fact: Westminster Abbey contains what is believed to be the oldest door in Britain, a wooden door that leads to the Chapter House. Tests showed that the wood for the door was felled in 1032, and that it was used for the door in the 1050s. It's hard to imagine how many people must have gone through it over the last 1,000 years!

THE TOWER OF LONDON

It has a grim reputation as the final waiting place before meeting an executioner's axe. The Tower of London has sat beside the Thames since the late eleventh century, a symbol of royal power and justice. People spent their last days in the Tower before meeting their maker, knowing that once they went in, they were very unlikely to come out again. And yet, some nobles who were held there over the centuries lived in relative comfort for weeks or months on end (under what was essentially house arrest), and were eventually released. So, what is the Tower, and why was it built?

The Tower site was chosen by William shortly after his conquest in 1066. By 1078, building began on the White Tower, the oldest part that still survives in some form. It was probably completed by 1087, and sat by the Thames, overlooking the surrounding lands. Unlike a lot of early Norman fortresses, which were built of wood, the Tower was built (or maybe rebuilt over the next few years) of stone. Indeed, it's the longest surviving stone keep in England. It was meant as a symbol of William's power, and to let the Anglo-Saxon people know that they had been conquered (he never stopped reminding them). William II ordered a wall to be built around the Tower in 1097, probably for extra protection; a whole lot of people were still pretty unhappy with being subject to a foreigner, after all!

But it wasn't meant to be a prison, or a torture chamber. It was actually a royal residence, and for centuries, kings lived lavishly within its walls. The prison portion of the complex was only one part of the structure. The "tower" is actually several buildings with two sets of walls, and a moat (now drained).

During the reigns of Richard I, Henry III, and Edward I, the Tower was expanded into a true royal residence. It has also served many other purposes over the centuries, including being an armory, a zoo (seriously!), a treasury, the Royal Mint, and the home of the crown jewels. And while it has a grim reputation due to the executions that occurred within, this was less the case before the sixteenth century, when it was more seen as a prison. Amazingly, only seven people were executed inside of its walls before the twentieth century, though a whole lot more met their ends outside on nearby Tower Hill.

Initially, it also served as a refuge for Jews, who were brought over by the Normans and offered protection. When antisemitic attitudes broke out at various points over the next 200 years, the Jewish residents of London were safeguarded in the Tower. But in 1290, King Edward I ordered them all expelled from England; the Jews would have no safety in the keep from then on.

The Tower saw its share of violence over the next few hundred years, including sieges and political intrigue, but it remained a crucial structure in the history of the British monarchy right up until the mid-twentieth century. Of course, it's now open to the public as a museum.

> **Corvid support fact:** The Tower is famous for its population of ravens, who are cared for by the Raven Master. Ravens have been associated with the area possibly as far back as Celtic times. A legend (which might have

been invented in Victorian times) says that if the ravens ever leave the Tower, the crown will fall soon after, and Britain with it.

LONDON BRIDGE

Want to know the truth? Scholars are not exactly sure when the famed "falling down" of London Bridge might have happened. So, what's the story behind this world-famous bridge?

Bridges across the Thames in the London area have been pretty common over the last 2,000-plus years. The Romans probably built some bridges in the area to make crossing much easier, and to move troops and goods over the river. In fact, a bridge of some kind was probably there before the Roman town of Londinium grew up around it. After the Roman period, London and its surroundings fell into ruins, and any bridge or bridges likely collapsed as well.

The Thames ended up being a border between the two Saxon kingdoms of Wessex and Mercia, and bridges connecting the two weren't high on the priority list, though Alfred might have ordered some kind of bridge to be built in the area. By 1016, there was definitely a bridge connecting the two banks in London. William the Conqueror rebuilt it again, as did other kings, always trying to improve on it, though it was always constructed out of wood, and therefore subject to fire and collapse.

Henry II commissioned a new stone bridge to be built. It was to be on a larger scale and in its center was a chapel dedicated to Thomas Becket (more about Henry and Thomas in a bit). This was often the starting point for pilgrims wending their way to Canterbury Cathedral. Work on the bridge started in 1176, but wasn't finished until the reign of King John, in 1209. From then, it became the classic London Bridge of history and legend.

One of the most famous features of the bridge were the houses that lined it. The ground floor of each home was almost always a shop, with rooms for living above. These houses extended out over the Thames in a feat of amazing, if nerve-wracking, engineering. At its height in the late fourteenth century, there were something like 140 houses on the bridge, and the bridge itself was one of the busiest shopping precincts in London (even though it wasn't technically in London). The bridge survived over the centuries, including the fire of 1666, but by the end of the eighteenth century, planners knew that it was time to construct a new bridge. This New London Bridge was completed in 1831, and the old one was, sadly, demolished, having lasted far longer than anyone could have imagined based on those that preceded it. But by the early twentieth century it was clear the new bridge was sinking and also needed to be replaced.

In the 1960s, the London city council hit on the idea of selling the bridge to raise money. Amazingly, this plan worked and it was bought in 1968 by Robert P. McCulloch for nearly $2.5 million. The bridge was dismantled brick by brick and shipped to the United States, where it was taken to Lake Havasu City, Arizona, and rebuilt. It's still there. Another London Bridge was built between 1967 and 1972, though many might say it's not all that impressive to look at.

Mistaken identity fact: Many people think that the Victorian neogothic bridge near the Tower of London is London Bridge, but it's not. It has the rather uninspired name of "Tower Bridge."

WILLIAM RUFUS: A MURDER MYSTERY?

O n a summer day—August 2, 1100, to be exact—King William Rufus (William II) was out hunting on horseback in New Forest, a wilderness in southern England. New Forest was a piece of land newly set up for use by the king and his people only. With William were various nobles, including one Sir Walter Tyrell, and William's younger brother, Henry. The group was not having the best time of it, and it was about to get much worse for the most important member of the party.

William and Tyrell went off chasing a deer. William took a shot with an arrow, but missed and asked Tyrell to give it a go. The knight did so, but missed, and his arrow struck William in the chest. William tried to pull it out, but this only made things worse, and he was soon dead. Tyrell insisted that it was a tragic accident.

So, what really happened?

Well, Henry was very unconcerned by his older brother's death. So much so that instead of taking care of his brother's body or calling for help, he rode off to the city of Winchester, claimed the crown for himself, and secured the royal treasury in the city. Three days later, he was the new king. Not suspicious at all, right? William's body was just left in the forest and found a few days later by a peasant, who put it on his cart and took it to Winchester. William was buried without much fuss, suggesting that everyone just wanted to forget about the whole thing.

Tyrell fled to France, but interestingly, some historians don't think he was the killer. They have suggested that another (possibly French) assassin was probably lying in wait for William, and shot the fatal arrow. The other nobles who had been in the hunting party immediately declared their support for their new king, Henry I, and everything just kind of went on as before.

But what *really* happened? Well, 900 years later, we can't know for sure, but William Rufus definitely had enemies, as he was in the habit of starting wars. He also seemed to have no interest in fathering children to produce an heir to the throne. He and his older brother, Robert, were often at odds. William the Conqueror had given Robert the lands of Normandy in France, and gave William England. The older William clearly thought that Normandy was the better prize, but Robert probably also wanted to be a king, and the youngest son, Henry, certainly did. William Rufus was also keen to invade France, while Henry couldn't be bothered with such an ambitious endeavor. So, did the French conspire with some of William's nobles to do him in? It seems possible, but again, being so far back in time now, we'll probably never know for sure. It does seem pretty likely that it wasn't just a case of, "Oops! Sorry about that!"

Whatever happened, Henry took the throne, an act that would come to change English history forever.

Getting a-head fact: William's bones are buried in Winchester Cathedral, but his skull seems to be missing!

MATILDA, STEPHEN, AND THE ANARCHY

Matilda (1102-1167) was the daughter of King Henry I (the fourth son of none other than William the Conqueror). She ended up marrying the Holy Roman Emperor, Henry V, in Germany (not to be confused with England's King Henry V). As such, she took the title "Empress," though after Henry died in 1125, she married (or more accurately, was married off to) Geoffrey Plantagenet, the Count of

Anjou. So, on paper, Matilda was well settled and she never had to worry about anything again, right?

Well, there was a minor complication. Her brother (and heir to the English throne) William Adelin died in a shipwreck while sailing back from France to England, in November 1120. The ship sank at the start of the short journey across the English Channel after hitting a rock, and everyone on board, save one person, drowned. This left Matilda as Henry I's sole heir, which sent England into a great confusion about who would inherit the crown. Matilda (who was also called Maude) claimed the throne, and her father supported this, but Norman law didn't allow for a woman to rule. What to do?

Her cousin, Stephen of Blois, wanted to be king, and claimed that Henry had changed his mind about Matilda inheriting the throne on his deathbed in 1135; how convenient. And who did Henry I prefer? Why, Stephen of course! And naturally, the Norman barons backed Stephen, since the idea of a woman ruling on her own was beyond their limited comprehension. But to her credit, Matilda refused to back down. Her father had nominated her, and she was quite certain he wasn't capable of changing his mind.

Thus, two factions formed and the two rival monarchs went to war, battling from the 1130s to the 1150s, a time known as "The Anarchy." They battled back and forth, and Matilda was captured more than once, but always managed to escape. Stephen himself was captured once, but let go, as was Matilda on another occasion. Obviously, the warring cousins were either too chivalrous, or they weren't very good at strategy.

Matilda's problem was that she wasn't as popular as Stephen; she was arrogant and demanding, unwilling to compromise, and those around her found her difficult to deal with. She was never able to rally the people to her side as well as Stephen could. In 1153, she agreed to give up her claim to the throne, but only if her son by Geoffrey—another Henry—could inherit it. Stephen agreed to these terms in what became known as the Treaty of Westminster. Ultimately, Stephen died just a year later, and Henry was crowned. He went on to become the legendary King Henry II (see the next entry), the first of the Plantagenet kings that would rule as a dynasty for more than 200 years. So, even though she was deprived of her birthright, Matilda had the last laugh, and managed to live until 1167!

> **Drunk and sunk fact:** Young William Adelin was returning to England after a military victory over the French, and his friends and other family were celebrating by drinking on the so-called "White Ship" as they crossed the Channel. This widespread inebriation likely led to the ship careening into a rock in the bay and breaking apart. The revelers were probably too intoxicated to even know what to do, though William did try to rescue his half-sister. It is said that after this tragedy, Henry I never smiled again.

HENRY II,
RULER OF AN EMPIRE

King Henry II (1133-89) was the great grandson of William the Conqueror, married to Eleanor of Aquitaine, and the father of two English kings, Richard I and John. He came to the throne as a result of an agreement between his mother Matilda and King Stephen (see the previous entry), which ended the miserable civil war the nation was locked in for nearly twenty years. With all of these other famous people around him, Henry himself can sometimes get a bit lost in the crowd. But he was an important king at a critical time in England's history, ruling lands from Scotland to the border of Spain. In fact, he ruled more of France than the French did!

Henry faced a divided and broken kingdom when he became king at the young age of 21, but he rose to the challenge and quickly started to repair the damage. Opposing forces in the civil war had built a number of castles to solidify their positions, but Henry had them torn down and made it law that no new castles could be built without royal permission. Keen to consolidate his power, Henry introduced new courts and judges that were answerable to him, whereas before, many of these institutions and authorities had been under the eye of the church. Of course, this move didn't please some churchmen! But it laid the foundations for English Common Law, the principles of which are still in force today.

Henry certainly made enemies, not only with rival nobles and the church, but even his own family. His most notorious conflict was with Thomas Becket, the Archbishop of Canterbury, during the 1160s and '70s (more on him in the next entry), a quarrel that eventually led to Becket's murder in Canterbury Cathedral in December 1170. Did Henry order him to be killed? Historians are still debating that, but a lot of people have believed that to be the case, then and now. Becket's death set off a crisis in the realm that took a long time for Henry to repair. Still worse, his own sons began to rebel against him in 1173.

Henry had intended to split his vast lands among his sons, but his oldest son, known as "Henry the Young King," (who co-ruled with him) objected to having the kingdom partitioned, a move that could potentially weaken its strength (you have to admit, he had a point). You know what royal siblings are like; if one gets too much, the others get envious and soon they're fighting amongst each other! Younger brother Richard joined in the revolt, along with some barons, and they had support from the Kings of Scotland and France. Worst of all, Henry's wife, Eleanor of Aquitaine (for more on her, see page 101) also joined the rebellion, which must have been the most painful betrayal. But they all underestimated Henry, who fought back and little by little reasserted his dominance until the rebellion was broken after a year. For her role, Eleanor was detained under house arrest for the next eleven years. Henry had shown his family, his kingdom, and all of Europe that he was not to be trifled with!

But alas, things continued not to go well for Henry, though he survived and struggled on. Henry the Young King died in 1183 after more squabbling with both Henry II and Richard, leaving the latter as the new heir to the throne. Henry's sons had wanted to keep his empire from being divided, but in their recklessness, they commenced the process of tearing it apart. Even his favorite son, John, joined in rebellion against him, which crushed Henry. He died on July 6, 1189, broken-hearted and bitter, his amazing accomplishments overshadowed by a never-ending family feud.

> Humiliating fact: After Becket's murder, Henry had no choice but to submit to the pope and ask for forgiveness. For his penance, he had to go to Canterbury Cathedral, dress in sackcloth, and allow the monks there to whip him. His attempts to dominate the church became less forceful moving forward, though he still tried to assert his own authority where he could.

THE MURDER OF THOMAS BECKET

By any account, Becket (1119/20-70) was an enigma. He seemed to live two completely different lives, one before he became Archbishop of Canterbury, and one after. And these two different personalities caused nothing but trouble for Henry II, who at one time had been his biggest supporter. So, what caused a rift between these two incredibly powerful men, and how did it change English history forever?

Becket was the intelligent and hardworking son of a merchant. As a young man he was a clerk to Theobald, the Archbishop of Canterbury, and in 1155, Theobald suggested that Henry II appoint him as Chancellor of England. Becket and the king became fast friends due to their similar ideas about government. They ate and drank, hunted, and played chess together, and set about reforming England's laws. One of Henry's concerns was that priests and other members of the clergy could pretty much do whatever they wanted and not be tried in a secular court; they were always tried in ecclesiastical courts, and often got away with whatever crime they'd committed. Henry wanted to do away with this practice and bring the clergy under his control. Becket seemed to agree with this perspective.

When Theobald died in 1161, Henry saw his big chance to enact his plan. He pushed for Becket to be made the new Archbishop of Canterbury and was delighted when Becket was elected to the post in May 1162. But almost immediately, Becket seemed to have some kind of religious conversion, and started taking the church's side in all things. He also adopted a much more ascetic lifestyle, drinking nothing but water and eating bland food. Henry felt betrayed, and grew increasingly furious as Becket set about undoing everything they had worked for. Things boiled over in 1164, when Becket refused to go along with the king's new proposals, and he was convicted of contempt for royal authority. Becket fled to France and stayed there until 1170, when negotiators were able to mend things well enough for him to return to England. But that didn't stop Becket. Almost immediately, he went right back to being a pain in Henry's backside.

Henry was at his wit's end, and wanted something to be done. It's said that he complained about Becket out loud to his advisors. The most famous version of his gripe is, "Will no one rid me of this turbulent priest?" though that's probably a slick translation of what he actually said. In any case, four knights took it upon themselves to do just that. Whether Henry knew about it or not, they went to Canterbury Cathedral on December 29, 1170.

Finding Thomas in the cathedral, they tried to arrest him, but he refused to go. The knights left and retrieved their swords and when they re-entered the cathedral and found Becket, they stabbed him to death. One knight sliced off a part of the back of his skull, and some of his brains spilled out onto the floor (yuck!). As the news spread, all of Europe was shocked and many began to brand Becket as a martyr. Henry was certainly unhappy with what had happened, though he made no effort to arrest the murderous knights, who fled north to the small Yorkshire town of Knaresborough. In 1172, Henry negotiated a peace with the pope and vowed to be more nuanced when negotiating future power struggles with the church.

Tales of Canterbury fact: After Becket was canonized as a saint in 1173, Canterbury Cathedral became a major center for medieval pilgrims, not only from Britain but beyond. Claims of miraculous cures and healings abounded following these pilgrimages, so people increasingly began making long journeys on foot to go to Becket's shrine. Chaucer's *Canterbury Tales*, of course, follows a group of pilgrims on their way from London to Canterbury, who agree to tell each other stories along the way to pass the time (more on them in a later entry). Canterbury Cathedral remained a place of pilgrimage until the sixteenth-century Reformation, when during Henry VIII's reign in 1538, reformers destroyed the shrine and Becket's bones.

ELEANOR OF AQUITAINE

E leanor of Aquitaine (1122-1204) is arguably one of the most famous women in history. Though not English (she was thoroughly French), Eleanor was married (at different times, obviously!) to both the King of France (Louis VII), and the King of England (Henry II). She was Queen of France from 1137 to 1152 and then Queen of

England from 1154 to 1189; that alone is quite an accomplishment!

She was the daughter of William X, Duke of Aquitaine, and was raised in a brilliant court that celebrated art, poetry, and learning. She was highly educated and in time would become a patron to many poets and troubadours. William died in 1137, along with Eleanor's brother, which meant that she inherited vast amounts of money and land, and suddenly, every monarch in Europe wanted to marry her; picture *The Bachelorette*, medieval edition! Louis VII won the prize (let's be honest, Eleanor had no say in the arrangement), and the two were married that same year. But it wasn't a particularly happy marriage.

She accompanied Louis on a crusade in 1147, the so-called Second Crusade (the First Crusade had wrested Jerusalem from Muslim control back in 1099). Unfortunately for Louis and his knights, his crusade ended in disaster for the Christian forces, which further eroded relations with Eleanor. Along the way, the couple had two daughters, but no son, so they divorced in 1152.

Wasting no time, she allied herself with Henry of Anjou and married him only a few months after divorcing Louis. As per the agreement between Matilda and Stephen, Henry was in line to become King of England, and did just that in 1154. Eleanor was now Queen of England, which was a vast domain under Henry's rule (see page 97 for more). And, unlike her marriage with Louis, the union was a fruitful one, producing five sons, including the valiant Richard and the villainous John, both of who would go on to become kings of England in their own time.

But, as in her previous marriage, she and Henry were often at odds. For many years, Eleanor helped Henry run the vast empire, but she moved away from him in 1167 to Poitiers in France, possibly because of his endless infidelities. There she established her legendary "Court of Love" where poetry, music, and literature flourished. In 1173, she sided with her son Henry in a rebellion against his father. Afterward, her estranged husband had her imprisoned in various castles for the

next eleven years. She lived in luxury, but was not free. She was then given a partial release, and freed fully when Richard came to the throne after Henry II's death in 1189. Eleanor resumed her duties in England, and even helped raise a huge ransom for Richard after he was captured while returning from the Third Crusade.

By the time her son John became king in 1199, Eleanor was very old and could not mend the numerous misfortunes caused by her son's bungling. But throughout her life, she was a force to be reckoned with, and no one who had encountered her true power wanted to cross her.

Failed crusade fact: Louis VII was seen as a weak and ineffective military leader during the Second Crusade, while Eleanor was praised for her intelligence and wisdom. This obviously didn't go over well with the king, and only added to their marital tension.

A WELSH PRINCE SAILS TO AMERICA?

Welsh Prince Madog ab Owain Gwynedd, commonly known as Madoc, did something incredible in about 1170, at least according to some legends: he sailed to North America. Not only did he go and then return, he took a good number of folks with him, who reportedly settled as colonists in the New World, centuries before that term came to be.

The story presents Madoc as the son of the great Owain, king of Gwynedd. When Owain died in 1170, his sons and family began to fight over who would succeed him. Madoc and his brother Rhiryd wanted no part of the struggle, and, perhaps out of fear for their lives, they and a band of followers set off from Wales to explore the great ocean to the west. They sailed far and eventually discovered a vast and abundant land, where the group of men, women, and children decided to stay and start a new life. At some point, Madoc returned to Wales and convinced more than 100 people to join them. They went west again and never returned.

Legends later claimed that the group explored the Americas, and might have landed anywhere from Nova Scotia and Florida to the Yucatan, Panama, or the mouth of the Amazon River. It's a fantastic story, but is there any evidence for it? Well, the tale might have existed in the Middle Ages, but the earliest surviving versions date from the late fifteenth century. The story became better known in the sixteenth century, when Humphrey Llwyd published his book, *Cronica Walliae*. The idea that the Welsh had already been to America and set up colonies was appealing to the Elizabethans with the Age of Exploration getting into full swing. The Tudor monarchs were Welsh, so if Welsh royalty had already established New World colonies, Queen Elizabeth I had a greater claim to portions of North America than the Spanish, who were also exploring the continent.

So, was the Madoc story just a bit of propaganda? Possibly. A Madoc story of some kind had existed for centuries, but there were no early references to him landing on a whole new continent. No archaeological evidence has been found of Madoc and his followers, but, allegedly, there were Native American legends about the group, describing how they had intermarried with the local populations, and even continued to speak Welsh. There were occasional stories that English traders and explorers in Virginia would meet with Native Americans whose languages resembled Welsh, but these claims were never really proven.

The possibility was revived again in the nineteenth century, as some historians found the story intriguing, and probably wanted to use it as proof that some sort of earlier "civilizing" had occurred among various Native American groups. They even went so far as to claim that certain peoples, such as the Cherokee, had legends of a people called "Welsh" who had settled in the area, though these claims have never been backed up with concrete evidence.

> **Plaque fact:** Plaques were once put up in various American locations (such as Georgia and Alabama) claiming that these sites were visited and/or colonized by Madoc and his people, but most of these have since been removed, owing to the lack of evidence.

RICHARD I: RARELY AT HOME

Richard the Lionheart is, for many, the essence of chivalry. In the popular imagination, Richard is known as the English king who went away on a crusade and had his kingdom stolen by his evil brother, Prince John (more on him in the next entry). As we all know, Robin Hood and his Merry Men in Sherwood Forest stood up to John and his scheming. Richard finally came back, reclaimed his throne, pardoned Robin and the other outlaws, and made everything right again.

The problem is, it didn't really happen that way. Even though there's a statue of Richard outside Parliament in London, and even though he was born in Oxford, he wasn't really interested in England as anything more than his personal bank. Richard identified far more with his French heritage. In addition to being King of England, he was also the Duke of Normandy, Duke of Aquitaine, Duke of Gascony, Count of Anjou, Count of Nantes, Overlord of Brittany, and Lord of Ireland. That's a whole lot of titles!

He preferred to be in Aquitaine in southwest France, and used taxes from England to finance his military operations, including the major outlay that was his crusade. Being the son of King Henry II and Eleanor of Aquitaine, he followed in his father's footsteps as a military leader, and in his mother's by going to the Holy Land. Richard went on crusade in 1190, but wasn't able to retake Jerusalem. He and the great Islamic leader Saladin pretty much battled to a standstill. During their struggle, they came to admire one another, and agreed to a three-year peace treaty; then Richard left.

On the way back, he was kidnapped and taken prisoner in Germany, and his mother had to come up with a huge ransom to secure Richard's release. Guess where a lot of that money came from? Exactly, English taxes! As you might imagine, the people weren't actually all that thrilled to see Richard return to England. He spent a bit of time there, fixing any messes John might have made (which probably is a source for some of the Robin Hood legend), and then went off again to fight more battles in France.

Richard continued this bellicose lifestyle until March 1199, when he was struck by a crossbow bolt while trying to take over an enemy castle known as Chalûs-Chabrol. The wound became infected and he died, but not before forgiving the young man who had shot him, insisting that he be given money and freed. But after Richard died, that same young man was skinned alive and hanged. So much for chivalry and grace!

Richard left England to John (and what a mess that became!), who started screwing things up straight off. Perhaps benefitting from comparison with his brother, Richard began to be remembered fondly for his heroism, courage, and chivalrous behavior, even if this wasn't always precisely the case.

Afterlife fact: Interestingly, in the thirteenth century, the Bishop of Rochester said that after his death, Richard spent thirty-three years in purgatory, being cleansed of his sins, and finally went to heaven in March 1232. We don't know how the bishop figured this out, but he seemed pretty confident about it.

KING JOHN:
AS BAD AS EVERYONE SAYS?

Was King John as bad as everyone says he was? The short answer is yes. The longer answer is: absolutely. The even longer answer is: yes, he was, but it helps to keep a few things in mind. King John (1166-1216) was the youngest son of Henry II, and was never meant to be king. He took the throne only because his older brother, Richard the Lionheart, died. And yet, he was Henry II's favorite son, even though he wasn't particularly good at much, and seemed to be kind of obnoxious even when he was young.

One thing he did do better than Richard, though, was stay put. While Richard wanted to be out fighting wars in France and the Holy Land, attempting to cover himself with glory (and enemy blood), John was more than happy to stay in England. He took much more of an interest in the day-to-day running of his kingdom than his late, great brother, and he did try to improve the justice system. But overall, he wasn't well-liked, and he did some really bad and foolish things, such as:

- **In his seventeen-year reign, he managed to lose almost all of the lands his father and brother held in France. He wasn't a great military leader, and his continual screw-ups made him very unpopular.**

- **He might well have ordered the murder of his young nephew, Arthur of Brittany (son of John's older brother, Geoffrey), who had a good claim to the English throne. No one can prove it, but it seems like the kind of thing John would do.**

- **He managed to get into a huge argument with the pope over who should be appointed the Archbishop of Canterbury. Eventually, the pope got tired of John, excommunicated him, and put the whole nation of England under an**

interdict, which meant that priests were not allowed to conduct religious services for anyone. This made a lot of people furious, especially when John started taking away church lands for himself.

He also made a lot of his barons very angry with his antics, so much so that they decided to create a document to rein him in, the famous Magna Carta (see the next entry). John was forced to attach his seal to this document on June 5, 1215, at a place called Runnymede, west of London. It basically gave the barons a whole bunch of rights to regulate the king as they saw fit. If John agreed to all of it, they would give him their loyalty again. Of course, this wasn't welcomed by John or his supporters, and a civil war erupted between them and the rebellious barons. Things got so bad that many barons started to support the French prince Louis, saying they would make him their new king.

Things kept getting worse for John, and by the autumn of 1216, he was dying from a stomach ailment. One last indignity happened when he apparently managed to lose the crown jewels while traveling in an area called the Wash on the eastern coast of England. The tide came in and swept a whole lot of his baggage out to sea. Not everyone agrees that he lost the jewels then, but it makes a good story and a fittingly ridiculous end to a reign that was mostly a disaster.

> Heir-y fact: John's son inherited the throne and became Henry III. Henry had his own problems, to be sure, but he managed to hang on to the crown for an incredible fifty-six years!

MAGNA CARTA

Everyone knows about the Magna Carta, or likes to think they do. Politicians in both Britain and the United States like to extoll its virtues as a founding document of "freedom" against oppressive tyrants, while a lot of everyday folks vaguely know that it has something to do with King John, the bad guy from the Robin Hood stories. But what was the "Great Charter," why was it drafted, and what makes it so important, then and now?

As we've seen, John was not exactly the nicest fellow. He screwed up constantly and managed to alienate just about everyone around him. He was one of those monarchs who insisted on his absolute right to rule, and, as we've seen, his nobles got pretty tired of it after a while. Rebellion was brewing, and the barons managed to capture London in May 1215. John had no choice but to negotiate with them, if he was to have any hope of regaining his authority, much less peace. But these barons weren't interested in conquest for conquest's sake; they came up with an idea to check their weak king and make him do their bidding: Magna Carta.

This document, written in Latin, spelled out the rights and duties of the king, the nobles, and the church in sixty-three clauses. Many of these clauses were designed to give the barons power over the king, and demand relief from excessive taxation, but one important clause is still relevant in Britain and beyond: the right to a fair trial. The clause specifically states:

"No free man shall be seized or imprisoned, or stripped of his rights or possessions, or outlawed or exiled, or deprived of his standing in any other way, nor will we proceed with force against him, or send others to do so, except by the lawful judgement of his equals or by the law of the land. To no one will we sell, to no one deny or delay right or justice."

Now, the barons were not exactly social reformers that were concerned about the welfare of the peasants, but this clause, along with the others, suited them politically. Seeing himself backed into a corner, the angry king had no choice but to agree to their terms (he didn't actually sign it, by the way; he affixed his royal seal to it). But as soon as the agreement was made, John wrote to Pope Innocent III in Rome, whining and complaining. Remember, this is the same John who pissed off the pope and had England placed under interdict, so he was clearly desperate. Happily for him, the pope agreed that Magna Carta was illegal and "shameful," and he declared it null and void forever. Of course, that's not how it worked out. With John back in the driver's seat (or so he thought), it wasn't long before a full-on civil war broke out, and John died, broken and miserable the following year.

His son, Henry III, recognized the potential value in the Magna Carta and reissued a much shorter version in 1225 as his coronation charter. The English people would gradually come to see their monarch as ruling with the consent of the governed, a wild and crazy idea that other European nations mostly laughed at. But the idea persisted until it blew up in the royals' face once again in the English Civil War of the seventeenth century.

> Donation fact: At the beginning of World War II, Winston Churchill wanted the copy of Magna Carta owned by Lincoln Cathedral to be donated to the United States in the hopes of cementing a British-American alliance. Instead, the document was stored in the safety of Fort Knox and returned to Lincoln after the war.

THE ROBIN HOOD LEGENDS

L ike King Arthur, everyone knows of Robin Hood. The stories of Robin, Little John, Marian, Friar Tuck, Will Scarlett, and the rest of this band of outlaws living in Sherwood Forest and fighting against the evil Sheriff of Nottingham are so ingrained in Western folklore that it's impossible to imagine modern culture without them. According to legend, Robin saved England from the clutches of the wicked Prince John, who ruled England cruelly while his heroic brother, King Richard I, was away on crusade, and eventually his band of Merry Men were pardoned by the king upon his return to England. It must have some basis in truth, right? Well, yes, but not in the way most people think.

We've already established that Richard was far less interested in ruling England than in using it to fund his wars, and John, while definitely not a good guy, actually took a far greater interest in England's affairs and its legal and political systems. So, even if the story were true, it's very unlikely that Richard would have known what this band of outlaws was doing in Sherwood Forest, much less cared enough to pardon them.

The earliest surviving story of Robin and company comes in an original manuscript called *Robin Hood and the Monk*. It contains some of the familiar parts of the Robin mythos, including being set in Nottingham and Robin and the sheriff being enemies. There is no Marian, but there is a lot of killing. There were mentions of Robin Hood in earlier, fourteenth-century English texts, but only in passing. Still, these brief appearances prove that the character was already a part of British folklore. In addition to Nottingham and Sherwood, there are a number of locations in Yorkshire that lay claim to various Robin Hood legends.

But did he actually exist? Maybe, in some form. One of the earliest mentions of a possible candidate comes from 1199, of a man named

Robert de Hodelme who had deserted his service to King Henry II. There is an account from York in 1226 that mentions a "Robert Hod" who became an outlaw. "Robin" was a common nickname for "Robert" and "hod" means "hood," so this seems like a good possibility. But while the man is deemed an outlaw, there is no mention of him robbing others. In the 1260s, a man named Roger Godberd was hiding out in Sherwood Forest and fighting against King Henry III. He was said to have been able to summon 100 men or more to his service if he needed them. Godberd was eventually captured and died in 1276. Roger's life seems a very likely influence on the Robin Hood stories.

It also seems that the name "Robin Hood" might have been slang for an outlaw: "He's on the run; he's a 'Robin Hood' now." The term appears in a few English legal documents in the later thirteenth century, but it is unknown whether the slang term came first and was taken up later by writers of Robin Hood stories, or if there was a Robert or Robin who was famous enough to have given his name to all outlaws.

> **Well-hidden fact:** Robin is said to be buried in a forest near the ruin of the Priory of Kirklees. A small monument marks the spot, but it's on private land and is not open to the public. In order to see it, you'll have to become an outlaw yourself!

OXFORD AND CAMBRIDGE

Two of the most revered universities in the world, and two of the oldest, Oxford and Cambridge began in the twelfth century and came into their own in the thirteenth century, though the concept of these schools at the time was not what we expect a university to be now.

Though they were centers of learning, the number of subjects was limited; you didn't go to medieval Oxford to get a degree in journalism, for example. Both universities emphasized the study of the *Trivium* (grammar, logic, and rhetoric), and the *Quadrivium* (arithmetic, music, geometry, and astronomy), which were seen as essential steps on the way to the study of theology. Indeed, the main purpose of study was for (male) students to immerse themselves in theology.

History has largely settled on 1096 as the date a group of clerics or monks gathered in the town of Oxford for learning, but an exact founding date (if there ever was one) is unknown. By 1167, students were beginning to flock to the institution, since King Henry II had forbidden them from going to Paris to study (it was part of the king's quarrel with Becket). From then on, students and masters came to the town in large numbers, and by 1231, the masters were officially recognized as a *universitas*, a kind of corporation, and, of course, where we get the word "university" from. Henry III granted the university a royal charter in 1248, and it only grew in reputation from there.

But early on, relations with the local people were not always good, the classic "town-gown" conflict. In the decades following 1167, students began to gather into colleges and halls for protection, shelters that were often organized by where students hailed from.

Students could get rowdy and obnoxious even back then, you see, and in 1209, when faced with violence, a group of Oxfordians fled east to another location: Cambridge.

That year, three Oxford scholars were hanged by the leaders of the town for allegedly murdering a woman. These leaders didn't consult the church authorities, who, of course, would never have permitted the executions to happen. Fearing for their safety, some scholars fled to Paris, while others went to a new location that was beginning to attract students and teachers because of the learning going on at Ely Cathedral: Cambridge. It's sometimes said that in Cambridge, the town is the university, and it's true. It grew as a response to the possibility of a new university, even though there had been settlements there since Roman times. Cambridge succeeded in gaining a royal charter from Henry III in 1231, seventeen years before Oxford! Thus began a rivalry between the two institutions which continues to this day.

> **Etymology facts:** "Oxford" comes from the tenth-century Old English word, *Oxnaforda*, or "where the oxen ford." Similarly, "Cambridge" comes from the eighth-century Old English word, *Grontabricc*, the "Bridge on the River Granta."

FEUDALISM AND SERFDOM: THOSE AT THE TOP AND THOSE AT THE BOTTOM

You've probably heard both of these terms bandied about when people are talking about the Middle Ages, and knowing what they mean is crucial in understanding how medieval societies were set up in the West. For the record, feudal doesn't mean "futile," and serfs were not slaves (and had nothing to do with catching the waves). As far as Britain is concerned, the Normans brought the feudal system with them in 1066, when William realized that he needed his most loyal men to govern parts of the country for him. The practice of feudalism grew over the next few centuries, becoming very much part of the fabric of English society.

Feudalism is based on a military structure. At the top of the pyramid is the king, who gives out big tracts of land. High-ranking nobles and lords then offer knights and others of lower rank a piece of that land,

or a "fief," in exchange for military service and loyalty. The knight that accepts the land becomes a vassal of the lord, who was also called a liege. The king starts the process, but it moves down the ranks, so that different nobles have different henchmen in their service in exchange for the lands those henchmen received. The big problem with this arrangement is that a vassal to a lord above him can also be a liege to someone beneath him, making the social structure very complicated! And while all of these lords and vassals are technically loyal to the king, there isn't much to stop them from going to war with each other, which means that petty conflicts and battles could (and often did) easily break out.

At the other end of the system reside the serfs. Without them, the whole system would begin to collapse, which is exactly what started to happen following the Black Death (see later in this chapter). Serfs were laborers tied to a specific piece of land. They worked for who-ever owned the land (aka the "landlord"), and were not free to go to another plot of land or noble if they didn't like their situation. This was also true for their descendants, so if your parents were serfs to a particular lord, you automatically were, too. In this way, they were little more than slaves, but serfs could own property, and could band together to improve their living conditions. They had to pay rent to their landlords in the form of crops produced in their farms, and in return that lord was supposed to offer them protection and try to make sure they didn't suffer or starve, even though they often did.

In Western Europe, serfs were most often known as *villeins*, which meant they were below knightly status. However, it also meant that they were seen as crude and beneath the upper classes. As you may have guessed, the word "villain" comes from this archaic term.

The whole system was set up to benefit the few at the top, and ensure that not much changed. And for several centuries, nothing did. But, like any restrictive system, feudalism eventually broke down. In England and Britain, war, pandemics, the rise of a new and wealthy middle class, and other factors undermined feudalism and serfdom, leading to far more economic freedom and, ultimately, a more egalitarian society.

Bad feudalism joke fact: In a democracy, it's your vote that counts. In a feudal system, it's your count that votes!

THE MEDIEVAL FEAST

In Medieval Britain, food was a very different experience for the various social classes. The poor frequently ate bland fare that also wasn't very nutritious, while the rich got to indulge in new and exciting dishes, and impress their friends and neighbors. And feasts for the wealthy were often lavish and expensive, especially at the holidays. As with modern banquets, these meals were commonly divided into courses. Three courses was typical, but there are records of as many as twenty! But instead of a salad or a soup, a main course, and a dessert, each course usually featured a mixture of meat and vegetables.

These courses could be quite elaborate, with everything from a peacock that was plucked and roasted and then had its feathers stuck back on, to a gigantic pie from which birds were released when the pastry was cut open. All kinds of imaginative dishes were served at these feasts, including weird concoctions like the cokyntryce, which was a capon (rooster) and a pig cut in half. Then the back part of the pig was sewn to the front part of the rooster (and vice versa), stuffed with other foods, and roasted. Apparently, medieval diners found this very appealing!

Musicians, acrobats, dancers, and actors were all common sights at grand feasts too, and each of them could make a pretty penny offering up entertainments. Of course, sometimes things went horribly wrong: performers caught fire, or crashed into each other, or whole sets came tumbling down!

One of the more common misbeliefs about medieval food was that people used a lot of spices to hide the terrible flavor of rotten meat. This comes from the idea that without refrigeration, meat would go bad very quickly, especially in hot weather, and so the only way to hide the offputting flavors was to pile on black pepper, cinnamon, ginger, and other spices. But this doesn't seem to be the case. Yes, meat would spoil quickly back then, but the animals were usually killed just before being prepared, so there wouldn't have been time for it to go bad. And it was common to kill a certain number of cattle as cold weather came on, and then smoke, salt, and dry the meat so that it could be eaten over the winter; basically, people made jerky. Eating rotting meat would have been just as unappealing and dangerous then as it is now.

Even more importantly, spices were not easy to come by. They were imported from faraway lands, rare, and very expensive, so that only the very wealthy could afford them. There is no way that anyone (even the most decadent people) would have dumped a heap of cinnamon or cloves on a lump of rotting meat just to make it taste better. Okay, maybe it happened once or twice, but it certainly wasn't common!

Flaming food fact: Cooked birds, pigs, and fish were sometimes made to "breathe fire" at feasts by dousing a piece of cloth in alcohol, stuffing it in an animal's mouth, and setting it on fire just before bringing it to the table!

MINSTRELS
AND MORE

You might think of minstrels as fellows in tights and pointy shoes who danced into towns strumming their lutes and singing songs about knights, true love, talking donkeys, food fights, or whatever else comes to mind. Indeed, the word "minstrel" comes from the Old French word *menestral*, meaning "entertainer" or simply, "servant." Many picture them as medieval pop stars, constantly touring. This is only kind-of, sort-of correct. Actually, it's just barely correct.

There were a good number of professional musicians throughout the Middle Ages, both in Britain and abroad. But there were definitely some types that were not common in England, most notably the troubadours. Troubadours were a class of poets and musicians who primarily lived in what is now southern France. They were often nobles or even royalty, and they were skilled poets, whose words were sometimes set to music. While it's possible a few of them ventured as far north as England at some point, it's very unlikely.

There were other kinds of musicians, such as trouvères (the northern French version of the troubadours), jongleurs (French entertainers who might perform acrobatic tricks, as well as music), minnesingers (German poet-musicians), and goliards (often student musicians who liked to sing about drinking and getting into trouble). Any or all of these types might have ended up in England at one point between the twelfth and fourteenth centuries, depending on what rich patrons they were working for.

Minstrels themselves were a big deal, especially by the fourteenth century. They would hold big gatherings (MinstrelCon 1310, perhaps?), meet old friends, swap new tunes, purchase instruments, and jam for days. They were also very popular with the English kings, especially Edward III, who hosted quite a lot of them, and paid them

handsomely. Sometimes the minstrels had to do odd things, like dance naked at Christmas celebrations, which must have been a blast in December!

Henry II had one special entertainer named Roland the Farter. It is said that each year, at the king's Christmas celebrations, Roland was required to perform *Unum saltum et siffletum et unum bumbulum*, which is Latin for "one jump and whistle and one fart." Apparently, everyone thought this was very entertaining. The king was so pleased with his *bumbulum* that he gave Roland a large house and thirty acres of land, a huge property for a commoner at the time!

> **Starving artist fact:** Minstrels were a large part of the entertainment of the time, but they always wanted to work for the rich, rather than trying to make a living among the lower classes. It could be a rough life for any musicians that didn't have a noble or royal patron backing them, and people often looked down on these struggling artists as loafers—unfortunately, musicians have been urged to get "a real job" for a long time!

ROBERT THE BRUCE: THE *REAL* BRAVEHEART

Most people, if they hear "Braveheart," will think of the Hollywood movie that racked up Oscars back in the 1990s. On the whole, the film is well-liked, but it is absolutely loathed by historians, since it's filled with so many mistakes and downright untruths. One historian pointed out that there are no less than ten errors in the first two minutes of the film! So what's wrong with it? Just about everything, from the kilts (worn backward and from the wrong time period) to the blue face paint (not worn since the time of the Picts, if at all), to the age of

William Wallace (who would have been younger) to the age of Princess Isabella (who would have been *way* younger), and dozens of other mistakes. This is too bad, because the true story of William Wallace is amazing, and didn't need a bunch of Hollywood types making up a bunch of nonsense to try (and fail) to make the story more "epic."

There's even a problem with the film's title. While the movie relates a highly fictionalized version of Wallace's life, Wallace was never known as "Braveheart." That moniker belongs to another Scotsman, a noble-man named Robert the Bruce (1274-1329), who eventually became king of Scotland and beat the English at the Battle of Bannockburn in 1314. Bruce witnessed Wallace rise up against the English and eventually be brutally executed by them (at least that part of the film is reasonably accurate!) in 1305.

While dealing with a lot of Scottish in-fighting over who was best suited for the throne of Scotland, Bruce came out on top and was crowned king on March 25, 1306. The last thing he had any intention of doing was submitting to King Edward I, or his son, Edward II, after the elder Edward died on July 7, 1307. Robert wanted Scotland to be free of any English meddling, and started a war that lasted for several years, with Bruce's forces gradually taking back more and more Scottish land.

The war came to a head in June 1314, when the two forces met at Bannockburn, a river surrounded by marshes. Robert's forces were able to catch the English off-guard and keep them from using their archers. In a very dramatic scene, an English knight on horseback, Sir Henry de Bohun, spied Robert sitting on a small horse and carrying only a battle axe. Henry decided to try and take Bruce out with a lance. He charged directly at the Scottish king—the last mistake he would ever make.

Robert waited until the last moment, stepped his horse to the side, stood up in the stirrups, and brought his axe down on Henry's helmet. The blow was so strong that it split the helmet, and poor

Henry's head, in two! Needless to say, this was quite the show of strength, and Robert's forces routed the English the following day, causing Edward II to retreat in humiliation, and establishing Scotland as a sovereign nation.

Name origin fact: After his death, Robert's heart was taken on crusade to Spain. During one battle, Sir James Douglas threw it at his enemies, shouting, "Lead on brave heart, I will follow you!" And that's where Bruce's nickname came from. The heart was later returned to Scotland, and buried at Melrose Abbey.

THE HORRID
BLACK DEATH

One afternoon in June 1348, an Englishman, Roger the Rat Catcher, didn't feel so well. He'd woken up feeling a bit off, and had gotten progressively worse as the day went on. He lived in Weymouth on the south coast of England, where some merchant ships had recently arrived. Apparently, some of the men on board also felt sick, but that wasn't too unusual. Still, something about this particular malady seemed different.

Before too long, Roger retired to bed with a fever and chills. His head began to pound and his stomach ached, maladies that were accompanied by pain in his arms and legs. Over the next few days, things got worse. Large, painful lumps that leaked pus began to grow on his neck and in his armpits. Poor Roger knew he was done for, and as he lay dying, he heard that many others in town had also come down with this mysterious sickness—including the rest of his family. A few days after he'd fallen ill, Roger died, most likely in agony.

Poor Roger is fictional, of course, but his story is exactly what happened to many people living on the south coast of England in that fateful summer of 1348. And his job gives a clue as to the source of this awful disease. What came to be known as the Black Death was actually the bubonic plague, a terrible bacterial infection carried by fleas living on rats and other rodents. These days, the disease can be treated with antibiotics (yes, the plague is still around!), but back then, there was no defense at all.

The plague had come from rats living on ships traveling to England from the Mediterranean. And before that it had come from rats on ships that had sailed to and from the Middle East. Whenever these ships docked at a new port, some rats would scurry ashore, taking their fleas with them. The fleas would then jump off the rats and onto humans, biting them to feed, and infecting them with the bacteria. This plague seems to have originated in central Asia, possibly in the thirteenth century, but upon reaching Europe in the late 1340s it began to spread like wildfire. There were different forms of it, the most common being the bubonic plague, so-called because it causes the growth of "buboes" or swollen lymph nodes in the neck and armpits. Another form that some historians think must have been present was the pneumonic plague, which was spread by coughing and sneezing, like a head cold. Given how fast the plague advanced over Europe, some of it must have been this version.

It was a pandemic of apocalyptic proportions. It's estimated that between one-third and one-half of Europe's population died between the years 1347 and 1353, when the plague finally subsided, though it would return over the following centuries in smaller outbreaks.

Social upheaval fact: The Black Death forever changed the makeup of society in Europe, transforming economics, politics, beliefs, and just about everything else. From Scandinavia to southern Italy, no region was left untouched by its death and misery, not even islands like Iceland or Britain.

THE BLOODY AND VIOLENT PEASANTS' REVOLT

E ngland, like the rest of Europe, went through a lot during the plague. With so much of the population wiped out, there were shortages of workers, food, and much more. In response to these issues and the potential chaos they could cause, some powers-that-be tried to control things like wages and who could work where. Wages were kept low, and people didn't have the freedom to take their labor where they wanted to.

To make matters worse, England was in the middle of a very long war with France, the so-called "Hundred Years' War," which actually lasted for 116 years, from 1337 to 1453, but who's counting! And of course, wars are expensive, what with paying soldiers, weapon manufacturers, armorers, and so on. And where did that money come from? As usual, from taxes—which most people couldn't afford. And with far fewer people actually alive to pay taxes, the remaining people had to pay more. The public was hit with poll taxes in 1377, 1379, and 1381, and it was the 1381 levy that was the last straw.

Many just tried to get out of paying the tax, which often didn't go so well for them. When representatives of the young King Richard II (who was only 14 years old in 1381) tried to collect taxes at several villages in southern England, people basically refused, and at the charmingly named village of Fobbing, they attacked and killed the tax collectors. Other villages heard about this and decided to join in on the fun!

Led by a man named Wat Tyler and a priest named John Ball, the anti-tax movement grew at an alarming rate, drawing the attention of the king and the church. On June 13, the rebels entered London, killed several merchants, and destroyed a palace belonging to John of Gaunt, who was the Duke of Lancaster and the young king's chief advisor (or his puppet master, some would say!). King Richard II really had no choice but to negotiate with the peasants. He met with them outside the city and promised that he would end forced labor and serfdom, and allow cheap land and more freedoms. It seemed like the rebels had won an incredible victory.

But—there's always a "but"—while the king was out of London, the rebels struck again, and got a bit too enthusiastic and too violent. They went to the Tower of London and forced the chancellor, Archbishop Simon of Sudbury, and the treasurer, Sir Robert Hales (who had created the hated Poll Tax) to come out. When they did, the mob beheaded them. Brutal, yes, but it certainly got the point across!

Richard and Tyler met again the next day, and the mayor of London killed Tyler, though the king was able to convince the remaining rebels that he would honor his promises if they went home. Of course, Richard had no intention of doing so. Over the next few weeks, the remaining rebellion was quelled by the king's soldiers and all of his promises were conveniently forgotten. So, the Peasants' Revolt wasn't the start of a great revolution, but it's worth noting that there were no more poll taxes afterward; perhaps the king made a significant concession after all.

> Unexpected outcomes fact: The labor shortage *did* eventually allow for people to charge more for their work, which led to the rise of a new English middle class in the fifteenth and sixteenth centuries.

GEOFFREY CHAUCER

C haucer (early 1340s-1400) is the greatest early English poet. Indeed, he chose to write in the English language at a time when it was still much more fashionable to write in French or even in Latin. His works helped make English a "literary" language, capable of producing masterpieces. By Chaucer's time, English had been evolving away from Old English for centuries. It had absorbed thousands of French words, and was spoken more and more by people of all social classes. But French was still the main language of the English court, so Chaucer was taking a bit of a risk writing in English for his royal patrons: Edward III, Richard II, and Henry IV.

Although remembered as a writer, Chaucer was also a civil servant and diplomat. He seems to have traveled widely, including to the continent. He worked through good times and bad, all while writing poems. And what poems they are! He might have even written some of them to distract himself from the terrible things going on all around him (such as the Peasants' Revolt). Works such as *The Parlement of Foules*, *Troilus and Criseyde*, and *The Legend of Good Women* are still read and admired to this day. But one work stands above them all as his masterpiece: *Canterbury Tales*, which he began writing in the late 1380s.

This wonderful collection tells the story of a group of pilgrims heading across southern England to visit Canterbury Cathedral and the shrine of Archbishop Thomas Becket (killed during the reign of Henry II; for more on this incident, see page 99). It was the most popular pilgrimage to take in England at the time, with thousands flocking to Canterbury each spring and summer. Chaucer's magnum opus provides a remarkable cross-section of late fourteenth century English life, fashioning vivid characters such as the Wife of Bath, the Knight, and the Miller, who told each other stories to amuse themselves during their long journey. The prize for the best story was a free meal back at the Tabard Inn at Southwark, London, where the pilgrims started from. There are twenty-four stories in all, which is only one-fifth of what Chaucer originally intended to write (120 stories). Sadly, Chaucer never finished this massive undertaking, but we're lucky to have the chunk that we do!

These tales are a mixture of pious, serious, sad, funny, and outrageously risqué, providing an amazing view into Chaucer's world and time. *The Canterbury Tales* was a hit in his social circle right from the start, and after his death, several other copies were made by hand (printing hadn't been invented yet). Within a few decades, the work achieved a kind of best-seller status, and later poets praised Chaucer as the greatest of them all. The *Tales* have continued to entertain and delight readers ever since.

Sad food fact: We have no idea who won the free dinner!

AMAZING MEDIEVAL WOMEN

U nfortunately, history has often been written by men and intended for men, and as such it's filled with all of the things manly men did for manly reasons. Of course, much of this has to do with the systematic exclusion of women from participating, or even having any say, in the world's grand events. But some medieval women rose to positions of great power, simply because they were already noble by birth, and stepped up at the right time. Here are some of the more impressive and amazing women from the medieval period. We're cheating a little by going back to the Anglo-Saxon period to start, but here are four medieval women who should be better known. Thankfully, in recent years, more studies are being made into their fascinating lives.

Queen Emma of Normandy (c. 984-1052): Emma had the distinction of being married to two kings of England, the Anglo-Saxon Æthelred the Unready and the Danish Cnut the Great. She was queen when Æthelred ruled from 1002 to 1016, though for a few months, the Danish Sweyn Forkbeard was declared king, from December 1013 to February 1014 (when he died). After Æthelred's death in 1016, Emma did the logical thing: she married Sweyn's son, Cnut, and became queen of England again! By the time Cnut died in 1035, she was queen of England, Denmark, and Norway! She outlived her second husband as well, and continued to be prominently involved in English politics until her own death in 1052.

Licoricia of Winchester (early thirteenth century-1277): This woman with the fantastic name is almost unknown now, but she was very important in the middle of the thirteenth century. A Jewish woman, Licoricia inherited her husband's business after he died in 1244, and became extremely wealthy and influential, eventually dealing with King Henry III himself. While Jews were forbidden from working in certain kinds of business, they were very important in other trades and in money lending. Henry offered Licoricia assistance and royal protection, allowing her to grow very rich. But in 1277, her daughter, Belia, found Licoricia and the family maid stabbed to death in their home. The motive was probably robbery, and while at least one man was accused, there is no record of him being brought to trial for the crime.

Julian of Norwich (c. 1342-approximately 1416): A famed English mystic, in her own time and now. Though, as you might expect, her life is shrouded in mystery—historians are not even sure if Julian was her real name. She suffered a severe illness at the age of 30, and had a series of religious visions that would make up her book, *Revelations of Divine Love*, which is the earliest known work in the English language by a woman. Julian then became an anchoress, which is to say that she lived in isolation in a small stone cell (room), attached to St. Julian's Church in the town of Norwich (and from where she probably gets her name). This may seem like an incredibly lonely life, but she used her isolation to read, write, pray, and meditate. Julian wasn't exactly a hermit, because she could receive visitors (they stayed on the other side of the wall and would talk with Julian through a window), and she had her food and other needs delivered. Her writings are still widely read, and remain highly regarded.

Mother Shipton (c. 1488-1561): Though born at the tail end of the Middle Ages, Mother Shipton is unique enough to deserve a mention here. Her real name was Ursula Southeil, and she became well-known as a prophet and soothsayer. She was said to have been born in a cave outside the Yorkshire town of Knaresborough. Ursula's father is unknown, but many would whisper that he was the devil himself! As she grew up, she became known for offering healing herbs and potions, and somehow managed to escape being persecuted as a witch. She is best known for her prophecies, some of which spoke of the turbulent times brought about by King Henry VIII. Her cave near Knaresborough is still a popular tourist attraction, and the town even has a pub named after her.

> **Educational fact:** Medieval literacy was obviously much more common among those in the upper classes and in service to the church, but even

here there was often a divide along gender/sex lines. At various times and places during the Middle Ages (in England and beyond), it's quite possible that more women were literate than men.

HENRY V AND AGINCOURT

"**W**e few, we happy few..."

Most people are familiar with the rousing speech King Henry V gives to his troops before the Battle of Agincourt, a battle which Shakespeare immortalized in his play of the same name. Hopelessly outnumbered, Henry rallies his faltering army to meet the French at a site in northern France, and, with an assist from God, scores a stunning upset that humiliates the French and proves once and for all that England is superior! Except, that's not quite what happened, of course.

What we do know is that Henry V was convinced that he had a claim to the throne of France (English kings had been claiming this for a while, to be honest). In 1415, he decided it was time to do something about it. The reigning French king, Charles VI, wasn't exactly the most stable ruler. He struggled with mental illness throughout his life, and sometimes forgot who he was, or thought he was St. George. For a time, he was afraid that he was made of glass and would shatter if anything bumped into him. Considering Charles's fragile state, Henry probably thought he had a good shot at taking the French throne.

Henry and his troops landed in northern France in August 1415 and laid siege to the city of Harfleur. While they eventually took the city in September, many English soldiers were killed or became sick during the siege. Henry decided to move his army to Calais and head for home, but he was cut off and had to take a detour. The French were waiting for him near the village of Agincourt. With no choice, Henry and his men had to fight for their lives. The French expected an easy victory, but they got a nasty surprise.

Historians argue over what the numbers of each army really were. Of course, the English like to say that the French outnumbered the English by five to one, or even more; there were allegedly up to 30,000 French and only 6,000 English. The actual numbers were probably much closer, anywhere from 5,000 to 9,000 English and 12,000 to 15,000 French. But almost everyone agrees that the English were outnumbered and underdogs. None of that mattered, though, because Henry's forces won the day and inflicted a humiliating defeat on the French. How did they do it?

The French were in full, heavy-plate armor, which was great for deflecting blows from swords and arrows, but much harder to move around in, and also made it difficult to see. The battlefield at Agincourt was muddy and wet, and thus easy to get bogged down in. And getting bogged down is exactly what happened to a lot of the French knights. Many fell into the mud and simply couldn't get up, which made them easy prey. The English began to rout the French forces, including their nobles, knights, and commanders. The male line of entire French noble families were wiped out during the battle, along with thousands of French knights. It was a stunning victory that earned Henry a sterling reputation, and gave England something to brag about for centuries.

Royal missed-the-boat fact: Henry V was eventually named king of France, but died before he could be crowned.

THE WARS OF
THE ROSES

How can you summarize a conflict like the Wars of the Roses in a single entry? You can't, but here we go anyway! These wars were really one civil war fought in England between 1455 and 1487, a series of skirmishes between two English aristocratic houses, Lancaster and York, for the crown and control of the nation. They were known as "The Civil Wars" at the time, and for a century or more after. The much more memorable moniker was formulated much later, a reference to the symbols representing the two houses: a red rose for Lancaster, and a white rose for York.

The conflict had its origins in Henry IV's usurping of the throne from Richard II and his family. While the following king, Henry V, was a strong leader and renowned for his victory at Agincourt, his son, Henry VI came to the throne as an infant and failed to improve much from there, remaining a weak and ineffective ruler throughout his reign. A very pious man, Henry VI would probably have been happier as a monk in a monastery, but fate wouldn't let him enjoy that life. As a child, he was advised by unpopular and corrupt advisors, who clearly manipulated the youth to achieve their own designs.

With France gaining the upper hand in the Hundred Years' War, Henry's ineffective rule became even more obvious. Henry's cousin, Richard, the Duke of York, had a strong claim to the throne—he was a great-grandson of King Edward III—and Henry's supporters knew it. Henry began to suffer mental health problems in the early 1450s, and eventually, he was so far gone that he was judged unfit to rule. Richard stepped in to become Lord Protector and decided to try and get rid of the undesirables populating Henry's court. But Henry got better and his wife, Queen Margaret, forced Richard from his position. Richard then assembled a small army and succeeded in capturing Henry in May 1455, the first skirmish of the war. But by this time,

Margaret had given birth to a son, which weakened Richard's claim to the throne. Despite this reality, Richard was soon reinstated as Lord Protector, and Margaret and her son fled into exile for their safety.

This led to a series of battles and skirmishes at the end of the 1450s, with each side angling for control. Richard still insisted that he was the lawful heir to the throne, but he was killed at the Battle of Wakefield in December 1460, and his head was then paraded around topped with a crown made of paper, mocking his claim.

Richard's son, Edward, Earl of March, took up his father's cause and the fighting resumed. At a battle near Towton, North Yorkshire in March 1461, something like 28,000 soldiers died in one day, the single largest loss in English history. The Yorkist side was victorious, Edward succeeded in having himself crowned as Edward IV, and a tense peace descended over the country throughout the 1460s. But Margaret had no intention of giving up, and with the help of some traitors to Edward IV and a significant army, the Lancastrians succeeded in defeating the York side and sent Edward IV fleeing to Flanders in 1470.

But he wasn't done, either, and invaded England in 1471, once again taking the throne back (got whiplash yet?). Henry finally died in May 1471 (some believe Edward IV might have had him murdered), and Edward IV's claim to the throne seemed settled. The next twelve years brought relief from the endless fighting, though the throne was by no means secure. Edward had two sons, who would become the tragic "Princes in the Tower" (more about them in a bit).

Edward IV died in 1483, and again there were questions about succession. A new Duke of York, also named Richard, eyed the throne for himself. He was destined to become the infamous King Richard III, and because of his reign, the Wars of the Roses were not quite yet over.

Family feud fact: The civil war was also known early on as "The Cousins' War," simply because the members of the York and Lancaster houses were mostly all descended from the sons of King Edward III, though most historians would say that the York faction had a stronger claim to the throne, even though it was the Lancastrians that occupied it. The whole thing was just a big family squabble!

RICHARD III: EVIL OR NOT?

P retty much everyone has heard of Richard III, one of the most famous of all medieval English kings, and arguably the last one. But what is fact and what is fiction in his case? Many people's opinions of Richard III are influenced by the Shakespeare play, whether they've seen it or not. In this version, Richard is a monster, a grotesque hunchback who plots, murders, and schemes his way to the throne in a series of increasingly worse crimes, including murdering the young sons of King Edward IV to make sure the oldest one does not become king. The people hate him for his crimes and long for someone to save them. It's only when the heroic Henry Tudor invades England and meets Richard's army at the Battle of Bosworth Field on August 22, 1485, that the tyrant is killed and peace is restored to the land. Henry is crowned as Henry VII, the first Tudor monarch.

It's a great and dramatic story, but there's one big problem: Shakespeare wrote his play between 1592 and 1594, at a time when Queen Elizabeth I was still on the throne. And who was Elizabeth? None other than Henry VII's granddaughter! So that meant any version of the story, whether on stage or in print, had to make the Tudors look good. There was no other option. Now, this doesn't mean that Richard III was an angel and that it was really Henry VII who was the monster. Both were kings, and both could be ruthless and cruel while trying to gain and hold onto power. But was Richard all that much worse than those monarchs who came before or after him? Here are some facts:

There is no evidence he was a hunchback. His skeleton shows signs of scoliosis (a curve in the spine), but this wouldn't be enough to change his body shape. This legend can be tied to the Tudors, who wanted to present Richard as a (literally) twisted monster.

He wasn't all that unpopular. In fact, he seems to have been well liked and seen as a capable leader. When he was crowned king in 1483, he even recited his vows in English rather than Latin, so that the people could understand them.

He probably didn't murder the princes in the tower. Despite being saddled with this horrible crime for centuries, there's no real evidence that Richard killed the boys or ordered them to be murdered. Henry VII had just as much motive for wanting them dead, it must be pointed out. And there were others that might have killed them after they were put in the Tower of London for their own protection.

The princes might not have been able to inherit the throne anyway. It seems that Edward's sons were born from a marriage (to Elizabeth Woodville) that was not properly ratified. This wouldn't mean much to most people, but for monarchs it was crucial that everything be in its right place, and it's possible that the princes were not eligible to inherit the throne. This would have made Richard the next closest heir. Also, after years of civil war, the nobles probably wanted a strong, capable adult on the throne, rather than a child—another point in Richard's favor.

> **Archaeological damage fact:** Richard's skeleton was discovered under a car park in the city of Leicester in September of 2012. The area had once been the site of a monastery, where Richard's body was taken after Bosworth. Archaeologists said that the skeleton showed signs of "humiliation injuries," meaning that his body was defaced after death.

CHAPTER 5

THE TUDORS

(1485-1603)

HENRY VII:
THE FIRST TUDOR MONARCH

S avior of England from tyranny, or a scheming opportunist? Rightful King of England, or an underhanded usurper? Many questions about Henry Tudor (later Henry VII) remain, but if you listen to the Tudors of the time, he was pretty much the greatest thing since sliced bread (except sliced bread hadn't even been invented yet, so Henry was alone at the top of the heap!) Many people learn about Henry through Shakespeare's play, *Richard III*, where Richard is presented as an evil mastermind, murdering and committing other crimes all the way to the throne. Henry steps in to set things right in the end, and takes the crown for himself. But of course, this was Tudor propaganda. What's the *real* story?

Henry (1457-1509) was the son of Edmund Tudor, the Earl of Richmond and half-brother of King Henry VI (he died before Henry was born). His mother was Lady Margaret Beaufort, Countess of Richmond, who was the great-granddaughter of John of Gaunt (King Edward III's fourth son). As you can see, Henry's eventual claim to the throne was a bit distant, but he definitely had royal blood in his veins. He was born into a world of turmoil, as the Wars of the Roses flared up all around him, which meant that he was anything but safe. In 1471, when Edward IV regained the throne, Henry, his uncle Jasper, and various other Lancastrians escaped to Brittany, where they lived in exile for the next fourteen years.

Trouble was brewing back home, for while Richard had his supporters, there were many who were also against him. In 1485, with the support of the French, Henry made his move. Though outnumbered, he met Richard's army at Bosworth Field (to the west of the city of Leicester) on August 22, 1485, and won a decisive victory. Richard was killed and Henry was able to seize the crown for himself.

Henry declared himself the new king by right of conquest, and was crowned on October 30 in the same year. To secure his claim, he married Elizabeth of York, daughter of King Edward IV and sister to the missing Princes in the Tower. The famed Tudor seal, the overlaid red and white roses, would soon symbolize the uniting of the formerly at-odds houses of Lancaster and York. While Henry faced various rebellions and plots over the years, he weathered the storm with a surprisingly calm and successful reign, such that, when his son became Henry VIII following VII's death, no one really challenged it.

But was Henry VII the legitimate king? What about the Princes in the Tower? Henry had a distant claim to the throne, it's true, but he was not the first example of a king taking power despite limited family connections. His victory over Richard III was as good a claim as any. And yes, it would have been in Henry's best interests for the young princes to be out of the way. But did he have them killed? Most scholars think they were probably dead already, framing it as a lucky break for Henry rather than the result of his scheming.

A capable administrator throughout his time at the helm, Henry brought stability back to the nation. But even he couldn't control his destiny. His oldest son, Prince Arthur, the heir to the throne, died in 1502, screwing up Henry's plans for the succession. He then had to turn to his next son, Henry, who would change British history forever.

Fancy flag fact: Henry VII flew the flag of the red Welsh dragon of Cadwaladr as he went into battle at Bosworth, and later added the green and white background colors (the Tudor livery) that are still seen on the Welsh flag today.

HENRY VIII'S
MANY WIVES, PART I

M ost people today think of Henry VIII as the portly tyrant with the flat cap who chopped off his wives' heads. But in truth, as a young man, Henry was educated, handsome, and athletic, and had much of Europe swooning. It was only later that he descended into the bloated and petulant monarch that history remembers. Henry came to the throne in 1509, after the death of his father, Henry Tudor (Henry VII). As we've seen, Henry became king because his older brother, Prince Arthur, died, leaving him next in line. The prince's death was such a disappointment that it gave birth to a messianic superstition: no royal son named "Arthur" can ever ascend to the throne, because there is only one "real" Arthur, who will return in Britain's hour of greatest need.

In any case, Henry VIII soon set about doing kingly things. In 1509, he married Catherine of Aragon (1485-1536), daughter of King Ferdinand and Queen Isabella of Spain (and Columbus fame). Catherine had previously been engaged to Arthur, because that's just how things were done among royals in those days. And Henry would later use this fact as reason to end the marriage via annulment. By 1533, Catherine had not produced a male heir, only a daughter, Princess Mary, and Henry, antsy about his lineage, moved on.

He was also having affairs with other women, and set his eyes on Anne Boleyn (c. 1501-36). Anne was a bridesmaid to Queen Catherine, so she was always around Henry's court. But the pope would have none of this second marriage talk, so Henry broke with the Catholic Church, declared himself head of a new Church of England, had his marriage to Catherine declared null and void, and married Anne in 1533. Needless to say, the pope and Catholic Europe were not amused. Still, this one rash decision changed English history forever.

Henry married Anne, but she gave birth to a daughter, Princess Elizabeth, which didn't please Henry at all. So, he looked for a way to end their marriage and found it, accusing her of adultery and other crimes. Was she really guilty? That's one of those hot questions that historians will kick around forever, but for Henry, she was definitely guilty, and in his court, that meant death.

Anne was executed in 1536, by which time Henry had already moved on to the woman who would become his third wife, Jane Seymour (1508-37), who had been the maid of honor for both Catherine and Anne; Henry obviously liked picking his new wives from this select group! Henry married Jane very soon after Anne's execution, and she finally gave him what he wanted: a son. Little Prince Edward was now the male heir to the throne and Henry was delighted. He truly seemed to love Jane and it could have been a lasting and happy marriage, but a terrible tragedy was visited on them. On October 24, 1537, only twelve days after Edward was born, Jane died of complications from the birth, leaving Henry devastated.

Multi-marital fact: While Henry would live for only a little over ten more years after Jane died, he would have three more wives!

HENRY VIII, THE CHURCH OF ENGLAND, AND THE DISSOLUTION OF THE MONASTERIES

H enry wasn't just a ladies' man—he also kept himself busy dissolving England's hundreds of monasteries. Even though he had created his own church, he was not technically a Protestant, and still considered himself a Catholic. But greedy Henry saw that multitude of monastic houses as a source of great wealth for the Crown. These monasteries and abbeys were closed on Henry's order and the monks and nuns were basically turned out into the cold to fend for themselves. Many of the buildings were left to crumble.

On November 28, 1534, the Act of Supremacy was put into law, which basically gave Henry supreme command of a new Church of England, denied any power to the pope, and said that Henry was the highest authority, second only to God. As such, he could pretty much do anything he wanted in England. And what he wanted was the wealth of the monasteries. England had been at war with France from 1532 to 1533, and this conflict had drained the national coffers, so this seizure would give Henry and the country a quick and convenient injection of cash.

Henry started the process in 1536, and it continued for four more years. The main problem with the policy was that these monasteries were places of charity and hospitality. They fed the poor, provided travelers with places to stay, employed people to work their lands, and offered medicines (such as they were at the time) and care, along with a dozen other services. Monasteries and abbeys also held large libraries, holy relics, and many other treasures. They were very important to society and culture, so a lot of the faithful saw Henry's move to shut them down falling somewhere between a disaster and an outrage. Indeed, the policy unleashed a tsunami of social change in England.

Henry's chancellor, Thomas Cromwell, conducted a census of these monasteries to figure out just how much wealth they held. He also went looking for any real or imagined slights against the king, evidence of disloyalty, corruption, and so on. He was able to determine that all of the monastic houses had a total income of something like $150 million in modern money, a sum that Henry wanted for himself. Cromwell spun the situation as though the monasteries were taking in vast amounts of money, and keeping most of it for themselves. If Henry had control of this income, he would, of course, put it to better use for society. Sure, that seems likely!

While a segment of the English people were already leaning toward the new Protestant religion and didn't care what happened to the monasteries, a sizable portion of the population was horrified when they began to be closed. In October 1536, a group of priests, nobles, abbots, and others who wanted a return to the Catholic Church organized a protest that quickly swelled to number tens of thousands of people. It became known as the Pilgrimage of Grace, and Henry quickly realized that this could be a huge problem. The king sent his troops to confront the angry swarm, and persuaded them to disband on the promise of pardons and reforms to meet their demands. Of course, he had no real intention of keeping those promises, and when the protests flared up again in January 1537, he took the opportunity to arrest and execute several of the leaders. After that, there were no more protests, and Henry's plan to relieve the monasteries of their cash continued.

> **Monastic stats fact:** There were about 800 monasteries and abbeys in England and Wales at this time, most of which had been there since the Middle Ages. Many were already in decline by Henry's reign, however, and there were far fewer monks and nuns than there had been even a century earlier.

HENRY VIII'S MANY WIVES, PART II

D evastated by the loss of Jane Seymour, Henry remained single for two years, but his advisors realized that a king needed a queen, and thought that a political marriage would be a good idea, so the search for a wife began anew. His minister suggested that he marry one of two German noblewomen, Anne or Amelia, who were sisters of the Duke of Cleves. Either would make a good match, and would also align Henry with the duke. Henry agreed and requested that portraits of the two sisters be sent to him. He chose Anne (the original swipe right?), and a union was arranged.

Unfortunately, Anne of Cleves (1515-57) had no say in this arrangement, and as a pawn in a political marriage, she had to do her duty and go to England. Only there was a problem. When she arrived, Henry discovered that she didn't look like her portrait (the original misleading profile picture?), and he wanted nothing to do with her. But plans for the marriage were already well underway, so it had to proceed. The marriage was purely symbolic, and only lasted for six months. Henry became genuine friends with Anne and remained so through his life, but they never lived as husband and wife. When he offered her an annulment to their marriage, she was happy to accept. He set her up with lavish homes and plenty of money, and she lived as "the king's sister" until her death in 1557. Of all the wives, she did the best for herself!

Henry's gaze then turned to Catherine Howard (1523-42), a lady-in-waiting to Anne of Cleves. She was only about 18 at the time, and for pervy old Henry (aged 49), the potential union must have been a dream come true. He married her only nineteen days after his marriage to Anne was annulled! But Catherine, while thrilled by the chance to become queen, had no interest in Henry, who could barely walk by this time. She enjoyed flirting with other men, and probably messing around with them, too. Three men were said to be involved with her at different times: Thomas Culpeper, a nobleman at Henry's court, Henry Mannox, Catherine's music tutor, and Francis Dereham, who had known Catherine before. All three denied the charges, but all three were executed. Catherine was convicted of treason by way of adultery, and also executed, on February 13, 1542.

You would think that would have been enough wives for Henry, but there would be one more: Catherine Parr (1512-48), who had already been married three times herself. But it was a good match, and Catherine became a good companion to Henry. Importantly, she took a great interest in all three of his children, and even convinced him to restore Mary and Elizabeth to the line of succession, meaning that they could inherit the throne someday. Henry, knowing that Edward would be king, agreed, never imagining that both Mary and Elizabeth would be queens of England eventually! Catherine outlived her husband, dying a year and a half after him, on September 5, 1548.

> **Wife facts:** The stories of these six women are amazing, inspiring countless pieces of art (including progressive rock keyboardist Rick Wakeman's hit 1973 album, *The Six Wives of Henry VIII*). Living with Henry could not have been easy, and not all of them prospered in their times as queens. Anne Boleyn and Catherine Howard met terrible ends for no good reason, while Anne of Cleves and Catherine Parr were fortunate to make something of their marriages. But all deserve to be remembered for navigating the tricky and often horrible world of early Tudor politics.

HENRY VIII: NOT-SO-YOUNG AND HEALTHY, AND EDWARD VI

By 1547, Henry was in terrible shape—sick, overweight, suffering severe pain due to gout, and generally miserable. This late image was quite the contrast to the young, athletic prince who had dazzled Europe and England forty years earlier. But he'd really let himself go, and was now paying for his indulgences. Henry died on January 28, 1547, at only 55 years old.

At least he had the satisfaction of knowing the son he'd had with Jane, young Edward, would succeed him as king. Edward showed promise as a potential ruler, and was appealing to reformers because of his Protestant beliefs.

Except his star didn't shine for long. Edward became king at the age of nine, but, obviously, he was far too young to do much on his own, and the kingdom was primarily run by his advisors, a standard practice until a monarch came of age. But it also meant that the advisors had lots of chances to scheme and try and secure their own goals, which usually involved giving themselves more wealth and power. In short order, the country was beset by economic problems, riots and insurrection, and a failed war with Scotland—a lot for a boy king to have to deal with!

Unlike his father, Edward was a committed Protestant, and supported making this new faith the official religion of England. Needless to say, the move didn't sit well with many Catholics, who, following Henry's tyranny, were very eager to hand the English Church back to Rome. Edward's wishes might have prevented that, but he didn't live long enough to see it through. Though healthy as a boy, he fell ill with a fever in January 1553, and got progressively worse. He died in July, possibly of tuberculosis, though some more suspicious folks believed that a group of Catholics had poisoned him.

In his last days, Edward's advisors convinced him to name Lady Jane Grey as his successor, to prevent his half-sister Mary from taking the throne. Jane was a granddaughter of Henry VII and was Edward's cousin. Most importantly for them, she was also a Protestant. Mary, of course, would have none of this, and rallied troops and people to her side. Jane was technically Queen of England for only nine days before the councillors conceded that Mary was the lawful queen. Poor Jane was executed at the age of sixteen or seventeen, the tragic pawn of far more powerful people.

Ruler fact: From 1547 to 1558, England had five different monarchs!

MARY TUDOR:
A SHORT AND TROUBLED REIGN

Mary (1516-58) was the fifth child of Henry VIII and his first wife, Catherine of Aragon, and the only one of their brood to survive infancy. She ascended to the throne after Edward's death and the disruption caused by Jane Grey and her supporters, no doubt feeling that she was finally being given what she was entitled to. Being a faithful Catholic, she immediately set about trying to restore England to its former religion, a move that was relief to many people, and which aroused the fury of many others.

Mary also married King Philip II of Spain, an unpopular decision (including with some Catholics), and began rounding up Protestants and burning some of them at the stake, an even more unpopular decision! Her tyranny earned her the nickname "Bloody Mary."

By most accounts (even those written at the time), Mary's reign was a disaster. In 1558, she managed to lose Calais, England's last little toe-hold on continental Europe, a huge comedown from the days when Henry II ruled from the far north of England all the way to southwest France and the Spanish border. To say the least, Calais was a humiliating defeat.

While Mary may not have been the tyrant that some later Protestant writers tried to portray her as, she was definitely not winning over hearts and minds, either. Crop failures and other social problems meant that many people who at first welcomed her started to turn against her. Some of them began to look to her younger sister, Princess Elizabeth, as a better alternative. But before any kind of revolt could happen, Mary became ill (possibly with cancer) and died. She had at first thought that she was pregnant, but in reality it was far from a blessing. Henry's oldest surviving child had her time on the throne, and made something of a mess of it. Could her controversial sister do any better?

> **Lukewarm reaction fact:** When he heard Mary had died, King Philip, who was living abroad and away from Mary for long periods of time, was said to have written, "I felt a reasonable regret for her death."

ELIZABETH I: A NEW HOPE?

When Princess Elizabeth took the throne on January 15, 1559, and was crowned Queen Elizabeth I, the country let out a sigh of relief. After all, her sister Mary had been rather horrible as a ruler. But was Elizabeth, just 25 years old, up to the enormous job of ruling a nation that was in trouble, split along religious lines, in danger of foreign interference, and not far from being broke. Few believed that she was. At the time, the misogynistic belief that women could not be good rulers was very common (even among women), and Mary had done nothing to dispell it. A lot of Elizabeth's advisors simply hoped that she would marry someone soon and hand over the running of the country to a man—but she proved far more intelligent and crafty than they ever imagined.

One of her first big challenges was the religious issue. Her father, Henry VIII, had broken with Rome and created his own church, but basically remained Catholic in private. Her brother, Edward VI, was a devoted Protestant, but died too soon to do much in terms of establishing this belief as the nation's religion. Mary was a devout Catholic, and launched a reign of terror against Protestants, which made everyone, Protestants and Catholics alike, loath her. Obviously, Elizabeth was going to have to navigate a careful route through this mess. She was able to work with Parliament to solidify an official Protestant Church for England, while allowing it to hold onto some Catholic elements, which angered strict Protestants to no end. But for the time being, the gambit worked. Catholics were allowed to practice under a kind of "don't ask, don't tell" policy, as long as they remained loyal to the queen.

As for marriage, her advisors and courtiers tried to get her to marry for the next three decades! There was no shortage of noblemen and kings from other countries who lined up for the chance to marry a queen and become ruler of England. And there were times when Elizabeth definitely considered it. But, ultimately, she always decided that she was "married to England" and couldn't allow a man to share her power and responsibility. While it meant that she never had any children to carry on the Tudor line, it proved to be the right decision, and under her wise guidance, England became *the* world power by the end of the sixteenth century. For almost forty-five years, Elizabeth was the ruler that no one thought she—or any woman—could be, and she is now seen as one of the greatest and most important figures in European history.

Pretender fact: In 1587, a young man who said his name was Arthur Dudley was arrested in Spain on suspicion that he was a spy. He claimed to be the illegitimate son of Elizabeth and her favorite nobleman, Robert Dudley. He was the right age to have been born in 1561, when Elizabeth retired from the public eye for a while due to a mysterious illness. Was she pregnant during this time? Most historians don't think so, and the Spaniards who questioned Arthur didn't either. But they seemed to have kept him in prison, and he was never heard from again. Did he take an astonishing secret with him to the grave?

SIR THOMAS GRESHAM AND THE ROYAL EXCHANGE OF 1571

G resham (c. 1519-79) was an English merchant who served under three Tudor monarchs: Edward, Mary, and Elizabeth. He spent a considerable amount of time in the "Low Countries" (modern Belgium and the Netherlands), and while there, he was inspired by the idea of a *bourse*, an "exchange" where merchants could trade, buy, and sell. After returning to England, and at the suggestion of Richard Clough, another merchant, Gresham offered to set up such an exchange in London in 1565—at his own expense. It would be modeled on the one in Antwerp. Queen Elizabeth was thoroughly impressed, and agreed to the proposal.

With the queen's permission, it was to be known as the Royal Exchange, and she opened it on January 23, 1571. It contained merchant stalls for fine goods, and all manner of businesses were present. Perhaps most importantly, the queen gave the Exchange a license to sell alcohol, which no doubt greatly increased its appeal; imbibe while you shop!

In a sense, it was England's first shopping mall, and eventually, it took shape as a large courtyard with a colonnade walk around all four sides. Above this was a second floor containing shops selling wares of all kinds (a third floor was later added). In addition to shopping, merchants could meet and trade news stories from their varied travels.

The Exchange thrived into the seventeenth century, even surviving the trials of the English Civil War, but it was destroyed in the 1666 London Fire (more on that tragedy in the next chapter). A second Exchange was built, but it also burned down, by an 1838 fire that was caused by an overheated stove in a coffee house in the market. Happily, this fire didn't destroy the rest of London, though it could be seen as far away as Windsor, some twenty-four miles to the west! A third version (which is still standing) was opened by Queen Victoria in 1844. It was remodelled in 2001, and now includes an upscale bar and restaurants, as well as luxury retailers.

> **Stock fact:** In Elizabethan times, and well into the seventeenth century, the Exchange did not allow stockbrokers to trade there, because they were considered rude and disruptive. Make of that what you will ...

PLOTS AGAINST QUEEN ELIZABETH I AND FRANCIS WALSINGHAM'S SPY NETWORK

When Elizabeth ascended to the throne, it was a relief for many, but not all. Following the brief reign of her sister Mary and the return of the Catholic religion, many English Catholics now feared retribution and the aggressive Protestantism being forced on them. And so, some people started thinking about removing the new queen from the equation. For them, the lawful queen of England was the Catholic Mary, Queen of Scots, descended, like Elizabeth, from Henry VII. From the very early days of Elizabeth's reign, some plotted in secret to have her assassinated and place Mary on the throne. Always canny, Elizabeth knew that if she was going to survive, she needed a network of spies to keep her safe.

By the 1570s, Francis Walsingham was in charge of a spy network that trumped anything seen until modern times. His informants and double agents abounded in England and beyond. Walsingham was the eyes and ears of the court, and if something was afoot, there was a good chance he would know about it soon. Indeed, he foiled many attempts against the queen's life until his death in 1590.

Some of the plots against Elizabeth include:

The Ridolfi plot of 1571. In 1571, A banker and nobleman from Florence, Italy, Roberto Ridolfi, helped English conspirators hatch a plot wherein Thomas Howard, the Duke of Norfolk, would wed Mary, Queen of Scots. Elizabeth was to be assassinated and Mary would take the throne. Ridolfi even informed the pope and King Philip II of Spain of his plans. Eventually, the plot was uncovered and Norfolk was executed, but Ridolfi himself was safely far away in Italy, and ended up living into old age, dying in 1612 at 81.

The Throckmorton plot of 1583: Named for Sir Francis Throckmorton, an English Catholic who wanted to see Mary on the throne of England. His plan was grand, and even included a full-scale invasion of England led by Henry I, Duke of Guise, a French nobleman who was very eager to see Protestants of any kind removed from power. But Throckmorton was sloppy and Walsingham was able to suss out his intentions and obtain incriminating information while searching his house. Throckmorton would later confess under torture, and was executed in 1584.

The Parry plot of 1585: William Parry was actually a double agent working for both Elizabeth and Mary, and confessed as much to gain Elizabeth's pardon and some rewards. But, somewhere along the way, he seemed to have decided to try to kill Elizabeth for real. When his would-be co-conspirator, Sir Edmund Neville, ratted him out, that was the end of Parry's intrigues, and he was executed in 1585.

The Babington plot of 1586: The plot that changed the course of English history, a plot which would bring down a monarch and start a war (see the next entry).

And who was the common factor in all these plots? Mary, Queen of Scots, to whom we now turn.

> **Tuneful fact:** Walsingham sometimes employed musicians as spies, because they could travel to other countries, entertain, and mingle with powerful people without causing much suspicion.

THE EXECUTION OF MARY, QUEEN OF SCOTS

A s you might have noticed in the previous entry, quite a few of the plots against Queen Elizabeth involved trying to place her cousin, Mary, Queen of Scots on the throne. But why was Mary so important, at least to groups of plotters and conspirators?

Well, like Elizabeth, she was a granddaughter of Henry VII, which gave her a claim to the English throne. And, being Catholic, those who wanted to erase the new Protestant religion from England saw in her a chance of accomplishing their aim, after Mary Tudor failed to accomplish anything at all. Elizabeth and her advisors were very well aware of the potential threat that Mary posed, but even after arresting her, Elizabeth could not quite bring herself to execute her royal cousin.

Mary had been wrapped up in a civil war in Scotland, and had to flee to England in 1568. At first, she hoped Elizabeth would help her to regain the Scottish throne, but Elizabeth was very cautious about providing too much aid. Instead, Mary was detained and eventually held against her will in England, being moved around to various castles and homes over the next two decades. As we've seen, during this time, several plots against Elizabeth were hatched, often in support of Mary, but it's hard to tell whether Mary was aware of them, much less formulated them. Elizabeth's advisors and spies always insisted that Mary was behind these plots, but Elizabeth still remained reluctant to execute her cousin—that is, until the Babington plot was uncovered, which seemed to show beyond doubt that Mary was indeed involved in a conspiracy to kill Elizabeth.

The Babington plot is in reality a convoluted mess that still has historians scratching their heads. But, essentially, in 1586, Mary began to receive communications—coded letters hidden in beer barrels—from a Catholic loyalist named Anthony Babington. He told Mary that he and a group of conspirators were planning to assassinate Queen Elizabeth and put Mary on the throne, and asked for her support. She replied that she wanted more details, but that was all. That letter was intercepted by Walsingham's network, and Babington was outed. He and his cronies were arrested, as was Mary. It seemed like there was an airtight case against them.

Walsingham had wanted to condemn Mary for a long time, and had been monitoring these letters all along. When she sent the reply to Babington and his squad, Walsingham intercepted the letter and forged a postscript, asking for the names of all the conspirators. Walsingham's insertion made it look like Mary was agreeing to the plot.

Mary was eventually put on trial, and she denied ever agreeing to a plot to assassinate Elizabeth, which technically was true. But the fact that she was writing to these conspirators at all was enough to condemn her. Elizabeth knew that she needed to order Mary's execution, but still hesitated. When Mary was finally beheaded, on February 7, 1587, Elizabeth was furious, and later claimed that her council had carried out the execution without her authority. This might have been a deliberate plan on the council's behalf to make Elizabeth look less responsible for her cousin's death, but, either way, Mary, Queen of Scots was eliminated.

What happened next would change the course of English, and world, history.

> **Gory execution fact:** Beheading was the most common form of execution in England, and Mary was no exception. But it took three swings of the axe to separate her head from her body. The executioner then tried to lift up her severed head to show those assembled, but ended up only holding her red wig. Her head fell to the floor, its lips allegedly still moving!

THE SPANISH ARMADA

Mary, Queen of Scots was dead, executed (reluctantly) at Queen Elizabeth's behest. Needless to say, Catholic Europe was outraged, vowing to take revenge on the "heretic" queen. The following year, King Philip II of Spain sent a huge armada, consisting of his entire navy, to invade England and depose Elizabeth, with the goal of finally restoring Catholic rule to the island. While Mary's execution was one reason for the invasion, Philip was also tired of English pirates such as Sir Francis Drake (more about him on page 163) harassing his ships and plundering his wealth; Drake had also launched a preemptive strike against the Spanish fleet in Cadiz, where he damaged or destroyed several ships that were under construction. Elizabeth didn't

approve this attack beforehand, though she was probably secretly pleased with the results.

King Philip was also alarmed by the growing political power of England both in Europe and farther afield—England was eyeing the New World for colonies of its own, after all. In reality, Philip was probably planning an invasion of England as early as 1584—Mary's execution just provided the perfect excuse to put that plan into action.

The Spanish fleet was made up of about 130 ships, and could well have spelled doom for Elizabeth and the English. Indeed, there was a great sense of impending disaster on the island, with people anxiously awaiting the news that the Spanish ships had set sail. In July 1588, that dreaded day finally arrived.

But the combination of English fighting spirit and the famously unpredictable English weather conspired to win the day for England. After several days of stalemated fighting, the Spanish fleet broke off to wait for reinforcements from the Netherlands that would be used in a land invasion. The English took advantage of this and, by night, launched a series of "Hell Burners," old ships that were covered in flammable material, set alight, and guided into the Spanish fleet. The Spanish retreated, but the English were able to trap them in the English Channel, leaving the armada no choice but to sail north, toward Scotland, with the goal of heading around Ireland before heading back to Spain.

This is where the wild weather came into play. A fierce storm battered the Spanish fleet in northern Scotland, and by the time the remnants of the armada reached Ireland, those sailors that went ashore were quickly killed by the Irish, who were also Catholic, but had no love for Spain. The Spanish fleet was decimated, having lost at least sixty of its ships and three-quarters of its men.

The victory would open the way for England to become a major European power, inaugurating the Elizabethan "Golden Age." The

Spanish defeat was seen by Protestants as a sign from God that Elizabeth was meant to reign and England destined to prosper. Spain, and the rest of Catholic Europe, were too stunned to make anything of it.

> **Chewy fact:** It's also thought that wood-eating sea creatures, called shipworms, might have been chewing on the Spanish ships for some time, weakening them and making them more likely to sink when battered by storms.

SIR WALTER RALEIGH AND SIR FRANCIS DRAKE

They are probably two of the most famous men from the Elizabethan era, both renowned as explorers, with Raleigh more known as the courtier, and Drake the fearless sailor.

Sir Walter Raleigh (c.1552-1618) was a courtier, statesman, gifted poet, and all-around Renaissance man. A favorite of Queen Elizabeth's, Raleigh also made many enemies, due to his arrogance and reckless-ness. He was known for his explorations of the American continent, and efforts to create colonies there, as well as his military prowess in Ireland. In both cases, those actions have caused many to now see him as an advocate for colonialism and exploitation. Raleigh is credited with bringing the potato to Europe (especially Ireland), but a lot of historians now think it was introduced by someone else. He definitely helped popularize tobacco, however, and soon it became all the rage for the upper classes in England and Europe. It was touted as a medicinal plant that could help the lungs and respiration (!)—even Queen Elizabeth was known to smoke on occasion.

But Raleigh managed to fall out of favor both with Elizabeth (by secretly marrying one of her attendants) and her successor, King James (by possibly being a part of a plot against him in 1603). James sent him to the Tower, where he lived in limited luxury until 1616. James then released Raleigh to send him on a mission to South America, but the king came to suspect that Raleigh was trying to incite a war between England and Spain. His patience exhausted, he had Raleigh executed in 1618.

Sir Francis Drake (1540-96) was an acclaimed sailor, explorer—and, yes, pirate—who made life on the high seas hell for Spain and Portugal, raiding and looting their ships and sinking them afterward. King Philip II of Spain hated Drake so much that he offered up to 20,000 ducats (about £4 million today) to anyone who could kill him! But Drake always got away.

Drake also circumnavigated the globe from 1577-80, becoming the first Englishman to sail around the world. He sailed as far as the west coast of America, right up to the San Francisco Bay and just north of it, claiming it for Elizabeth and naming it Nova Albion ("New Britain"). Upon returning, he continued being a pain in Spain's backside, and helped to destroy the Spanish fleet at Cadiz in 1587, an attack that was later branded as "singeing Philip of Spain's beard." Those ships were to have been a part of the Spanish Armada, but Drake's attack delayed the launch of the fleet by up to a year, and probably saved England from an invasion that would have likely over-whelmed it.

During a venture to Puerto Rico in early 1596, Drake's attacks against the Spanish didn't go as well as they usually did, and he contracted dysentery, which killed him in January of that year.

> **Game and cloak facts:** Drake is said to have refused to sail out to meet the threat of the Armada until he had finished a game of lawn bowling, saying that there was time enough for both! This story is apocryphal, but it's also a good one. As for Raleigh, there is no evidence that he ever

threw his cloak over a puddle so that Elizabeth could walk across it without getting her feet wet. It's a charming, chivalrous tale, but nothing more than that.

THE ELIZABETHAN UNDERWORLD, CRIME AND PUNISHMENT

As London's population grew throughout the second half of the sixteenth century, it was inevitable that crime of all kinds would blossom along with it. Pickpockets, muggers, murderers, conspirators, smugglers, confidence men, and more became common in the streets and taverns of the city. There were "good" areas and "bad" areas, just as in any urban setting, and the seedier side of life was usually found on the south bank of the Thames, where people could operate beyond the jurisdiction of the London authorities. As we'll see in the entry on page 167, playhouses were also built in this neighborhood, and were often places where criminals gathered to pick the pockets of theatergoers, or plot bigger scores.

So, how did London deal with this burgeoning underworld? There was no police force at the time, which meant that it was easier to get away with all kinds of mischief and mayhem. The best hope for justice when getting mugged or pickpocketed was to shout as the criminal ran away, and hope to raise enough of an alarm that others would intervene and try to stop them. As you can probably imagine, this didn't have a high success rate, so more often than not, thieves disappeared long before they could be collared. Organized crime operated similarly then as now, and included extortion, protection money, threats, and so on.

What happened if a criminal did get caught, and was taken in by authorities? Well, the punishment depended on the crime, but almost always, punishments were far worse than what criminals today might expect. Minor crimes might be dealt with by punishments like pulling the offender through a crowd in a cart and shaming them for their act, or putting them in the pillory (stocks) and letting others hurl verbal abuse and various objects at them.

More serious offenses usually involved brutal punishment such as having body parts (ears, nose, hands) cut off, or just as often, being put to death. Hanging was the preferred method of execution, and it was done differently than in later centuries, where the neck is broken by the noose as the condemned person falls from a platform. In Elizabethan times, hanging was performed by fastening a rope around the neck and pulling the person up, often over the large limb of a tree. The victim would then struggle and kick as they suffocated. The preferred hanging spot was at Tyburn, a spot outside of London on the way to Oxford. The hanged were said to be "Dancing the Tyburn Jig," meaning that they kicked their legs as they strained for air.

Crimes such as treason would usually lead the individual being tortured, hanged, drawn, and quartered. What are these last two, you ask? The offenders were hanged but taken down before dying. Then the stomach was cut open and their intestines removed while they were still alive. The body was then cut into four pieces, with the head removed and placed on a spike so that others could see the fate of traitors. And yes, this gruesome style of execution was almost always done in public!

> **Picky fact:** There was a secret school in London for training pickpockets and petty thieves. If they "graduated," they would earn titles like "judicial nipper" or "public foister" for their skills in being able to cut loose a purse from a belt without being noticed. Class was held in Billingsgate, not far from the Tower of London.

ELIZABETHAN THEATER

I n the later sixteenth century in London, the theater exploded in popularity. Previously, there had been bands of traveling players who went from town to town around the country and performed in inns, but by the 1570s, permanent theaters were being built to house acting companies and their playwrights. Of course, there were some who didn't approve. Puritans saw these buildings as new shrines to old pagan gods (since the Romans had enjoyed plays, and there had been no theaters since Roman times), and were quick to condemn them. But up these playhouses went, and soon, they were attracting people from all levels of society, who were eager to spend a few hours inhabiting another world where they could be entertained by grand tales of love and war—or, better yet, revenge and murder.

One such playhouse, unimaginatively called "The Theater," was built in 1576, and would host plays for over two decades. The owner was smart in building it on the south bank of London, where the city authorities had no say in what occurred. That land was under the laws of the queen herself, who loved the theater. Other playhouses soon sprang up there, taking advantage of this loophole in the law. The Curtain Theatre opened in 1577, and, during the 1590s, that was where many of Shakespeare's early plays were performed. The famous Globe Theatre was built in the same area in 1599. These were all outdoor arenas, meaning that even if it started raining, the show still had to go on!

These theaters shared their environs with brothels, animal fighting pits, prisons, a house for the insane (Bedlam), and workshops for malodorous trades like tanning. No wonder some people hated the theater so much! But this motley company did nothing to keep the crowds away, and it was in places like this that Shakespeare and his colleagues produced and premiered their famous plays.

People didn't just sit (or stand) and watch these outdoor plays, but often laughed, clapped, jeered, and made rude comments; it must have been very annoying for the actors! Some audience members even sat on the side of the stage, playing cards or dice as the production proceeded!

Despite all of the surrounding chaos, the plays themselves had to be careful about the kinds of stories they told. A man with the wonderful name of "the Master of Revels" had to approve each play before it could be performed. This meant that the stories couldn't feature anything too antireligious, or speak out against Elizabeth's government.

Despite the restrictions on what could be shown, and the disreputable reputation of these entertainment houses, people flocked to theaters to see new plays, which sometimes changed weekly. In a time before movies, television, and the internet, they really were the hottest thing going!

> **Unappreciative fact:** Unlike in modern times, actors in Elizabethan England were not seen as celebrities and were not paid well. They were often viewed as little more than criminals, who could even be arrested if someone really disliked them. The actor's life has always been a hard one!

ROBERT GREENE,
THE VAGABOND PLAYWRIGHT

Greene (1558–92) was the grand man of London playwrights in the 1580s and early 1590s. He was well educated, having received degrees from both Oxford and Cambridge. He was well aware of his exalted place, and happy to lord it over those who were less educated than he—a group that included a young man named William Shakespeare. But, despite his credentials, Greene had no interest in a scholar's life, much less one in the church. No, he loved debauchery and drinking too much, and would spend hours in taverns telling wild tales about his adventures across Europe, which may or may not have been true—in fact, they probably weren't.

Greene claimed that as a young man he married, but soon left his wife for London. On his way to the city, he met an actor who told him about the playwright's life, and the money and wild times that could attend it. Greene joined this actor, set up residence in a brothel, took a mistress whose brother was a master thief (and would later be hanged), and set about writing plays and telling wild stories. These acts caused others to brand Greene a liar, a thief, and a cheat who had wasted his education.

He seemed to be aware of this disrepute, and tried more than once to reform and repent, but he always slid back into his old ways—probably because, among other actors and playwrights, he was sure to be the center of attention. Shakespeare spent some time with him, but was not interested in the wild and crazy lives of Greene and his buddies. And, since Shakespeare had no university degree, he wasn't all that welcome, anyway.

Greene took ill in August 1592, after a meal of wine and pickled herring, and was so poor that he existed solely on charity from friends in his final days. After his death, his last pamphlet was published, called "Greene's Groats-Worth of Wit." It featured Greene's opinions of his colleagues, including young Shakespeare, of whom he wrote:

> **"For there is an upstart Crow, beautified with our feathers, that with his Tygers hart wrapt in a Players hyde, supposes he is as well able to bombast out a blanke verse as the best of you: and being an absolute Johannes Factotum, is in his owne conceit the onely Shake-scene in a countrey."**

Greene was attacking Shakespeare for presuming to be as good as the university-educated playwrights such as Greene and his fellow scoundrels. The text implied that young Will was nothing but an imitator, and would never be as good or original as those he aped. Well, guess who had the last laugh!

> **Influential fact:** Greene might have been one of the models for Shakespeare's beloved Falstaff character, and a few of Greene's own plays could have influenced *A Midsummer Night's Dream* and *The Winter's Tale*.

CHRISTOPHER MARLOWE: GENIUS AND SPY?

Most people who know the works of William Shakespeare probably have at least a passing familiarity with his fellow playwright, Christopher Marlowe (1564-93). Marlowe, a Cambridge-educated writer, was active in the late 1580s and early 1590s. His plays include such masterpieces as *Tamburlaine*, *Doctor Faustus*, and *Edward II*. While these aren't exactly the touchstones that *Romeo and Juliet*, *A Midsummer Night's Dream*, and *Hamlet* are, they are magnificent plays that are still performed today, and hold up well after all this time.

Marlowe was an undoubted genius, and had he lived longer, his work might have even outshone the plays and poems of Shakespeare. But he was destined to die a violent death at the age of 30, in a tavern brawl caused by a dispute about the bill.

Or was there more to it than that? During his Cambridge days, it was obvious to many that Marlowe was more than just a typical university student. At some point, it seems he was recruited by Queen Elizabeth's government to engage in spying missions. As we've seen, danger abounded in the 1580s, and there were always plots against the queen's life. The queen's spymaster, Sir Francis Walsingham, was well aware of the perils she faced, and sought out intelligent young men who could keep the queen safe.

Indeed, in 1584 and 1585, Marlowe had several long absences from his studies, longer than what would normally have been allowed. He also seemed to have a lot of money to spend on food and drink, far more than a typical student would have. So where was he, and where did his cash come from? It's possible that the government recruited him to go on spying missions, and paid him well for his troubles.

Marlowe definitely went abroad a few times, and was even arrested in the Netherlands and sent back to England, but he suffered no punishment and was soon released.

He later got into trouble over rumors of being an atheist (a crime in Elizabethan England). In May 1593, while he was being investigated on this charge (and ordered to stay put and not wander far away), he found himself at an inn, where said argument over the bill broke out. One of the other men in the dispute stabbed Marlowe in or above the eye with a dagger, killing him instantly.

A lot of people thought that the timing of the incident was suspicious. Was it an accident, or did his espionage uncover certain secrets that powerful people wanted kept quiet? Did Marlowe even die at all? Some think that he faked his death so that he could secretly travel back to Europe and continue spying. Some even think that he continued to write plays in secret and send them to, you guessed it, William Shakespeare, who published them under his own name (more on the Shakespeare authorship controversy in a moment). These theories are all unlikely, but not impossible—Marlowe was intelligent enough to vanish into thin air.

Conflicting stories fact: Marlowe was accused of being an atheist by some, and of being interested in moving to France to be ordained as a priest by others. Maybe he actually did?

WILLIAM SHAKESPEARE, THE ONE AND ONLY

W ho doesn't know the name of William Shakespeare (1564-1616)? Well, maybe a few people, but over the last four centuries, history and fate have conspired to make old Will the most famous author in the English language. Generations of schoolkids have been made to study his plays and poems (and a lot of them have hated it!), and his plays are staged all over the world, thousands of times every year. Plays like *Romeo and Juliet*, *Hamlet*, *Macbeth*, and at least a dozen others remain immensely popular, and many actors train for years to be worthy of the starring roles. What is it about this humble actor from the English country town of Stratford-upon-Avon that makes his work so popular more than four centuries after he died?

There is no one good answer to that question. For some people, it's his brilliant use of the English language, even if some of it seems hard to understand at first! Shakespeare also invented a large number of phrases that we still use in our everyday speech: A "laughing stock" (*The Merry Wives of Windsor*), "Knock knock! Who's there?" (*Macbeth*), "It's Greek to me" (*Julius Caesar*), "Love is blind" (*The Merchant of Venice*), "Break the ice" (*The Taming of the Shrew*), "For goodness' sake" (*Henry VIII*), Jealousy is the green-eyed monster (*Othello*), "Heart of gold" (*Henry V*), "Wild-goose chase" (*Romeo and Juliet*), and many more!

For others, it's his characters, who often seem authentically complex and familiar: Hamlet, Juliet, Romeo, Falstaff, King Lear, Henry V, and countless others. They leap off the page and become every bit as real as the people we know in our own lives.

Shakespeare seems to have been popular in his own time, and well-liked by his fellow playwrights and actors, with the exception of Robert Greene, of course (see page 169)! Some of these friends saw to it that Shakespeare's complete works were collected together into a book called the *First Folio* (published in 1623), making sure that they would not be lost to time. Indeed, eighteen of his plays (including *Twelfth Night*, *Julius Caesar*, *Macbeth*, and *The Tempest*) were not printed anywhere else and would have been lost forever if they hadn't been included in this edition; imagine how horrible that would be!

The bard's works have never gone out of style, even if some changes have been made to them over the years. Several theater groups and writers in the eighteenth century, for example, changed the endings of *King Lear* and *Romeo and Juliet* to happy ones, thinking that audiences would like them better! There was even an edition in the nineteenth century called *The Family Shakespeare* that took out all the dirty jokes in his plays, but where is the fun in that?!

Shakespeare's plays may be a product of his own time and culture, but they speak to people across all ages, and will continue to do so for a long time to come.

> **Skulduggery fact:** Shakespeare's skull seems to be missing from his grave! The question is, who stole it, and when?

SHAKESPEARE AUTHORSHIP CONSPIRACY THEORIES

Given how popular Shakespeare's plays still are, and how much he is revered to this day, it might surprise you (or not) to learn that a small number of critics and self-styled experts believe that he was not the author of his own works. The idea has been around since the nineteenth century, and the basic premise is that these undoubted works of genius could not have been written by a man from a country town who never attended university and never traveled widely (at least not out of Britain, as far as we know). Therefore, the plays must have been secretly written by someone else, and Shakespeare the actor agreed to attach his name to them in order to enhance his own reputation. Why would someone want to remain anonymous? Because plays were seen as "low" entertainment—despite Queen Elizabeth's fondness for them—and those of noble birth couldn't be seen to stoop that low.

So, who might have written them, if not Will? There have been more than eighty (!) candidates over the years, which makes this is a pretty flimsy conspiracy theory, but the three most popular ones are:

Sir Francis Bacon: Bacon was an important statesman, philosopher, and scientist, who would never have lowered himself to writing plays, at least not publicly. He was one of the early candidates for being the "real" Shakespeare, with some nineteenth-century writers claiming to find coded messages in the plays that revealed Bacon as their author. But these claims always fell apart on closer inspection. Mark Twain, among others, thought that Bacon was Shakespeare, but other supporters started claiming that he wrote pretty much everything that made it into the canon from the Elizabethan Age; then again, some of them insisted he was Queen Elizabeth's secret son, too.

Christopher Marlowe: As we mentioned on page 171, Marlowe was a playwright of undoubted genius and talent, and some think he simply faked his death, moved to the continent to continue spying for the English government, and wrote plays in secret, which he sent to Shakespeare to publish under Shakespeare's name. No evidence for this has ever been produced, but it makes for a dynamite story.

Edward de Vere, the Earl of Oxford: The current darling of many conspiracy theorists (known as "Oxfordians"), Edward de Vere is seen as the man with the education, travel experience, and artistic inclination to be the true bard. But he only became a serious contender beginning in 1918, when a schoolmaster named J. Thomas Looney (he insisted that it was pronounced "Loney," to give you an idea of how pleasant he was to hang out with) offered up the earl as the most likely man behind the famous plays and poems. Most Oxfordians insist that the plays are autobiographical, containing references to Edward's life. The thing is, autobiographies were not really a thing in the Elizabethan age, but they were huge in Looney's. Wishful thinking, maybe? Looney also insisted that the plays were staunchly pro-monarchy, while Bacon's supporters insisted that the same plays were very much in favor of a republic.

Shakespeare's plays contain references to things like leatherwork and tanning, things that Shakespeare, as a glove maker's son, would have known about. But one of Oxford's big pursuits, tin mining, never comes up once anywhere. Would Oxford really have needed to hide his identity? He was one of the most powerful earls in England and could pretty much have done what he wanted, as long as his work was not blasphemous and/or seditious. And further, he could have simply had the plays published anonymously. Why attach them to Shakespeare?

Of course, the biggest stumbling block to Oxford being the author is the inconvenient fact that he died in 1604, and Shakespeare continued to write plays for years afterward, which referenced then-current events. Some Oxfordians argue that he had written so many plays that they continued to be published after his death, but this fails to account for those pesky references to current events. Others simply deny that Oxford or Shakespeare wrote some of the later plays at all. And so the rationalizations continue, getting sillier and sillier.

Another inconvenient fact for this so-called conspiracy is that it was somehow perfectly covered up for hundreds of years until Looney "miraculously" figured it out in the early twentieth century. People during Shakespeare's time would have known about the faking, and it would almost certainly have slipped out. But for the actors who worked with him, and even his sometime rival, Ben Jonson (who also had no university education, by the way, and no one questions the authorship of his works), there was no doubt that the man from Stratford wrote his own plays.

Court records from 1604-05 list Shakespeare as the author of several of his plays. Would everyone really have been conspiring to keep a dead earl's secret?

Some people have a hard time accepting that genius can manifest anywhere in anyone. The Shakespeare authorship controversy isn't really a controversy at all, but an example of people's willingness to believe all sorts of nonsense to support an elitist attitude.

> Royal secrets fact: Another contender for the author of Shakespeare's plays is none other than Queen Elizabeth I herself! But this is even less likely than any of the other candidates, and there's that annoying little fact of her death in 1603, which would make it hard for all of Shakespeare's later plays to exist at all.

BEN JONSON: PLAYWRIGHT, SOLDIER, AND CRIMINAL

Jonson (1572–1637) might be considered the third of the Elizabethan playwright "trinity," along with Marlowe and Shakespeare. He was fortunate to have a good education as a youth, and was set to attend Cambridge University. But fate intervened and he ended up being apprenticed to his stepfather, a mason, instead, which must have been a bitter disappointment for the bright youth. Before too long, Jonson abandoned the bricklaying life and joined the military. He was sent to the continent, and later claimed that he killed an enemy in hand-to-hand combat and took his weapons as trophies.

As an ex-soldier living in London, Jonson found work as an actor, and eventually began writing his own plays. His first big hit was called *Every Man in His Humour*, produced in 1598. But soon Jonson found himself in legal trouble, accused of killing an actor named Gabriel Spenser. Spenser had acted in a play (co-written by Jonson) called *The Isle of Dogs*, that was banned and destroyed. We don't know what was in it, but it might have satirized Queen Elizabeth, which was a complete no-no! Spenser spent two months in prison for his role in the production, but Jonson got off with little more than a warning. Maybe Spenser resented this, since he challenged Jonson to a duel. But duels had been outlawed since 1571, and after Jonson stabbed Spenser to death, the playwright had no choice but to confess.

Jonson should have been executed, but he saved himself by a strange legal trick known as "benefit of clergy." This loophole said that if you could read Latin (mainly the Bible), you could legally be classified as a member of the clergy, and were therefore not subject to the laws of a secular court. Ecclesiastical courts had no death penalty, and since Jonson could easily read and understand Latin, he was released. He did get branded on the thumb, however, and warned that if he transgressed again, he would not get off so easily.

Ever the rebel, Jonson converted to Catholicism while in prison, a brave move considering that Catholics were forbidden to practice their religion openly. But this conversion lasted only ten years, and then he reverted to Anglican belief.

Jonson was destined to get into more trouble, first with his fellow playwrights from 1599 to 1602, who satirized him and he them, leading to some heated arguments. Then in 1605, he was thrown into prison—again—for co-writing a play that made some anti-Scottish remarks. James, the new king, was Scottish, so they didn't go over well! Jonson faced having his ears and nose cut off over the incident, but because he was also of Scottish heritage, he managed to talk his way out of a terrible fate yet again. One thing is clear: for all his faults, the man certainly had a talent for keeping his wits about him!

Final resting fact: Jonson lived until 1637, and managed to get himself buried in Westminster Abbey, where, bizarrely, he was buried standing up.

TUDOR COMPOSERS

Queen Elizabeth's father, Henry VIII, was a great lover of music, a skilled musician, and something of a prolific composer. While his daughter didn't have quite the same devotion to the musical arts, she could play various instruments, loved to dance, and was also fond of music. During her reign (and into that of King James) English music experienced a "golden age," fostering numerous composers that would leave their marks on music history. Here are just a few of the most notable.

Thomas Tallis (c. 1505-85) served under Henry VIII and all of his royal children, especially as a composer of choral music. Tallis successfully navigated the tricky waters of religious reform and counter reforms that tore England apart in those decades, though he seems to have remained a loyal Catholic throughout his life. One of his greatest works is his *Spem in alium*, a choral piece consisting of forty parts!

William Byrd (c. 1543-1623) was arguably the greatest of the Elizabethan composers, showing a mastery of many different genres and styles over a career that spanned from the reign of Henry VIII into that of King James. Byrd was a devout Catholic, but composed exquisite music for both the Catholic and Anglican masses. He always managed to avoid trouble and controversy and come out ahead during his long life, which stretched past the age of 80.

John Dowland (1563-1626) was arguably the greatest composer for the lute in any age, writing about ninety solo pieces for the instrument, as well as other works. Dowland was especially known for the melancholy and even bitter nature of some of his song lyrics, which might have reflected his actual disposition. He was a Catholic in a nation of Protestants, and sometimes blamed his lack of artistic success on that. At one point, he was also employed as a spy in the queen's service.

Thomas Morley (1557-1602) is credited with introducing the madrigal, a song form for solo voices in three to six parts that was first developed in Italy, to England. In English hands, the madrigal became something sublime, reaching its pinnacle in the early years of the seventeenth century. Morley, like Marlowe and Dowland, was also engaged in espionage, and one time got caught while spying on the continent. He talked his way out of it, or rather, cried his way out of it; his captors took pity on him and let him go. Not exactly James Bond in terms of keeping cool, but, hey, it worked!

> **Cornering the market fact:** Music could be big business even way back in the Elizabethan era. In 1575, Queen Elizabeth granted Tallis and Byrd a twenty-one-year monopoly on the printing of music and manuscript

paper. Monopolies were a big deal at the time, and getting one from the queen could make someone quite rich! Byrd later passed the monopoly on to Morley.

ELIZABETHAN MUSIC AND THE BARBERSHOP

L ike theater and literature, English music during Elizabeth's reign went through a "renaissance" of its own. Great musicians and composers seemed to come out of the woodwork, writing beautiful music that is still enjoyed today. Pop musician Sting even recorded a whole album of songs by John Dowland (see the previous entry) in 2006. As Queen Elizabeth encouraged music-making, especially during the last fifteen years or so of her reign, the popularity of secular music reached an all-time high.

People sang and played instruments everywhere, from the wealthiest of courts to the most common inns, and music featured in stage plays, holiday entertainments, important political events, and just about everywhere else—including barbershops!

Contrary to what you might think, these establishments weren't just for haircuts back in the day, though you could certainly get one if you wanted. In fact, barbers were usually known as barber-surgeons, and if that thought kind of horrifies you, it should! You could go to the barber to get a tooth pulled, for example, and sometimes barbers were called on to perform more grisly operations, like amputations. But one of the more common reasons that people went to a barber was to be bled. Wait, what? Yes, it was a common belief in ancient, medieval, and Renaissance medicine that the human body was governed by the four humors. These had nothing to do with being funny, but rather, described a person's makeup and temperament. These personality types and the substances associated with them were choler (yellow bile), phlegm, sanguine (blood), and melancholy (black bile).

These substances interacted in the body in various ways, and an excess of one or the other could result in poor health, it was thought. And one of the best ways to reduce this surplus was to have a barber surgeon gently open a vein in one's arm and let the blood pour out for a bit. Or, they might stick a leech on your arm and just let it feed for a while! After this treatment, the patient would allegedly feel better. The red and white stripes on a barber pole reflect these bygone days, with the white representing bandages and the red signifying blood, by the way.

So what does this all have to do with music? Well, one of the ways that patients could pass the time while they were waiting to be bled was to make music. Many barbershops had sheet music and instruments ready so that patients could make a spontaneous composition to take their minds off of the "treatment" they were about to receive. There was even a popular slow dance, called the *Gregory Walker*, which was named after a well-known hairdresser and musician.

> **Bloody fact:** So, do these Elizabethan horror shops have anything to do with modern barbershop quartets? No. That style originated in the later nineteenth century in African American barbershops.

ELIZABETHAN FOODS

L ike so many people throughout history, the Elizabethans loved a good meal! And for those who could afford the best, they got to enjoy some amazing (and bizarre) foods. Tudor food for both the upper and lower classes really wasn't all that different from what was consumed in medieval England, but there was a greater variety of spices available, thanks to increased and improved trade. The Elizabethans also had the advantage of being able to sample some of those unfamiliar new foods imported from across the ocean, like tomatoes and potatoes.

Breakfast was less common than you might think. It might be not much more than bread and ale (to get the day started right). The ale was very mild, by the way, nothing like the potent IPAs of today!

The two main meals of the day would be lunch and dinner, though lunch was also often called dinner, which is a bit confusing.

Foods were a bit more varied than in previous centuries, but again, the rich got all the best stuff, and the poor had to make do. Though even poor folks usually had an okay selection of things to eat, unless they'd been reduced to the status of beggars. Quite a few fruits and veggies were now available, even if some of them were still rare, coming from other continents. The rich delighted in oranges, lemons, figs, pomegranates, and other unusual produce.

Meats included all the typical farm animals, but also unusual birds like peacocks, swans, cranes, and partridges, and wild animals like deer, boars, and even hedgehogs!

Technically, Wednesdays, Fridays, and Saturdays were designated as "fish days," but this was less for religious reasons than to help stimulate the country's fishing industry. And the definition of "fish" was very broad: pretty much anything that wasn't technically beef. So venison, poultry, and other game all counted as "fish." So did beavers, because they lived in the water most of the time!

Ale was a drink that everyone enjoyed a lot of each day. As mentioned, it was brewed very mild and was often safer to drink than water that hadn't been boiled. The upper classes also loved to drink wine, especially if it was imported, though they tended to put sugar in it, a practice which would horrify modern wine connoisseurs!

> Sweet tooth fact: Queen Elizabeth *loved* sugar, which was rare and expensive at the time. In fact, she loved it so much that over time (and minus proper dental hygiene), it turned her teeth black. She was probably a bit embarrassed about this (though not so much that she gave up eating sugar), but one interesting side effect was that her darkened teeth started a fashion trend, with many ladies at the court artificially blackening their teeth. Why? Well, to imitate the queen, of course, but also to show to others that they were wealthy enough to afford sugar. It just goes to show you, people have a long history of involving themselves in all sorts of stupidity just to project a certain image to others.

THE LAST YEARS OF THE QUEEN

After the defeat of the Spanish Armada, England truly came into its own as a force to be reckoned with—on the seas, and everywhere else. The threats to the nation didn't stop; Spain plotted more invasions, and the spying and intrigue continued. But England was finally able to prove that it was a burgeoning superpower, one that enemies had better think twice about before crossing.

The last fifteen years of Elizabeth's life, from 1588 to 1603, were, as we've seen, the time when the arts flourished as never before. Theater, of course, made a huge impact on the country's language and culture, thanks in large part to the genius of William Shakespeare, and music also flourished as a new era of composers created masterpieces greater than anything seen before, and which continue to connect with audiences today.

While the sun had never shone brighter throughout the Elizabethan world, the source of that light, Elizabeth herself, was beginning to decline. The effects of age and stress had taken their toll, and she now hid under thick layers of makeup and wigs, even as her courtiers still praised her beauty. But the queen's mind was as sharp as ever, and she was aware that many in the court were now waiting for her to die. As the queen was childless, the question of who would rule after her had never been settled, and more and more people were growing nervous about what would happen. Elizabeth had hinted that the Protestant King James VI of Scotland, Mary, Queen of Scots's son, was the logical and legal heir, though this had not been formally established.

Some in her court even tried to hasten Elizabeth's exit, most notoriously the young Robert Devereux, Earl of Essex, who had become her favorite courtier in her last years. Essex was ambitious but not very competent. He bungled several tasks and military missions assigned to him in Ireland, came back to London, and tried to raise a rebellion against Elizabeth in 1601, which went about as well as you might think. He failed and was executed, but his death greatly upset Elizabeth, and might have contributed to her own decline.

At the end of her life, the queen grew terribly afraid of dying, and often stood for hours at a time, believing that if she lied down, she might never get up again. Eventually, she suffered from an illness that took away her ability to speak. When asked again if James would succeed her, she is said to have made a circular motion above her head, as if drawing a crown. Her advisors took this to mean "yes."

Elizabeth had worn her coronation ring for her whole life, but doctors insisted on removing it as she failed. She died on March 24, 1603, within a week of the ring's removal.

She left her nation far stronger and more respected than she found it, and established herself as one of the greatest monarchs in history. The Elizabethan age was over, and a very troubled seventeenth century was soon to follow.

Toxic fact: Some scholars think Elizabeth died of blood poisoning, brought on by the lead in the huge amount of makeup she wore. Lead was a common ingredient in cosmetics at the time, as no one knew how dangerous it was.

CHAPTER 6

THE STUART AND HANOVER CENTURIES

(1603-1837)

KING JAMES I
OF ENGLAND

J ames ascended to the throne of England after Elizabeth's death. He was the son of Mary, Queen of Scots, who, as you'll recall, also had a claim to the English throne. Since Elizabeth had no heir, the next closest relative was James. By 1603, he had already been king of Scotland (as James VI) since 1567, at the age of 1 year old! Obviously, he didn't do a whole lot of governing for many years, but the point is, he'd had plenty of experience as a king. So, when the English throne opened up, James was only too happy to move down to London and claim it.

Not everyone was thrilled with the idea of a Scottish king, even though James followed the "correct" religion, Protestantism. But a lot of folks were relieved that James was married and had children, including two sons, which meant that his government wouldn't have to be so stressed out about who would succeed him, as they had been with Elizabeth.

Let's be honest: James wasn't the greatest monarch in British history. But while he didn't have Elizabeth's brilliance (Did anyone?), he wasn't a total screw-up, either. During his reign, two of the most famous books in the English language were published: the *King James Version* of the Bible (yes, it was named for him, see the next entry), which was printed in 1611, and the *First Folio* (the complete collection of Shakespeare's plays), printed in 1623. James loved the arts, and took over the patronage of Shakespeare's acting troupe. They were renamed the King's Men, and went on performing for many years.

Another momentous occurrence during James's time on the throne came when the Pilgrims sailed to what they called Plymouth Rock in Massachusetts, and established the first permanent English colony in North America.

One curious thing about James was that, as a young man, he had a very strong fear of witches. He believed that witches in Scotland had sent storms to try to sink his ship on at least one occasion, and he even wrote a book in 1597 called *Daemonologie*, which was a study not only of witches, but also of demons, vampires, and werewolves! The book was reprinted in 1603 when he came to England, but it seems that as he grew older, he (wisely) became more skeptical about whether witches really were out to get him.

Still, the king's interest in the subject is believed to have partially inspired the three witches in Shakespeare's tragedy *Macbeth* which was first performed in 1606. As we've seen, *Macbeth* is considered to be an unlucky play, and you should never say the title out loud, unless you are acting in a production of it. Generations of theater actors and directors have believed this and have come up with all sorts of weird rituals to ward off bad luck and evil spirits. James, ever suspicious, would likely approve.

> **Smoky fact:** In addition to hating witches, James was not fond of pipe tobacco, which was becoming ever more popular. In 1604, he wrote a short book called *A Counterblaste to Tobacco*, in which he described tobacco as, "A custome lothsome to the eye, hatefull to the Nose, harmefull to the braine, dangerous to the Lungs." He would no doubt have been tickled by the warning labels on modern tobacco packages.

THE *KING JAMES* BIBLE

The *King James Version* of the Bible is the best-known English edition, and, regardless of one's beliefs, it's a masterpiece of literature.

The idea to commission a new English translation of the Bible grew out of the seemingly never-ending religious tensions that had been plaguing England since Henry VIII broke with Rome back in the 1530s. For much of Elizabeth I's reign, the conflict between Catholics and Protestants was a constant concern in the country, but as her reign went on, another group, the Puritans, gained power and influence. These believers were hardcore in their determination to break with Rome, and they strongly objected to the "Roman Catholic lite" approach of the Anglican services.

By the time James became king in 1603, Puritans wanted a new, authoritative English translation of the Bible, and after they (and others) petitioned him in 1604 for this project, he agreed in principle. English Bibles already existed, of course; the first translations went all the way back to the fourteenth century, when a reform-minded English theologian named John Wycliffe and others illegally translated the Bible into English from Latin (a big no-no at the time). But this new Bible was to be an authorized version, one that everyone could read (or have read to them) and understand. The project took teams of scholars (working together and separately) seven years to complete, but in the end, they produced a masterwork of continuity and poetic language that still resonates with readers today. Some have even theorized that William Shakespeare might have contributed to a portion of it. And while the King James Version never had quite the influence on the English language that the Bard's writings did, quite a few common phrases made their first appearances in its pages, including "give up the ghost," "salt of the earth," and "put words in my mouth."

The result seemed to satisfy both Anglicans and Puritans, which benefitted James politically. The new Bible was printed and sold throughout the land, and both churches and private individuals could own copies. And yet, it would still take decades to firmly establish itself as the definitive Bible for English-speaking Protestants. By the reign of Charles II, the King James Version was universally acknowledged, both in Britain and in the American colonies, and it would not lose its hold until the Revised Standard Version of the Bible was produced in the late nineteenth century.

> **Amusing typo fact:** In the so-called 1631 "Wicked Bible," a printing of the King James Version, there was a glaring typo that amused many, but outraged others. The word "not" was accidentally left out of the seventh commandment, meaning that it read "Thou shalt commit adultery." The authorities were not pleased and apparently the printers faced a serious fine!

THE EAST INDIA COMPANY

The East India Company was founded in 1600 as a joint-stock company (i.e., shares could be bought and sold by shareholders) with the intention, as the name implies, of doing business with India, a desire that grew out of Sir Francis Drake's adventures while circumnavigating the globe, as well as the aftermath of the defeat of the Spanish Armada. English merchants and sailors saw the opportunity to sail into the East Indies, cripple the Spanish and Portuguese trade monopolies there, and take some goods for England. Queen Elizabeth I was eager to press the advantage as well, and gave her permission for the company to form.

In 1592, Sir Walter Raleigh helped to confiscate the wares of a Portuguese ship, the *Madre de Deus*, which was stuffed with treasures, including gold, jewels, textiles, tapestries, spices like cinnamon, cloves, pepper, nutmeg, and more. While we can easily get these spices at a local grocery store today, throughout the Middle Ages and Renaissance, they were rare, precious, and outrageously expensive. The taking of this ship fired imaginations about what riches might lie to the east, and soon, plans were being drawn up to increase British trade missions at the expense of Iberian ones.

In 1599, a group of merchants convened in London with the idea of forming a company to sail to the East Indies under a royal charter. In the next year, they succeeded in obtaining the queen's support, and on December 31, 1600, they were allowed to operate under the rather long name of "Governor and Company of Merchants of London trading into the East Indies." The company received a fifteen-year monopoly on trade and ventures, with anyone operating outside of it facing the possibility of fines and imprisonment. The company allowed its employees (i.e., merchants and sailors) to operate on the side, as long as the EIC received a cut of the profit. This policy kept the EIC in compliance with the monopoly, while shutting out competition from other potential companies. As we've mentioned before, monopolies were a big deal in the Elizabethan and Jacobean years, and if you could obtain one, your fortune was as good as made.

In time, the EIC would grow to be one of the world's first multinational corporations, as well as one of the most influential ever. It raised money by selling shares and promising buyers a portion of the profits later on, a practice that still dominates the business world. Shareholders could attend meetings, which on occasion got very raucous as people demanded returns on their investments or lodged other complaints. But soon, profits and goods starting rolling in, and items (especially spices) that had once been prohibitively expensive were now available to a much larger customer base. And, as you might imagine, more customers meant even more money.

At the time, India was ruled by the Mughal Empire, and the EIC had to act as diplomats as well as merchants, getting in good with its rulers by bribing them or offering military support, or simply by exploiting weaknesses for various goods that the rulers wanted. Infuriatingly, the company also relied on slaves to do much of the labor, expanding the slave trade in that part of the world. The Mughal Empire's rulers were more focused on the Indian interior, which meant that the EIC could take control in coastal cities and territories, effectively making these areas sovereign nations.

In time, as the Mughals weakened (and collapsed in the eighteenth century), the EIC saw an opportunity, and began to dominate affairs in India, eventually leading to Britain imposing colonial rule on the whole of the subcontinent. In 1784, Parliament passed the "India Act" (put forth by Prime Minister William Pitt), which allowed for the British government to rule over the EIC's territory in India. As Britain's empire expanded, the EIC's importance waned—but the former was impossible without the latter.

> Small business fact: Despite its size, the EIC had relatively few employees. Its first governor, Sir Thomas Smythe, operated the whole company out of his home for the first twenty years of its existence, aided by a staff of just six people. Even by 1700, the company still had only about thirty-five full-time employees.

THE GUNPOWDER PLOT

"Remember, remember!
The fifth of November,
The Gunpowder treason and plot;
I know of no reason
Why the Gunpowder treason
Should ever be forgot!"

The opening lines of this famous poem are well known in Britain and by quite a few on the other side of the pond. Every November 5, also known as Bonfire Night, fires are lit across Britain to commemorate the failure of a massive assassination attempt against King James I, one of the boldest and most outrageous such plots in British history.

But what really happened on this notorious night?

A group of Catholic conspirators led by Robert Catesby, whose family had been persecuted for their beliefs, decided that it was well past time to restore Catholic rule to England. King James had not been as tolerant as they had hoped he might be, and he even ordered all remaining Catholic priests out of the country. So, the conspirators created a plot with the most astonishing goal: they intended to blow up the House of Lords with the king and the entire government inside!

The conspirators rented a cellar that happened to run under the House of Lords' building: no way would that happen today! And on the night of November 4, they began filling it with barrels of gunpowder, three dozen in total. But one of the plotters, named Guy Fawkes, was discovered down there. He was the man who was going to light the gunpowder on fire. He was arrested and tortured and finally confessed, naming his co-conspirators.

But how was Fawkes found out? It turns out that a Catholic nobleman named Lord Monteagle, brother-in-law to one of the conspirators, received an anonymous letter (probably from one of the other

conspirators, if not his own brother-in-law), warning him to stay away from Parliament on November 5. While they probably thought they were doing a fellow believer a favor, they didn't count on him being loyal to the Protestant king. Monteagle alerted James and his security, who began to search the area. That led them to the cellar, which led them to Fawkes. The plot was foiled only hours before it was set to go off. And, obviously, if the king and the entire government had been killed, England would have plunged into chaos.

Fawkes and the others were sentenced to be executed, but at his execution, Fawkes jumped from the scaffold and broke his neck, killing himself before authorities could receive the satisfaction of killing him. November 5 was later declared a day of public thanks for the safety of the realm, and the holiday is still celebrated annually.

> **Explosive fact:** That many barrels of gunpowder, if exploded, would have levelled everything for 130 feet in every direction, and partly destroyed buildings up to 360 feet away!

THE FIERY FATE OF SHAKESPEARE'S ORIGINAL GLOBE

The Globe itself is nearly as famous as the works of Shakespeare. An outdoor playhouse, it was an institution for London's theatergoers in the late sixteenth and early seventeenth centuries, and many of Shakespeare's greatest works were premiered there. It was O-shaped, allowing for people to stand in front of the stage, and provided covered seats around the edges.

The big problem was that buildings like these had no safety codes at all. They were built in a hurry to attract audiences, and were basically just wooden buildings with straw roofs, which means they were very vulnerable to fire. And, as you can imagine, there were no real plans for evacuation in an emergency.

Just such an emergency happened on June 29, 1613, during a performance of Shakespeare's *All Is True* (later retitled *Henry VIII*). The Globe had a cannon that would fire whenever the action in a play called for it (such as during battles). The cannon was kept in an attic, near the straw roof. You can see where this is going...

On one particular day, after the cannon was fired, some sparks flew out of it and onto the nearby straw, starting a fire. One playgoer, Sir Henry Wotton, provided an eye-witness account of what happened next:

Now King Henry making a Masque at the Cardinal Wolsey's house, and certain cannons being shot off at his entry, some of the paper or other stuff, wherewith one of them was stopped, did light on the thatch, where being thought at first but idle smoak, and their eyes more attentive to the show, it kindled inwardly, and ran round like a train, consuming within less than an hour the whole house to the very ground. This was the fatal period of that virtuous fabrick, wherein yet nothing did perish but wood and straw, and a few forsaken cloaks; only one man had his breeches set on fire, that would perhaps have broyled him, if he had not by the benefit of a provident wit, put it out with a bottle of ale.

So, one man saved his own behind by pouring ale on it! Incredibly, it seems that no one else was hurt, and everyone was able to get out of the burning playhouse in time. Since there was no organized fire-fighting force in London at the time, there wasn't much that people could do. The theater burned down in about two hours, taking with it costumes, and possibly some original manuscripts of Shakespeare's plays. The Globe was rebuilt the next year, but by then, Shakespeare had pretty much retired, and he died just two years later, in 1616.

Globe fact: The new Globe lasted until 1642, when the Puritans closed it after they banned all plays. A few years later, it was pulled down to make room for new houses. And that was it for a few centuries, until a new Globe was opened in 1997 that recreated the look and feel of Shakespeare's original, but with a lot more safety features built in—plus a gift shop.

THE SAD FATE OF PRINCE HENRY

Although some had mixed feelings about King James I (which they would have kept to themselves, of course), his son Henry seemed to be the gleaming hope who could unite England. Henry (1594-1612) was educated, devoted to culture and art, good looking, and charismatic. He danced well and played music, and was all-around "princely." He was so popular that at times he outshone his father, who seemed to actually be annoyed by it!

In short, Henry was cultured and intelligent, with a passion for learning and beauty. Most people had no doubt that the prince, the future King Henry IX, would be a great ruler. And, were it not for an unexpected tragedy, he probably would have been.

In addition to his other talents and affinities, Henry was also athletic and enjoyed various sports and games. He had for a long time wanted to learn to swim, but in 1607, two of King James' earls cautioned the king that not only was swimming unsafe, it was also not appropriate behavior for a future king. The thing is, being a teenager, Henry went ahead and learned anyway, and slipped away for a dip now and then. It so happened that in the late summer of 1612, he took to the water more than a few times, and it turned out his father's advisors were right to be concerned. After one of these swims, Henry fell ill, and by October, it was clear that his life was hanging in the balance. While some feared that he had been poisoned, most historians now think that he had contracted typhoid fever while in the water. He died on November 6, 1612, at the tender age of 18, sending the kingdom into shock. One can only wonder how the events of seventeenth-century England might have played out under King Henry IX rather than King Charles I.

> **Beyond the grave fact:** One week after Prince Henry's death, a man who was probably insane went to St. James' Palace and claimed to be Henry's ghost. As distraught as the court likely was, no one went for the ploy.

THE PILGRIMS

The story of the Pilgrims ("religious travelers"), between their flight from England, the landing at Plymouth Rock, their encounters with Native Americans, and the first Thanksgiving are an essential part of American mythology, one that has been relayed for generations. Images of men wearing black clothing and tall, buckled hats, and carrying muskets in the wilderness of New England are instantly recognizable to people throughout the United States. But, as always, the story we receive and the facts don't always line up. So, what really happened here?

Many of those in the group that would become the Pilgrims were Puritans who pushed back against King James and his support for the

Church of England. As James had also married Anne of Denmark, who had strong Catholic sympathies, he had little interest in the more extreme of his Protestant subjects. Many Puritans left England and sought refuge in the Netherlands, but they proved equally unhappy there, fearing they were losing their identity.

Then James saw a solution. He was eager to populate the new English colonies that were springing up in the Americas, and he was eager to be rid of Puritans at the same time. He offered them the chance to leave and go practice their faith as they wished.

And so, on September 6, 1620, the legendary *Mayflower* set sail from Plymouth, England. Originally bound for a settlement near present-day New York City, weather forced them northward, and by November 9, they spotted the tip of what is now Cape Cod. The crew decided to land farther inland, but since this was not the original destination, it technically didn't come under the king's charter. Thus, leaders had to hastily draw up one of their own, which would later become the Mayflower Compact. After landing in a natural harbor on November 16, the Pilgrims set foot on land and began constructing a simple town. The first winter was brutal, and a combination of disease, exposure, and food scarcity meant that only fifty-two people from that first voyage survived.

By March 1621, the colonists were approached by a Native man who spoke English. Tisquantum, commonly known as Squanto, was a surviving member of the Patuxet tribe, which had been wiped out by disease. Tisquantum had learned English from other traders, and had also been kidnapped and taken to Europe as a slave at one point. But eventually, he was freed and returned to America.

The Pilgrims began to learn the intricacies of the region's politics and discovered that they were by no means the only people living there. They signed a peace treaty with Ousamequin (known to the Pilgrims as Massasoit), leader of the Wampanoag, where each side agreed to aid the other in mutual defense. It was this treaty that led to the fabled first Thanksgiving the following November (to which the Wampanoag weren't initially even invited!), and the alliance would last in various forms for about fifty years, before the forces of colonialism overwhelmed it. Still, it was not always a peaceful coexistence by any means. And many settlers were only too happy to deal violently with enemies of the Wampanoag.

Thanksgiving was not a thing in colonial America or the decades that followed. It was only declared a national holiday by Abraham Lincoln during the American Civil War as a way to promote national unity, and, at that time, there was no mention of the Pilgrims. After the war, the legend was used by Protestants who were worried about the large numbers of Catholic and Jewish immigrants arriving in the United States. They felt that if they could tell the story that Native Americans had "willingly" given up their lands to these Puritan settlers who then founded the nation, it would give these Protestants a kind of assumed cultural superiority over new immigrant populations. It was a way of saying "we were here first," even though Native people had, of course, lived on the American continent for thousands of years.

As you might have guessed, the myth of the Pilgrims that survives today says far more about American identity than it does actual history.

> **Bloody fact:** Historian David Silverman, professor of history at George Washington University and author of *This Land is Their Land*, has noted that signs of violence were everywhere in the settlements of both the Pilgrims and their Native neighbors. "If you walked into either the Plymouth colony or a Wampanoag village during the 1600s, the first thing you'd see at the entrance would be severed body parts and decapitated heads." Yet another element you won't see in modern Thanksgiving celebrations!

OLD TOM PARR, A TRUE STORY?

Thomas Parr is a difficult man to categorize; does he fit in this book's medieval chapter, the Tudors, or the Stuarts? I ask because, if certain accounts are to be believed, he was born in 1482 and died in 1635, at the ripe old age of 152! Now, this immediately sounds like nonsense, and it probably is. But Old Tom's story is a pretty fun bit of British folklore. Since we know when Parr died, let's have a look at the mysteries surrounding when he was born. Is it possible he lived as long as some maintain?

Parr was born in the village of Alberbury in Shropshire, near the Welsh border, allegedly in either 1482 or 1483, at the time when the Wars of the Roses were coming to an end. He lived a simple life as a poor and humble man, and his diet was said to be "subrancid cheese and milk," along with bread and sour whey. William Harvey (the physician who discovered the process by which blood circulates through the human body) wrote that, "On this sorry fare, but living in his home, free from care, did this poor man attain to such length of days."

Tom seemed to live a life of vitality and happiness, marrying and fathering children at the age of eighty, and again at the age of 122! This second wife, Jane Lloyd, would claim that her elderly showed no signs of aging or slowing down. Word spread about this amazing man and his longevity, and he was brought to London to meet King Charles I in the autumn of 1635. But it seems that this trip took a toll on Old Tom, between the excitement of the crowds thronging to see him and his being fed very rich foods. He died while he was still there. One wonders how much longer he might have lived if he hadn't made that fateful journey?

Harvey conducted an autopsy on Parr and found that his internal organs were in very good shape. The great physician also could not determine the exact cause of Tom's death. So what was happening? Was it at all possible that Tom was really that old? It's highly unlikely, of course. It's possible that his birth record was confused with that of his grandfather, who might have also been named Tom. A grandfather born in the 1480s would have been entirely realistic. It's also possible that Old Tom was actually born around 1565, instead, which would have put him at about age seventy when he died, which seems far more likely. Tom himself could not remember events from his early life, certainly nothing about Henry VII or Henry VIII, the Wars of the Roses, or anything else. In the end, it seems this mind-blowing life span was nothing more than a simple mix-up of birthdates, but Old Tom was apparently happy to go along with the ruse.

> **Royal approval fact:** King Charles I was impressed enough by the curious case of Tom that he ordered the old man (regardless of his age) to be buried in Westminster Abbey, alongside kings and queens, poets, statesmen, musicians, and other luminaries. Whatever the truth, Tom certainly got everything out of his life!

KING CHARLES I AND PARLIAMENT

With Prince Henry dead, his brother, Prince Charles (1600-49) ascended to the throne as King Charles I on March 27, 1625. Charles was intelligent and thoughtful, and he went on to be a great patron of both art and music; for example, he created the royal post of "Master of the King's Music," which still exists today. But he almost immediately found himself in conflict with Parliament and the government. There was increasing tension in the country between the Puritans, the hard-line Protestants, and the more mainstream

Anglicans, and Charles did his best to irritate the former, most of all by marrying a Catholic French princess, Henrietta Maria (who, interestingly, was never crowned queen, because she wouldn't participate in Protestant services). This made many of Charles's subjects angry and suspicious, and while the king had initially promised that official policy toward Catholics (i.e., persecution) would not change after his marriage, Henrietta insisted that English and Scottish believers in the older religion be left to their own devices, and this agreement was actually written into their marriage treaty. Catholic-helmed plots against Elizabeth I and James I were still fresh in many people's minds, and they saw this new accommodation as an ominous sign.

Yet Charles was deeply religious and favored the Anglican liturgy, something that his reform-minded subjects, both in England and Scotland, found increasingly distasteful. Next, Charles began to give his support to anti-Puritan preachers and secretly promised the French king that he would relax religious restrictions on Catholics in England.

In the eyes of Parliament, these moves were unfortunate but forgivable. What was more difficult to overlook was Charles's belief in Divine Right, which basically meant that the king was anointed by God, and could do whatever he wished. Given that England had experience with tyrannical kings going back to John in the early thirteenth century, Charles's stubbornness on this issue didn't make him very popular (that whole "consent of the governed" thing).

The king's dismissive attitude toward Parliament only made things worse. He dissolved the governmental body more than once, and moved to do so permanently in 1629, leaving himself as the sole authority in England. Charles imprisoned his main Parliamentary opponent, Sir John Eliot, in the Tower of London that same year, and Eliot remained there until his death in 1632. These moves caused this period to be branded the "Eleven Years' Tyranny" by some, a rocky stretch that saw Charles fund his reign with taxes, loans, the use of archaic forest laws, and a tax known as "ship money," all of which made him very unpopular with people who might have otherwise supported him.

These fiscal liberties were just part of the issue. Charles also tried to enforce an Anglican-style liturgy in Scotland and a riot broke out in Edinburgh in response, forcing the king to recall Parliament to raise money for a war; a Scottish king going to war against his own people! This was too much, not only for Puritans, but even for many mainstream Anglicans. Tempers flared again, and after Charles tried to have some members of Parliament arrested in 1642, an outright rebellion began. Soon the country sank into civil war.

> **Stammering fact:** Charles was sickly as a child, and while he grew to be a skilled horseman and fencer, he retained a stutter for the rest of his life, which certainly must have made him look weak in the eyes of some of his more resentful subjects.

THE ENGLISH CIVIL WAR AND THE KILLING OF A KING

King Charles made it clear that he wasn't willing to negotiate with anyone who questioned his Divine Right to rule. This stubborn position (which his brother, Henry, probably wouldn't have taken, incidentally) meant that a full-on clash was inevitable. And so, England found itself embroiled in a civil war, the first since the Wars of the Roses nearly 200 years earlier. And, as in the multi-staged Wars of the Roses, it might be better to call the period of 1642 to 1651 the "English Civil Wars," since there were actually three wars fought during that tumultuous stretch, the first occurring from 1642 to 1646 (when Charles was captured), the second from 1648 to 1649 (which ended with Charles' execution), and the third spanning 1649-51 (which involved a failed invasion by Charles' son, Prince Charles; it wasn't yet his time).

Charles controlled northern and western England at first, but the Parliamentarians were able to forge an alliance with the Scots (whom, you'll recall, Charles had wanted to go to war with). On July 2, 1644, the Royalist and Parliamentarian forces fought at Marston Moor, west of York, and the Parliamentarians scored a crucial victory. The Battle of Naseby the following year (in June 1645) was the decisive win for the Parliamentarian side. Charles was defeated and surrendered to the Scots in 1646. He was handed over to Parliament, but he negotiated a secret peace with the Scots in 1648, and rallied the Royalist troops again. And so, a second civil war broke out. But Parliament's New Model Army, led by Oliver Cromwell (see the next entry), again defeated royal forces and took Charles into custody. The Puritans, now in control, decided that peace was not possible if Charles were to continue to reign, or even allowed to live!

It was an astonishing declaration; would a nation really kill its king? Even if Charles was obnoxious about his right to rule, most accepted that God decreed a monarch's place in the earthly order of things. If Charles were executed, would that offend God, who had placed him on the throne? Many rebels and loyalists wrestled with this question, and a lot of people, even politicians, opposed executing him. But Charles' opponents, led by Cromwell, won out, and the king was put on trial for treason, found guilty, and sentenced to death.

King Charles I was beheaded on January 30, 1649, in London, and his head was displayed like that of a common traitor. Needless to say, many were shocked and furious, but for now, the Puritans were in control, especially after Charles's son failed to take back the nation and reclaim power in the third leg of the wars. The Puritans would rule Britain very differently, as a Commonwealth with no king, and would often try to force their religious beliefs on the whole population. As you'll see on page 212, they weren't especially successful.

Grisly needle-and-thread fact: The day after Charles lost his head and it was displayed publicly, it was sewn back onto his body for burial.

OLIVER CROMWELL

C romwell (1599-1658) was a man both loved and despised, in his own time and ever since. He was responsible for bringing down the British monarchy and executing a king, and yet in time, Cromwell started taking on the trappings of a king himself, as he stepped into the leadership of a divided England as Lord Protector. So, who was this curious and complex man?

Cromwell was born to a minor landowning family near Cambridge, and was a descendent of Thomas Cromwell, a man who famously fell out with Henry VIII and was executed in 1540. Oliver was eventually educated at Sidney Sussex College in Cambridge, which had Puritan and Calvinist leanings. In the 1630s, he inherited some additional money and had a kind of spiritual awakening toward a deeper Puritan way of life, amid the growing turmoil and conflict between King Charles I and Parliament. Cromwell had been an MP for Huntingdon in 1628, but as the government's situation grew worse, he stood for Parliament and became an MP for Cambridge in 1640.

When the Civil War began in 1642, Cromwell was firmly against the king, and was soon the lieutenant-general of the Eastern Association army of Parliament. In 1645, he was promoted to second in command of the Parliament's main force, the New Model Army. His status was such that by 1649, when Charles was defeated and captured, Cromwell was one of the MPs who signed off on the king's death warrant. After Charles' execution, Cromwell pursued a military campaign in Ireland, defeating the rebellious Irish forces and occupying the country.

He also led a campaign against the Scots. After winning in both locations, he helped to establish the Commonwealth of England, Scotland, and Ireland, bringing about an end to the war. Cromwell was now Lord General, the commander-in-chief of the army.

In December of 1653, he was offered the role of Lord Protector. Parliament even offered Cromwell the crown, but he rejected it, preferring to think of himself as a "watchman" for the Commonwealth. Nevertheless, he ruled as king in all but name, even though he was constrained by Parliament. The new constitution said that he must receive a majority vote from the Council of State in order to call or dissolve Parliament, a precedent that was to remain in place after the Restoration of the monarchy and exists in Britain to this day.

While Cromwell ruled with considerable support, he was not without enemies, and many of his new government's laws were draconian and unforgiving. As you might expect from someone of Puritan persuasion, he did not extend religious toleration to Quakers and other minority religious groups, to say nothing of Catholics.

Cromwell's time at the top was brief, however; he seems to have suffered from malaria and kidney stones, and it wasn't long before his health began to fail. He died on September 3, 1658, probably of blood poisoning following a urinary infection.

> Inexperienced fact: For all of his importance as a commander during the war, Cromwell had very little military experience beforehand, having only served in a militia.

HOW "PURE" WERE THE PURITANS?

Modern imagination likes to think of the Puritans in England and America as dour, humorless people, dressed strictly in black, who banned pretty much everything that could be deemed fun. Although they weren't always the jolliest bunch, they were less severe than you might imagine.

Puritans believed in hard work, and weren't big on fun for fun's sake. When Cromwell took over the leadership of the nation, he closed all the theaters (as we've seen, Puritans had long hated plays), and discouraged or banned most sports. Cromwell's New Model Army helped enforce these new laws, and they did seem overly stern at times. Work was banned on Sundays, as it truly became a day of rest. And swearing was forbidden, too; it was something that could land you in jail! Women were not allowed to wear makeup and had to dress in plain colors, rather than bright ones, with their hair back and covered in a white cloth.

Cromwell also took the unpopular step of banning Christmas celebrations, something that had been enjoyed since the Middle Ages. He wanted Christmas to be a remembrance of the birth of Jesus and nothing else. Even decorations such as holly and other greenery were not permitted. On the day itself, soldiers would follow their noses and see if anyone in a given area was making a Christmas feast. If so, they would seize the food from the offender, the seventeenth-century Grinches!

And yet, Cromwell wasn't quite the joyless tyrant a lot of people think he was. He was actually fond of music and even dancing (which he allowed at his daughter's wedding). He also played bowls (bowling) and liked riding horses. He was known to enjoy alcohol, especially sherry and beer, and also liked smoking (given how tobacco was demonized by many Puritans only a few decades earlier, this is an amazing fact!).

Cromwell seems to have softened his views as he got older, probably because the reality of running a country meant that he couldn't impose every Puritan value on everyone if he wanted to have any chance of preventing rebellion and fostering constant resentment. He did change the structure of the English Church, but he didn't care as much what people believed as long as they conformed and didn't cause trouble, believing this to be an outward show of piety.

Cromwell, like most human beings, was something of a contradiction. He wasn't the humorless dictator that some people today think he was, but he was definitely not an enlightened, tolerant ruler, either. Toward the end of his rule, when he passed his authority on to his son, people were already pretty tired of the Puritans, and longed for a monarch. The country would soon get its wish.

> **Tasty fact:** Despite claims to the contrary, Cromwell didn't ban mince pies at Christmas (seriously, who would *do* that, anyway?!). Pies of all kinds were eaten all year long, and there were no Puritan laws that mentioned mince pies as being off-limits.

THE RESTORATION AND KING CHARLES II

The whole Commonwealth thing didn't work out quite as well as Oliver Cromwell and his Puritans had hoped. By becoming Lord Protector, Cromwell was king in all but name, and it must have had many thinking, "Why not just have the actual king instead?" And there was a potential "real" king, Charles I's son, who was also named Charles. Charles the younger had tried to save his father from the chopping block in 1649, but failed. Soon after, his supporters in England and Scotland declared him the new king, and this would-be Charles II went to Scotland to rally his troops. They invaded England, but were met by Cromwell's superior forces and lost.

After this defeat, Charles escaped and took refuge in France, Germany, and the Netherlands at various times. His supporters never gave up on him, and he never gave up on the idea of taking back the crown. As it turns out, he didn't have to launch another attack to do so. Oliver Cromwell died in 1658, and passed the role of leadership onto his son, Richard (just as a king would, incidentally). But poor Richard wasn't much of a leader or administrator, and soon the government was a bit of a mess. Richard was forced to resign, and it looked like war might break out again. As people were also tired of the Puritans being, well, puritanical, many started to look back longingly to the time when a king ruled England—even if Charles I was a bit of an ass.

The decision was made to ask the younger Charles to return to the country and become King Charles II, to which he happily agreed. He entered London on his 30th birthday, May 29, 1660, to much rejoicing. There were conditions, though: those who had acted against the crown were to be pardoned, and the rights of Parliament were to be upheld. The pardon didn't extend to those who had actually taken part in the condemnation and execution of Charles I, though. No, those poor fellows were rounded up (though a few escaped to Europe and America), tried, and executed, often by being hanged, drawn, and quartered in the brutal, medieval fashion.

The Restoration that followed was exactly that: a reinstatement of the older ways, while being more sensitive to the changes and challenges of the past thirty years. It was truly a new age. Charles II was a king in the grand sense, and determined to be a patron of the arts, sciences, and learning. He gave his backing to the new organization known as the Royal Society of London for the Improvement of Natural Knowledge, a group of scientists whose studies would change the world. The government soon stabilized, and many saw the quick turnaround as proof of divine workings, though there were still troubled times ahead.

Gruesome fact: To drive home the point that none but the anointed monarch should rule the land, Oliver Cromwell's body was dug up in 1661, hanged at Tyburn, and then his head was cut off and put on a pole at Westminster; it stayed there until 1685!

THE PLAGUE OF 1665-66

As if England hadn't been through enough with its civil war, the Puritan years, and seeing a Stuart king restored to the throne, nature had another nasty surprise in store. The country had been "plagued" by the bubonic plague for over 300 years, going back to the awful Black Death of the mid-fourteenth century. Outbreaks were common (about every ten years), but usually didn't spread too far. It was fairly common for them to strike in London, for many people to flee to the countryside, and then return a few months later, after cases dwindled back down. Shakespeare dealt with outbreaks on more than one occasion, for example, when the London playhouses would close, forcing his acting troupe to go on tour to support itself.

But this pattern of mild outbreaks changed drastically in the spring of 1665, when a new version of the plague paid a visit. By the summer, the illness was killing about 1,000 people per week, and King Charles II was compelled to leave the city, going first to Westminster and then moving onto Oxford for his own safety. The death toll continued to rise in September, and it seemed like the Black Death of old was back with a vengeance. It is from this time that images of doctors wearing terrifying long-beaked masks originated. Those beaks held various herbs that were thought to dispel the "foul airs" of the plague, and the fact that they wore these masks probably did prevent many of them from becoming infected—just not for the reasons they thought.

The famed writer and diarist Samuel Pepys (for more on him, see page 221) wrote on October 6, 1665:

> **"But Lord, how empty the streets are, and melancholy, so many poor sick people in the streets, full of sores, and so many sad stories overheard as I walk, everybody talking of this dead, and that man sick, and so many in this place, and so many in that. And they tell me that in Westminster there is never a physician, and but one apothecary left, all being dead—but that there are great hopes of a great decrease this week."**

Thankfully, the death rate went down as it grew colder, and over the next few months the pestilence seemed to go its own way, as it often had before. Still, it's believed that up to 100,000 people died because of this particular outbreak. By February 1666, Charles came back to London, which was a sign that it was safe for most people to come back, too. The plague passed away and everything returned more or less to normal. That is, until the night of September 2, 1666, when a baker named Thomas Farriner transformed the town in an instant.

True rat fact: As we Anglophiles know, the plague is spread by fleas that carry the bacteria and live on rats and other rodents (see page 125). One theory for why this particular outbreak of the plague went away was that the rats themselves were developing an immunity to the bacteria, meaning that they weren't dying and causing the fleas to leap off of them in search of other (i.e., human) hosts. If so, we can thank microevolution for slowing the outbreak!

THE FIRE OF 1666

Thomas Farriner lived above his bakery on the appropriately named Pudding Lane. His business was quite a success, and provided bread for the British Navy. But something went wrong in the early hours of September 2. Farriner was awakened by the smell of smoke coming from the bakery below. Knowing that a fire had started, he managed to get out, along with his wife and daughter. But the flames were already spreading quickly in the close confines of the neighborhood. London had nothing like a firefighting brigade at the time, so it was up to individuals to splash buckets of water on the flames, which obviously wasn't going to do much good on a straw roof engulfed by flames. The thing is, fires were fairly common in those days, and they were usually contained without much trouble. But it had been an unusually dry summer, which meant that the old wooden houses and their thatched roofs were little more than tinderboxes.

London's mayor, Sir Thomas Bloodworth, was roused from sleep and informed of this particular blaze, and is said to have replied, "Pish! A woman might piss it out!" His casual attitude meant that he didn't act quickly enough and order firebreaks, which would have pulled down buildings and prevented the fire from spreading. Because of this mistake, the flames spread rapidly throughout the old city, destroying most of the homes there (possibly as many as 13,000 of them) and tragically, the medieval cathedral of St. Paul's (its old lead roof melted in the extreme heat).

Samuel Pepys had not only observed plague-stricken London, but now also the conflagration that consumed it. He rushed off to tell King Charles II, who ordered that the houses in the path of the fire be torn down to create a firebreak, but by this point the flames were moving too swiftly for that strategy to pay off. Firefighters used gunpowder to try to blow up houses to create a bigger firebreak, but this only caused further panic, and a rumor quickly spread that the French were invading!

The fire was still raging on September 4, and by this point the king himself had joined the bucket brigades to try to get water passed from the Thames and into the city.

In the end, the fire burned from Sunday, September 2 to Thursday, September 6. Other firebreaks and a shift in the wind eventually caused it to die out. Only about one-fifth of the old city survived, while some 13,000 houses were destroyed. Officially, only six to eight people are recorded as having died, but the number was almost certainly higher than that. Rumors circulated that the fire had been started by French or Dutch spies, and poor old Farriner had to keep his head down amidst the confusion. A French watchmaker named Robert Hubert falsely claimed that he had started the fire and was hanged for it, though it was later discovered that he wasn't even in England, much less the city, at the time! London began the slow process of rebuilding under the direction of architect Christopher Wren, but sadly, much of its medieval and Tudor heritage was lost that week.

> **False rat fact:** The fire did not put an end to the plague by driving out rats, as many people often claim. The plague had already declined to very few cases by the time the fire started, and in any case, the flames didn't spread far enough to drive all the rats out of the city. No one at the time thought the fire had cured the plague, and no serious historian now thinks so, either.

JOHN MILTON

Milton (1608-74) was one of England's greatest poets, writing during a time of great upheaval and religious conflict. He managed to survive it all, experiencing the reigns of James I and Charles I, the Commonwealth, and then the Restoration of Charles II.

Born in London, Milton was educated at Cambridge for a time, and then embarked on a tour of Europe, mainly France and Italy. While he enjoyed encountering new cultures and learning from those who were different (he even had a meeting with the great astronomer Galileo during the trip), in 1639 Milton felt compelled to return to England, as word of civil war started to spread.

Despite his meetings with English and Italian Catholics, Milton came back as a firm supporter of Oliver Cromwell and the Puritans against King Charles I. So loyal was he to the cause that he ended up being employed by Cromwell's government during the Commonwealth, even as his eyesight began to falter. He was able to continue his duties with the help of others, but after Charles II came to the throne in 1660, Milton went into hiding, fearing repercussions. He was right. An arrest warrant was issued for his support of the Commonwealth, and though a general pardon was soon offered, he was still arrested. The intervention of friends and the paying of a fine got him off the hook, and he lived for a time in London, leaving only when the plague struck in 1665.

While Milton wrote many great works, he is best known as the author of *Paradise Lost* (published in 1667), an epic poem written in blank verse—aka poetry that doesn't rhyme, but still has a specific meter. In the second edition of the poem for 1674, Milton added an explanation for "why the poem rhymes not" to confused readers. Enthusiasts and English language scholars consider *Paradise Lost* to be one of the greatest epic poems in the English language—if not the greatest. It tells the story of Satan tempting Adam and Eve, and the couple's expulsion from the Garden of Eden, but it goes into far more detail about the story of the rebellious angels who were expelled from heaven. Satan, formerly Lucifer, is deliberately a morally gray character, with some readers seeing him as a villain, and many others arguing that he is actually a tragic hero.

Milton followed up this work with a sequel of sorts in 1671, *Paradise Regained*, though the scope of this poem is narrower, a retelling of Satan's temptation of Christ in the wilderness. While both of these poems were published when Milton was older, some researchers think that he might have started work on both as early as the 1640s. What is certain is that by the time they were refined and finished, he was completely blind, and had been forced to dictate his words to assistants, who transcribed them.

> **More new words fact:** Like Shakespeare, Milton introduced an amazing number of new words into English, more than any other writer. Among the approximately 630 new words formulated by Milton: pandemonium ("all demons"), unoriginal, earthshaking, enjoyable, terrific (but meaning something terrifying), fragrance, stunning, disregard, and space in the sense of "outer space."

SAMUEL PEPYS AND HIS DIARY

P epys (1633-1703)— by the way, his name is pronounced "peeps," like the little marshmallow birds that appear around Easter—was a member of Parliament and a navy administrator. He is best known these days for his detailed diary entries, which he wrote between 1660 and 1669. They offer a remarkable and invaluable glimpse into daily life during the early years of the Restoration and the reign of King Charles II, as well as recording details about those minor incidents that occurred during this decade, the plague and the Great London Fire.

Pepys's writings are quirky, amusing, and fascinating. For example, he mentions in 1660 that he was served a cup of tea, about the most British thing imaginable. But in this case, it's the first recorded instance of tea being served socially, rather than as a medicine. He wrote that after a meeting to discuss naval affairs, a certain Sir Richard Ford "did send for a Cupp of Tee (a China drink) of which I never had drank before."

Pepys admitted to having an excessive fondness for young ladies. He was married to Elisabeth de Saint Michel (1640-1669), who came from a family of French Protestant immigrants, but his wandering eye continued to wander, and he had several flings over the years. He even recorded these encounters in his diaries! But of course, the old male double standard kicked in, and when he became convinced that Elisabeth was having an affair with her dancing instructor in 1663, he became enraged. His anger turned to paranoia, and Elisabeth got sick of it, and his philandering. At one point, she even threatened Pepys with a hot poker, over his affair with their (former) servant, Deb Willet:

> "At last, about one o'clock [in the morning], she come to my side of the bed, and drew my curtaine open, and with the tongs red hot at the ends, made as if she did design to pinch me with them, at which, in dismay, I rose up, and with a few words she laid them down ... (January 12, 1669)"

That smoothed things over for a while, but Elisabeth was destined to die of typhoid in November of that year. Pepys genuinely mourned her death and was despondent about it. He never remarried, but at one point, he did have a lion as a pet. As you do.

Cheesy fact: During the 1666 fire, Pepys panicked about losing his most valued possessions. As the flames spread, he went outside of his home and dug a hole in the ground, figuring that he could bury things and keep them safe from damage. And what did he bury there? Gold, some of his writings, and a wheel of Parmesan cheese! Parmesan was rare, expensive, delicious, and had to be imported from Italy, so one can understand his concern!

TEA IN BRITAIN

Tea is, of course, the quintessential British drink, though some might argue that beer is a stronger candidate for that title. It's hard to imagine a time when tea wasn't drunk in Britain, and yet its introduction was relatively recent in the grand scale of history, only being first served socially in the seventeenth century, and establishing itself as the British drink of choice in the eighteenth.

Samuel Pepys may have recorded the first known serving of tea as a social drink, but that simply implies that it was already being done; he was just the first person to mention it. Tea was, of course, imported from China during this time and as such was very expensive, reserved only for the wealthy. But King Charles II's soon-to-be wife, Catherine of Braganza, was fond of the drink, and it soon became a hit at court. From there it slowly began to filter down (steep?) into the lower classes and become cheaper. And the rest is British history!

Sort of. In the later seventeenth century, coffee was all the rage (see page 240 for the lowdown on the rise of London's coffee houses), and it would be some time before tea truly hit its stride.

Tea had been drunk in China for over 2,000 years, and it then spread into neighboring countries like India at some time. By the sixteenth century, Portuguese and Dutch explorers were trading with China, and the first mentions of tea come from the 1550s. In 1610, a Dutch ship brought tea to Western Europe, and it seems to have been introduced to Britain by the 1650s. This was green tea, of course, though black tea would come to be the preferred version of the drink in the country.

The East India Company was eager to get in on importing this new drink, and Charles II greatly broadened their reach and powers to do just that (among other things). The EIC was finally able to establish trading posts in China itself in the early eighteenth century, and that was when the tea truly began to flow. Prices fell, allowing tea to be enjoyed by everyone. The EIC grew enormously in power through its tea monopoly (though smuggling was still rampant), and by the end of the eighteenth century, the global tea trade was pretty much in the hands of the EIC alone, which gave it tremendous political and economic power.

And, as we know, disputes over taxes on tea were one of the contributing causes of the American Revolution.

Most everyday Brits weren't too concerned about geopolitical affairs, though; they just wanted their cuppa. In 1717, Thomas Twining opened a tea shop in London, where patrons could buy the drink by the cup, or purchase dried leaves to take home. And unlike coffee shops, women were welcome, which only helped boost tea's popularity as the domestic drink of choice, a status it would never lose.

> Stomach-turning fact: In the early days of the tea trade, tea was often adulterated, i.e., mixed with other substances, to make the leaves last longer. Adulteration was usually done by the traders themselves, and could mean that the tea was mixed with substances like ash or willow

leaves, various kinds of flowers, sawdust (and old miller's trick) and even, wait for it ... dried sheep's dung. These substances were dyed to look like the tea itself. What this all meant (beyond being gross) was that more tea was consumed than was actually imported!

THEATER DURING THE COMMONWEALTH AND AFTERWARD

During the Puritan years, the arts definitely took a bit of a hit: theaters were closed, music composition was very tightly supervised, and overall, people couldn't be as free about such things as they had previously. But, as we've seen, Cromwell liked dancing and dance music, and it turns out that the Puritans did tend to look the other way about at least some artistic works.

One interesting fellow named William Davenant came up with some clever ideas in the 1650s of getting around the "no theater" law. Davenant was rumoured by some to be a son of Shakespeare, a rumor that he never denied, probably because it made him far more intriguing. He'd already been in trouble with Cromwell because of his theater associations, but he didn't let that stop him. First, he secretly converted a part of his home into a private theater, so he and his friends could perform their illegal plays to discrete audiences.

Later he came up with the idea of costuming his plays as music. Given that the Puritans didn't hate music nearly as much as plays, they were okay with this when they found out what he was doing. Basically, he was creating English operas, having his words set to music and having them sung. Davenant didn't invent opera, by the way; that had been done in Italy in the late sixteenth century. But his solution allowed for English-language operas. He even wrote some of the stories for these productions to support political and religious ideas that the Puritans preferred.

After King Charles II was restored to the throne in 1660, Davenant could come out of hiding and produce plays once again. He and another playwright, Thomas Killigrew, were given exclusive rights to control what was produced in the newly reopened playhouses. This gave them a lot of power, and of course, some other playwrights and producers resented it. But the two roared ahead with their plans, and they had a lot of them.

Killigrew might have been the first producer to allow women to act on stages. This was a big step, since women had never been permitted to do it before. Charles II made him the new director of the company that had once been associated with Shakespeare, which meant that Killigrew had control over producing those plays for the new London theater scene. He was even appointed to the role of jester for Charles, giving him the freedom to say all sorts of outlandish things, because he had the king's protection.

After being shuttered for almost two decades, theaters came roaring back to life in London and elsewhere, as people flocked to see plays, both old and new, often in fancier, indoor settings that were very different from the outdoor set-ups that reigned a half-century earlier.

> **Dramatic fact:** Killigrew took one of his old plays, *The Parson's Wedding*, which he had written way back in the 1630s, and staged it with an all-female cast, just to be daring and different!

ISAAC NEWTON

Possibly history's most famous scientist other than Albert Einstein, Newton (1642–1727) changed ideas about physics forever, made important discoveries about gravity, and invented a whole new mathematical system, calculus—high school students have been cursing at Newton for that ever since!

Born to a land-owning family in Lincolnshire, Newton's father died three months before he was born. His mother remarried a local minister, but he and the boy never got along. Indeed, Newton later admitted that he had once threatened to burn them and the house down! But he eventually found his way and became educated enough to take up a place at Trinity College Cambridge in June of 1661. He originally intended to study law, but he was also attracted to philosophy and the works of Galileo and Kepler. By 1663, he had become fascinated by mathematics and geometry. At this time, the Scientific Revolution was moving ahead at full steam, so Newton was in the right place at the right time.

In 1665, the university had to close because the plague was spreading in various areas (see page 215), so Newton returned to Lincolnshire, where he began work in earnest on his ideas about mathematics, astronomy, and physics, ideas that would revolutionize those fields. And he wasn't even 25 years old yet! The foundations for many of his most important works and discoveries were laid during this one break from Cambridge.

Newton also began work on creating differential and integral calculus, a mathematical system that would be independently invented by the German mathematician, Gottfried Leibniz, a few years later.

For those wondering: the famous apple scene is apocryphal. Unfortunately; no apple ever fell on Isaac Newton's head. But he did remark that he had seen apples fall from trees and wondered why they fell straight down instead of at an angle, an observation that led to his revolutionary study of gravity.

He returned to Cambridge in 1667 and was elected to a major fellowship in 1669 after obtaining his master's degree, which gave him the all-important privilege of dining at the Fellows' table! Over the next several years, Newton continued to produce works that would transform scientific thinking, and he developed a heated rivalry with fellow scientist Robert Hooke, who had criticized his work on optics and light. Newton got so angry over their disagreements that he had a nervous breakdown in 1678. The death of his mother the next year only made matters worse, and he broke off all contact with most people for the next six years.

During this time, Newton became very interested in planetary orbits, as were several other scientists, including Edmund Halley (of comet fame, see the next entry for more on him). Halley approached Newton in 1684 to discuss several topics, one of them the orbits of planets. Newton had already worked out that these orbits were elliptical, based in part on a theory by, ironically, Hooke. Halley offered to fund his research, and in 1687, Newton published his *Philosophiae Naturalis Principia Mathematica* (Mathematical Principles of Natural Philosophy), which is probably the most influential book on physics in history, even including Einstein's works. The work describes and defines Newton's three laws of motion and the theory of universal gravitation, which explained why planets orbit the sun in an ellipse, how the moon orbits the Earth, and so on. He applied mathematics to astronomy and physics in a way that changed the sciences forever.

Following this sensation, Hooke accused Newton of plagiarism, stoking the fires of their rivalry once more—even though Newton had only referenced Hooke's idea, and had fully credited him for it. No matter, Hooke was furious and spent the next several years trying to harm Newton however he could, even at the expense of his own career and reputation. By the 1690s, Newton was no longer the cutting edge of scientific discovery, and in 1696, he moved to London to become Warden of the Royal Mint. But he remained attached to the scientific world, and was elected as President of the Royal Society in 1703 (after Hooke's death). The remaining years of Newton's life were marred by controversy, and Leibniz also accused him of plagiarizing his work on calculus, though again, it seems that they both came up with their ideas independently. After dying at the age of 84, Newton became the first scientist to be buried at Westminster Abbey.

> **Unscientific fact:** For all of his incredible and ground-breaking discoveries, Newton was also deeply devoted to the study of alchemy, astrology, and prophecy. These were important subjects at the time, and not considered inappropriate subjects for an intellect of his caliber to pursue.

EDMUND HALLEY

Halley (1656-1741/42) was an English astronomer and mathematician. Born during that chaotic time of Puritan rule, he showed an interest in math and science from an early age. While still an undergraduate at Oxford, he had the audacity to write to John Flamsteed, Britain's first Astronomer Royal, and tell him that some of his published works about the positions of Jupiter and Saturn were wrong! But Flamsteed's project to catalog the stars encouraged the young man, and soon, Halley was involved in a project to catalog stars in the southern sky, with the support of King Charles II himself. In 1676, Halley sailed to the island of Saint Helena, off the west coast of southern Africa, where he created the first full account of the stars of the Southern Hemisphere.

Of course, Halley is best known for his observations of the comet that now bears his name, the one that has a huge orbit around the sun and can only be seen from Earth once every seventy-six years or so. Halley

wasn't the first to see the comet, of course. It's been observed by many people and cultures throughout history.

The earliest definitive mention of the comet came from China in 240 BCE, in a chronicle called the *Records of the Grand Historian*. Later mentions also appear in writings from Japan, India, and various places in the Middle East. One of the more famous sightings came in April 1066, six months before the Norman Conquest. The *Anglo-Saxon Chronicle* noted: "Then was over all England such a token seen as no man ever saw before. Some men said that it was the comet-star, which others call the long-haired star." Many of the English viewed the comet as an inauspicious omen for the newly-enthroned King Harold, while William the Conqueror himself seems to have believed it was a good luck sign for him. It turns out William was right! An image of the comet was even woven into the famed Bayeux Tapestry, which chronicled William's ascension to power.

In observing the comet, Halley was able to calculate that it was the same one that had visited Earth on many occasions in the past: in 1531, 1607, and 1682. Therefore, he predicted that the comet would next be seen in 1758, and he was right.

Despite his successes, Halley got himself in trouble for bringing scientific inquiry into established beliefs. He suggested that the Earth might be older than the Biblical account, for example (a view which prevented him from being appointed to a prestigious teaching job at Oxford), and he also suggested that The Great Flood might have been caused by the impact of a comet hitting the Earth. He was eventually appointed to another post at Oxford in 1703, when his main opponents were dead—which is one way to best them! Halley would remain in academia for the rest of his life and continue to expand his and our knowledge of the world and the cosmos.

> **Drunken fun fact:** It's said that Tsar Peter (the Great) came to England from Russia in 1698 and wanted to meet Isaac Newton, among other people. Newton was too busy and sent Halley instead. The two bonded over

discussions of science and the imbibing of good brandy. According to one report, both were drunk one night, and Halley ended up pushing the ruler of Russia around the south bank of the Thames in a wheelbarrow!

THE ACTS OF UNION

B y the early eighteenth century, England and Scotland had been ruled by the same royal family for a hundred years, with the exception, of course, of the Cromwell years! The Stuart line hadn't had been the best of times in governance, what with Charles I getting his head lopped off and then his younger son James II (who succeeded Charles II) getting into all sorts of problems, being deposed in 1688 for being Catholic, among other things, and trying to impose his will on Parliament and people, just as his father had done.

Throughout all of this, England and Scotland had different Parliaments under the same monarch, but some were starting to see this as a bit messy and too complicated; a wily king could play them against each other. James I had tried to unite the two countries under one Parliament way back in 1606, and had failed. There were other unsuccessful attempts in the seventeenth century, but by 1706, there was a pretty wide support for simplifying the government of the Commonwealth. But many in Scotland understandably did not want their nation to become just another English possession, and wanted to ensure that their rights were protected.

The Scottish Presbyterian Church, in particular, opposed the union unless it was granted full independence from the English Anglican Church. This was agreed, and the Scottish Church officially dropped its opposition, though some of the lower-ranking clergy still grumbled about the whole thing. Scotland retained its own courts and was given various trading and market rights as well as money (some would call these "bribes"), in exchange for agreeing to dissolve its own Parliament and allow the unified one to be based in London. Scottish peers (nobles) would also be seated in the House of Lords. Possibly the biggest concession was that Scotland agreed that the Stuarts would no longer have a claim to the throne (it was given to the Hanovers in Germany, instead, and the four Georges that would reign as a result).

This succession question really didn't sit well with some Scots, and rebellion began brewing within the country's borders. This unrest would last for decades, and result in some brutal recriminations. But despite all the complaints and protests, the Acts were ratified by both the Scottish and English Parliaments, and in 1707, the two nations officially combined to become the Kingdom of Great Britain (Wales was already under English rule by this time, and so came along for the ride, whether it wanted to or not). A single Parliament would govern the entire island until the late 1990s, when Scotland and Wales worked with England to create new "devolved" Parliaments and take back a degree of self-control for their own nations (see page 460).

> **Bribery fact:** "We're bought and sold for English Gold, Such a Parcel of Rogues in a Nation." The great Scottish poet Robert Burns (1759-96) is usually credited with writing this hot take in a poetic form, articulating a view that many Scots undoubtedly held, though these lines might have already existed in Scottish folk song form before him. In any case, the words spoke of the belief that Scottish noblemen had betrayed their people for titles and riches—essentially, they'd accepted bribes from the English to concede to a new union. Those in modern Scotland who want independence for their country still use these words to criticize the union!

THE HOUSE OF
HANOVER

H ow is it that a noble family of Germanic lineage came to be the monarchs of Britain? And continued to rule for over two centuries, all the way through the reign of Queen Victoria? The story of the Hanoverians is yet another fascinating twist in the history of British politics.

In fact, Britain had been ruled by non-English monarchs for a very long time: the Stuarts were Scottish, the Tudors were Welsh, and before them, there was a series of French houses: The Plantagenets, the Angevins, and the Normans. The last truly "English" king was Harold Godwinson.

Fast-forward to the seventeenth century, and Britain was in a crisis over the issue of James II, the Catholic Stuart monarch. Though James was ousted, the British feared the return of any other Catholic claimant to the throne, and so set about preventing it by law. The Act of Settlement in 1701 basically ensured that the crown could only pass to Protestants. But finding a legitimate heir who fit the bill would prove difficult. Anne Stuart (James II's daughter) was offered the throne, and reigned as queen until 1714. The crown was then meant to pass to Sophia, the Electress (princess) of Hanover (and James I's granddaughter). She was seen as a good, "reliable" Protestant Stuart, unlike the Catholic Stuarts and their sympathizers. The problem was that Sophia died before she could take the throne (two months before Anne, in fact), which meant that the crown then passed to Sophia's son, George.

At the time, George was something like fifty-second in line to the throne of Britain, but he was the closest eligible Protestant, being half-Stuart and half-Hanover.

The House of Hanover originated in 1635 as part of the House of Brunswick-Lüneburg, a duchy in northern Germany that grew in power throughout the seventeenth century. Alliances with other noble and royal houses secured its position, and gave some of its members claims to various thrones in Europe, even if they were fifty-two spots away!

What this all meant was that George was invited to become King of Britain in 1714, according to the provisions of the Act. He did so, and took up residence in London as the new monarch. Of course, supporters of the "true" Stuart line were enraged by this, and set about trying to install their own claimant to the throne over the next several decades (see page 236).

Despite the opposition in some quarters, George I ended up being the first in a remarkably long line of monarchs; George III and Victoria in particular lived very long lives and had long reigns. The eighteenth and nineteenth centuries were a period of relative political stability in Britain (George III's mental health issues notwithstanding). It was under the Hanovers that Britain transitioned from a potentially major player in Europe, to a world empire that controlled about one-fifth of the globe and one-fourth of its population.

> **Not fitting in fact:** Even though George I was king, he wasn't all that thrilled by life in Britain, and returned to Hanover whenever he could (and died there). He and his son George II were viewed as foreigners by the British. George I's English was not great (though he spoke several other languages), and his Lutheran religion rubbed some Anglicans the wrong way.

BONNY PRINCE CHARLIE AND THE JACOBITES

P rince Charles Edward Stuart was quite sure that the right to rule Britain belonged to his father, James III, son of King James II. James II was pretty unpopular, and very few wanted his descendants anywhere near the throne, even though he had already named his son, James III, as his successor.

James II was removed, and the throne was given instead to his daughter, Mary II, and her Dutch husband, William of Orange, and then to other Protestant Stuarts. Supporters of the "main" Stuart line never forgot this insult and were determined not to let it go. Calling themselves the Jacobites, they were mostly Catholic, though not all were Scottish (in fact, many Scots were tired of the Stuarts and didn't support them at all), and they launched several rebellions against the British government, beginning in 1689. Meanwhile, the baby James III was snuck out of the country by his mother, who disguised herself as a laundress and escaped to France, where James II joined them. Once there, they were given refuge by King Louis XIV of France, the famed "Sun King."

Catholic nations such as France and Spain, as well as the papacy, refused to recognize William and Mary as Britain's rightful monarchs, so James grew up in an environment where his right to rule was supported.

At one point, James III was even offered the chance to return to Britain—if he converted to Protestantism. He refused, so the throne passed to the German House of Hanover, an insult that the Stuarts and those loyal to them were determined to avenge. James III's son, Charles Edward Stuart was born in Italy in 1720, and plotted to regain the throne for his father. Branded "bonny Prince Charlie" because of his good looks and charm, Charles felt, as many Stuarts had, that

the throne was his family's by divine right (that again!), and that his grandfather had been unjustly shoved aside. In 1745, he finally returned to Scotland with James III's blessing. He rallied support from the Highlanders in the north, many of whom were Protestant, but still believed in the Stuarts' right to rule. This, of course, was a direct challenge to King George II. Charlie and his army took Edinburgh and other cities, and came within two days of marching on London, but Charlie's advisors suggested that he wait for French support, so he retreated back to Scotland. That would prove to be a fatal error.

The British rallied their forces and under the command of the Duke of Cumberland (King George's youngest son), and they met the Jacobites and Highlanders at Culloden, a marshy field near Inverness (of Loch Ness fame) on April 16, 1746. Charles's forces were cut down; something like 20,000 were killed by the British in less than an hour, ending the rebellion, and the hopes of restoring the Stuarts to the throne, forever. Highland culture (including the wearing of tartan) was suppressed by law, and Scotland suffered terribly under harsh punishments, despite never supporting Charles's challenge to the throne.

> **Cross-dressing fact:** Charlie escaped the battlefield and hid out in Scotland for several months, despite a wide-ranging attempt to find him. A supporter named Flora MacDonald disguised him as her maid, using the name "Betty Burke," and smuggled him out of western Scotland onto a ship bound for France. The plan worked and Charlie was able to avoid capture and returned to Italy, where he lived out his days, dying on January 30, 1788—139 years to the day his great-grandfather, King Charles I, had his head removed!

JOHN BULL, A SYMBOL
OF THE BRITISH

Though there was a gifted composer during the Elizabethan and
Jacobean eras named John Bull (1562-1628), the John Bull in this
entry refers to an everyman figure that first appeared in the early
eighteenth century as an avatar of Britain, somewhat like Uncle Sam
would become for the United States, though the British Bull is a more
humble figure from the country.

He seems to have been created by a Scottish scientist and political
satirist named John Arbuthnot (1667-1735). In a series of pamphlets
printed in 1712 called *The History of John Bull*, Arbuthnot described
Bull as a typical Englishman and as "an honest plain-dealing fellow."
His main adversary was the Frenchman Louis Baboon, a play on the
French House of Bourbon, the ruling family in France. Thus, Bull was
a kind of allegorical figure, one that could be used for political attacks
and satire against one's rivals and opponents.

Later writers and artists took up the figure of Bull and used him to
great effect. He was almost always shown as a portly English country
gentleman wearing a waistcoat and a long tailcoat. Later, the waistcoat would have a prominent Union Jack on it. Bull was frequently
drawn wearing a low topper (a kind of squat top hat) and depicted
with a bulldog next to him.

Practical and down-to-earth, Bull liked ale, country sports, dogs,
and all things British. By the early nineteenth century, he was a
dedicated enemy of Napoleon, with one cartoon even showing him
holding up Napoleon's head on a two-pronged pitchfork, articulat-
ing perfectly what many British though of the self-styled emperor
who loomed large across the English Channel! Indeed, Bull became
a symbol of British pride and resistance to the would-be conqueror
of Britain.

By the nineteenth century, Bull increasingly came to represent the common people, and satirists used him to indulge in criticism of the aristocracy. But this changed as the First World War dawned, when Bull was used to promote patriotism and the existing order. His popularity waned after World War II and the end of the British Empire, and while he still shows up occasionally today, he doesn't enjoy anything like the prominence and fame he once did.

> **Anthem fact:** The "real" John Bull was a gifted composer and player of keyboard instruments, and though he had to flee to the Netherlands in order to avoid some political and religious strife, it's believed that he wrote the melody that would end up being used for the British national anthem, "God Save the King/Queen." The fictional John Bull would no doubt be pleased.

LONDON'S COFFEEHOUSES

Just about everyone who loves coffee has their favorite local café. Coffee is a massive industry around the world, and vast numbers of people couldn't imagine getting their day started without it. Even though Britain is most often associated with tea drinking, coffee played a significant role in social activities and even the development of scientific and philosophical ideas during the seventeenth and early eighteenth centuries.

By the seventeenth century, coffee had been enjoyed in the Middle East for centuries. Visitors to cities such as Constantinople (modern Istanbul) noted that the locals enjoyed this dark, strong drink, but it wasn't much of a hit with Europeans, initially, judging by what an Englishman named George Sandys said during a visit in the early seventeenth century, saying coffee was "blacke as soote, and tasting not much unlike it." Not exactly a ringing endorsement! But eventually, merchants brought some beans to England. At first, as was often the case, coffee was touted as a medicine that was good for the brain—when this turned out to be true, and when English people realized this truth could be felt, the country's caffeine addiction was well on its way!

By the mid-seventeenth century, coffee was consumed in Oxford as a stimulant to aid in academic pursuits, and by 1652, London's first prototype coffeehouse was established by a Greek immigrant named Pasqua Rosée, who brought coffee from Turkey and set up a stall in a neighborhood called Cornhill. Initially, the beverage was a hit with intellectuals and the well-to-do, but it struggled to catch on much beyond those circles. Within about a decade, though, coffeehouses began to pop up everywhere, as people began to see them as a more "respectable" alternative to taverns and pubs. Indeed, coffee was seen as a cure for drunkenness, a reputation that it still carries today.

These places became hotspots of debate, gossip, ideas, and news, and it's thought that many great scientific and industrial ideas might have had their beginnings in coffeehouses, as intellectuals, stimulated by coffee and tobacco (pipe smoking was also common), sat and discussed their visions and plans. Certain houses became associated with certain types of business, or specific clients, and literary figures also thrived in these houses. Of course, the talk within sometimes turned to politics. King James II banned the circulating of newspapers in coffeehouses in 1688 to try to quell growing criticism of his government, but the power of the coffeehouse caused that move to backfire, and he was eventually deposed.

Women were generally not permitted in coffee shops, as such establishments were not considered "proper" for ladies. There's little doubt, however, that many wealthy women enjoyed coffee in the privacy of their own home.

By the mid-eighteenth century, the popularity of coffeehouses began to wane, as tea became much cheaper to import, and was considered more "respectable" for women and men. Tea would come to dominate British society at all levels, and coffee wouldn't regain its place as a popular social drink until the twentieth century.

> **Messy medical fact:** Isaac Newton once dissected a dolphin on a coffeehouse table, while other patrons presumably sipped their beverages and looked on.

HENRY PURCELL AND GEORGE FRIDERIC HANDEL, COMPOSERS

P urcell and Handel are two of the great names in English Baroque music. Purcell was English, while Handel was German, but their influence on the music of the times in Britain and beyond was immense.

Purcell (1659-95) was arguably England's greatest native composer between the Elizabethan and Jacobean artistic explosion and the late-nineteenth century. Like many other musical giants, Purcell showed a great talent for music in his youth, and might have been composing by the tender age of 9. By the age of 20, he was already the organist for Westminster Abbey, an amazing achievement! Later, he also served as an organist to the Chapel Royal, the private chapel of the monarch, so he was obviously in with the patrons who mattered.

Purcell is best known for his excellent theater music, as well as his one opera, *Dido and Aeneas*, but his talents ranged across a wide variety of musical forms. Unlike some composers who traveled widely and lived in many different areas, Purcell seems to have been mostly London-based, and lived in Westminster for the entirety of his short life.

Handel (1685-1759) was born in the same year as Johann Sebastian Bach, though the two were destined never to meet. One story says that Bach once journeyed to Handel's hometown for business, and was excited at the chance to meet Handel, but he found that Handel had left only one day before. What resulted from a meeting of these two Baroque giants would have been fascinating to hear, though at the time Handel was far more famous as a composer than Bach.

Handel was born in Halle, Germany, and though he loved music, his father would not permit him to have a career in it, thinking it would never earn him enough money (not much has changed for the aspiring artist, it seems!). But Handel's mother supported his dream, and saw to it that her son was able to study music in secret. He developed quickly, and started composing his own music by the age of 10 or 11. Still, he studied law (his father's wish) for a while, but eventually gave it up to pursue music full time. From there, things only got better for Handel. While touring in Venice in 1710, he heard about the exciting music scene in London, and was intrigued enough that he decided to go there and see it for himself. He would end up settling in England and working in the service of two other German transplants—King George I and King George II. Handel became a British citizen in 1726 and was known for his operas and such immortal pieces as *Music for the Royal Fireworks*, *Water Music*, and *Messiah*.

> **Death and darkness fact:** Purcell was said to have died after a night at the tavern with friends. His wife, disapproving of his behavior, locked him out of the house, forcing him to spend the night in England's

famously chilly weather. He developed a fever and died at the tragically young age of 36. Later in life, Handel developed eye problems (probably cataracts), and consented to an operation from a doctor, who had also operated on Bach for his failing eyesight. But the doctor was a quack and a fraud. The operation failed and Handel spent his last years totally blind. Also, Bach probably died of an infection after the same doctor failed to save his sight.

SAMUEL JOHNSON AND THE DICTIONARY

J ohnson (1709-84) was an author, critic, linguist, and lexicographer (someone who compiles dictionaries). He was born in Lichfield, in central England, and studied for a time at Oxford, though he didn't have the money to complete his degree. Having struggled for several years afterward to secure a solid position, Johnson admitted that he fell into a depression during this time, and become bothered by other health problems that would plague him for the rest of his life. He was known to have tics and involuntary movements that could be off-putting to some, and which were probably a sign that he had Tourette syndrome. Eventually, Johnson ended up in London working as a writer for *The Gentleman's Magazine*.

In 1746, he was approached by a group of publishers about compiling a new English language dictionary. Johnson agreed and was quite sure that he could have it finished in three years. It actually took eight years of work and six assistants to complete. Published in 1755, the *Dictionary of the English Language* contained about 40,000 words, and was an incredible achievement for the time. But Johnson had wanted to write, "a dictionary by which the pronunciation of our language may be fixed, and its attainment facilitated; by which its purity may be preserved," which is impossible, because language is always changing and evolving. Word definitions mutate and take on whole new meanings, new words are constantly being invented, and existing words fall out of usage. The best a lexicographer can hope for is a picture of language at the time, rather like a textual photograph.

Johnson didn't write the first English dictionary, though. In 1604, a man named Robert Cawdrey produced *A Table Alphabeticall*, and in 1702, John Kersey published *A New English Dictionary*. What made Johnson's unique was his meticulous attention to detail, and his colorful definitions, which were often accompanied by famous quotes that utilized the word being defined. Here are a few amusing entries:

Finesse: Artifice; stratagem: an unnecessary word which is creeping into the language. (Johnson was not fond of recent French loan words—never mind that English had long been a mix of French and English—and he even left out some, like Champagne!)

Lexicographer: A writer of dictionaries; a harmless drudge that busies himself in tracing the original, and detailing the signification of words.

Lizard: An animal resembling a serpent, with legs added to it.

Lunch: As much food as one's hand can hold.

Patron: One who countenances, supports or protects. Commonly a wretch who supports with insolence, and is paid with flattery.

Johnson's dictionary was intended for public use, rather than just in school rooms, and would be the standard for the English language until the Oxford English Dictionary appeared in the late nineteenth century.

Disability fact: Johnson was almost deaf in one ear and nearly blind in one eye, but these terrible obstacles didn't stop him from achieving amazing things.

CAPTAIN JAMES COOK

C ook (1728-79) was an explorer, cartographer, and a navy captain who is best known for his three voyages through the Pacific Ocean between 1768 and 1779, trips that included circumnavigating the islands that would come to be known as New Zealand, making the first recorded British sighting of the southeast coast of Australia, and establishing contact with the people of Hawaii (where he was eventually killed).

Cook was born in Yorkshire, the son of a Scottish farm laborer (also named James) and a local woman, Grace. His early life showed no signs of the promising naval career he would have. Cook had no formal education before his teenage years, but he soon learned well enough, and showed an aptitude for astronomy and charting that would serve him very well later on. In 1745, the family moved to the coastal village of Staithes (still pronounced by some locals as "Steers"), where he was apprenticed to a grocer. The grocer's life didn't suit him, and he soon moved to Whitby (also on the Yorkshire coast), where he was apprenticed to a family who were successful in shipping. Cook took to the sailing life at once, and spent several years on ships traveling between the north and London, all while immersing himself in mathematics and navigation. He then decided to enlist in the Royal Navy in 1755, where his actions during the Seven Years' War in Canada earned him the respect and attention of higher-ups.

In 1766, he was offered a commission as commander of the HMS

Endeavour, the ship on which he would make his famous Pacific Ocean voyages. While he officially sailed for astronomical observances, he was also charged with searching for a southern continent that many believed existed (and does, of course; it's Antarctica). On his first voyage, he stopped in Tahiti and then continued on to New Zealand to map it, before sailing up Australia's east coast, which he claimed for Britain and named "New South Wales." The locals, of course, were not consulted about the matter. Cook returned to Britain in July of 1771, but set out again the following year, commanding the HMS *Resolution* and still searching for that elusive southern continent. He came close to the coast of Antarctica, but his ships had to turn away due to the terrible cold and weather. Cook and his crew visited New Zealand once more before returning to Britain in 1775.

In 1776, Cook again commanded the *Resolution*, with the intention of looking for the fabled Northwest Passage, a waterway that many believed connected the Atlantic and Pacific Oceans (unlike Antarctica, it doesn't exist). After the disappointment of not finding it, Cook and his crew returned to Hawaii in January 1779, and stayed there for a month. At some point during that stay, tensions flared between the indigenous people and Cook's crew after the sailors stole some wood from a burial ground, and a group of Hawaiians stole one of the ship's small boats in response. In retaliation, Cook decided to kidnap the Hawaiian king, Kalani'ōpu'u, and hold him for ransom. As you might imagine, the locals didn't appreciate this at all. As Cook attempted to lead the king back to the ship, he was attacked, clubbed, and stabbed to death. His crew were compelled to make the journey home without him, though the Hawaiians did return some of Cook's remains so he could be given a burial at sea.

Although Cook was undoubtedly a brave and brilliant explorer, many native peoples in Polynesia and Australia see him as little more than a herald of the brutal colonialism that soon followed.

> **Diseased fact:** Scurvy, a disease caused by a lack of the Vitamin C found in fresh fruit and vegetables, was a scourge of the navy and ocean

explorers on long sea voyages in the eighteenth century. Cook managed to keep his crew scurvy-free on all three of his journeys by always purchasing fresh food at ports along the way, and by providing the crew with a healthy amount of sauerkraut—pickled cabbage—which he shrewdly noticed kept his sailors from getting sick. Everyone ate it every day, whether they liked it or not!

OLAUDAH EQUIANO, ABOLITIONIST

E quiano (c. 1745-97) was a former slave who lived in London and wrote an early and passionate argument for the abolition of slavery in Britain and beyond. Born in the Kingdom of Benin (now a part of southern Nigeria) around the year 1745, Equiano was taken as a slave and transported to Barbados, where he would be sold again, ending up in Virginia. There, Michael Henry Pascal, a lieutenant in the Royal Navy, bought him and renamed him "Gustavus Vassa," a name he would continue to use throughout his life. Pascal took Equiano back to the UK, and allowed him to improve his English and to learn to read and write. But by 1762 Equiano was back in the Caribbean again, now owned by Robert King, an American merchant, who eventually allowed him to buy his freedom, as well as learn the merchant's trade. Once Equiano was free, he decided not to stay on as a partner with King. Instead, he relocated to Britain in 1768.

Equiano would eventually work for the British Navy, and even joined an expedition to the Arctic in 1773. Afterward, he went to work, as a manager for a sugar plantation on Africa's Mosquito Coast, helping to manage the slaves and their work. After this, he returned to England and settled in London, where he began to work in earnest with abolitionist groups.

In 1789, he published his autobiography, *The Interesting Narrative of the Life of Olaudah Equiano; or, Gustavus Vassa, the African.* He recalled his youth among the Eboe people, and how in his village, his own people would sell others into slavery, though as he put it: "Sometimes indeed we sold slaves to them [the traders and other groups], but they were only prisoners of war, or such among us as had been convicted of kidnapping, or adultery, and some other crimes, which we esteemed heinous."

This arrangement hadn't kept him from being taken, of course, and would no doubt inform his own views about campaigning for slavery to be abolished. Equaino's book was insightful, detailed, and compelling, and it became a huge success, going through nine editions, and helping the antislavery movement gain momentum. Equaino put his elevated status to good use, becoming a prominent member of the Sons of Africa, a group of former slaves who advocated for abolition, and he also tried to improve conditions for free Africans already living in Britain.

Equiano died in 1797, sadly, before he could see slavery abolished in Britain. But his efforts absolutely contributed to it happening.

> **Accuracy fact:** Recently, a few researchers have suggested that Equiano might have been born in colonial America, specifically in South Carolina, instead of Africa. But others have countered that there is too much detail in his autobiography for it to have been invented, and there is more evidence that supports him being from Africa than not.

DIDO ELIZABETH BELLE, FROM SLAVERY TO HIGH SOCIETY

Dido Elizabeth Belle (1761-1804) had an unlikely and disadvantaged start in life, as the illegitimate daughter of a British Naval officer, Sir John Lindsay, and an African slave woman, Maria Bell. But Belle made the best of it, rising swiftly in both society and reputation.

Belle was born in the British West Indies, but in 1765, Lindsay took her with him to his family home, Kenwood House, just north of London. He later arranged for Maria to be freed and to inherit land of her own in Pensacola, Florida, near the north coast of the Gulf of Mexico.

Upon arriving in England, Little Dido was afforded treatment that was unheard of for a black person at the time. It would have been perfectly normal and expected that she would take on a servant's role in the house, but instead, she seems to have been brought up as a lady, right alongside her aristocratic British cousin, Elizabeth Murray. A surviving portrait of the two shows them dressed and smiling in finery, obviously standing as equals.

In time, Elizabeth married and moved away, and increasingly, Belle worked to assist Elizabeth's father, William Murray, First Earl of Mansfield, and Lord Chief Justice (the most powerful judge in Britain), taking dictation from him for his notes, letters, and other writings. She was obviously bright and well educated, and he trusted her with the job. Murray seemed to have a genuine affection for her, and just may have had his worldview transformed by young Dido.

As a judge, Murray ruled on many cases involving slaves, including one in 1772 involving an escaped slave. The slave's owner wanted to return him to the West Indies to be resold, but Mansfield ruled that slave owners could not force slaves out of Britain and to another country, saying that slavery is "so odious, that nothing can be suffered to support it but positive law." In other words, slavery did not exist within the framing of British common law. Abolitionists would take this ruling to mean that slavery either didn't exist at all, or that Mansfield had just abolished it. Of course, this was not the case, and full abolition wouldn't come until 1833. Still, this ruling was monumental, and marked the shift away from legal justifications for slavery in Britain.

Many think that Mansfield's relationship to Belle might have influenced his decision. When he died in 1793, he reiterated that she was a free woman, probably just in case anyone had any doubts, and left her a generous sum of money. She eventually married a Frenchman, John Davinier. They had three sons, and established a peaceful existence in London.

> Unkind fact: For all of the affection and support Belle received, she still got hid away from distinguished guests during dinner parties, and was only allowed to come out afterward to have coffee with a few of the more enlightened women.

THE AMERICAN REVOLUTION FROM THE BRITISH POINT OF VIEW

If you were raised in the United States, you probably know plenty about the American Revolution, beginning with stories about the colonists being unhappy with many policies of King George III and his government, and how this led to disagreements, and finally open conflict in a war for the colonies' independence. And you've probably mostly heard this from the American point of view, because why would it be otherwise? But it's interesting to step back and look at things from the other side, particularly since this is a book about Britain.

Just what did the British people think of the colonists and their revolution?

Certainly, the Americans had some justifiable complaints with the crown that needed to be addressed, and George III was definitely stubborn in assuming that he could just demand their loyalty. You would think that after what happened to Charles I and James II in his own country, George would have been a little less pushy about taking the "his way or the highway" tack. But he wasn't, and when war ensued, not everyone in Britain blindly supported the crown. One group of merchants who operated out of Bristol urged the king to give the colonists what they wanted. They were doing this not so much out of sympathy for the colonists, but out of a fear that a war would interrupt their trade and be a disaster for both them and the British economy. No good could come from this, they warned, and they were right.

Many nobles and other members of the upper classes were very concerned about the increasing antimonarchy attitudes from across the pond, and probably a little worried for their own heads. Even several politicians thought that a war would be terrible for the British economy and make things worse than they already were. One Member of Parliament, Thomas Townshend, First Viscount Sydney, wrote, "the Government and Majority [of Parliament] have drawn us into a war, that in our opinions is unjust in its Principle and ruinous in its consequences." Townshend knew he faced an uphill battle with this stance, since more politicians favored cracking down on the Americans than conceding to them, and the king was determined not to back down. Still, Townshend bravely voiced his opinions.

In the end, nothing else mattered—enough high-ranking men wanted to teach the American colonies a lesson, a motivation that ended up backfiring in a spectacular degree. As France became involved in the war and started supporting the Americans, the situation only got worse for the British, who eventually had to accept a humiliating defeat, and let the colonies go their own way.

Loyal royal fact: It's thought that between 15 and 20 percent of American colonists were loyalists, in other words, devoted to Britain and remaining under its rule. Many of these colonists even fought for the British. After the war, over 60,000 people still loyal to the crown left the new nation. Members of this strange diaspora emigrated to Canada, Florida (not part of the United States at the time), the Caribbean, and Britain itself.

MARY WOLLSTONECRAFT, ADVOCATE FOR WOMEN'S RIGHTS

Wollstonecraft (1759-97) was a writer and philosophe, who was a great champion of women's rights long before it was truly acceptable. She was also the mother of Mary Godwin, who as Mary Shelley would write one of the most important influential books in English history, *Frankenstein*. Wollstonecraft's best-known work is *A Vindication of the Rights of Woman*, written in 1792. A beautifully argued piece for equal rights between women and men, Wollstonecraft's tome is rightly seen as a watershed moment in the women's rights movement.

Born in London, Mary was an advocate for equality from a young age. The daughter of an abusive father, she helped her sister, Eliza, escape from a terrible marriage, hiding her sister away until a separation was agreed on. By 1784, the sisters had opened an all-girls school in North London that would allow them to be educated and to develop just as boys would, proving once and for all that there was no fundamental difference between them. While it only remained in operation for a few years, the school received praise for its commitment to excellence.

Despite the school closing, Wollstonecraft remained a passionate advocate for the education of women, arguing that learning was essential to make them equal to men, famously writing, "I do not wish them [women] to have power over men; but over themselves." She further noted, "Men, indeed, appear to me to act in a very unphilosophical manner when they try to secure the good conduct of women by attempting to keep them always in a state of childhood." In other words, women were kept in ignorance when they were perfectly capable of learning and thinking independently. This type of argument might seem pretty obvious today, but at the time, it was radical.

In 1792, Wollstonecraft traveled to France, which was dangerous, given that the Revolution was in full swing. She was a supporter of the idea of the revolution, but was dismayed to see that the new revolutionary leaders were not much better than the aristocrats they'd ousted. Still, she remained hopeful for a better future, despite the brutality of some of the revolutionaries' behavior.

While abroad, Wollstonecraft met an American merchant named Captain Gilbert Imlay. The two enjoyed a brief romance and she gave birth to a child from it, a daughter named Fanny. When Wollstonecraft came under suspicion and faced possible arrest, Imlay declared that they were married, which would make her American and therefore immune from prosecution—even though, of course, they were not. In any case, the fib probably saved her life. Imlay soon left her, and she was forced carry on by herself. Sometime later, in 1797, she met William Godwin, a man devoted to the idea of philosophical anarchism, the intellectual critique of power and authority. From their relationship came another child, Mary (of monster fame), but sadly, Wollstonecraft suffered complications from the pregnancy, and died just eleven days later, meaning that her poor daughter never got to know her. For a time after her death, Wollstonecraft was best known for the scandalous act of mothering a child outside of marriage. But by the early twentieth century, her importance as a founder of the women's rights movement was undeniable.

Fiction fact: Wollstonecraft also wrote a novel titled *Mary: A Fiction*. Though she wasn't overly pleased with it, its story of a female protagonist probably influenced the writings of Jane Austen and the Brontë sisters (more on them soon!).

ROBERT BURNS, SCOTLAND'S GREAT POET

K nown to his friends and fans as "Rabbie," Burns was more than just a Scottish poet—during his life and still to this day, he is seen as *the* Scottish poet. He wrote in a form of the Scots language, a tongue that is quite distinct from English. Burns wrote his Scots poems in a "lighter" version of the tongue, making it easier for English speakers to understand. But he also wrote in "standard" English, and proved to be a master of the idiom in both.

Burns was born in Alloway, Scotland, a town southwest of Glasgow on the west coast of the country, to a farming family. As a boy, he loved hearing stories of the supernatural from an elderly neighbor, and his imagination was fired by these tall tales of ghosts and legends. Burns helped out on the farm, and also received a decent education from a local school. He composed his first poem at the age of fifteen, the inevitable result of falling in love for the first time. In 1784, his father died and Robert and his brother tried to maintain the family farm, but faced all kinds of hardships and financial problems. Burns considered moving to Jamaica for work, and published his first collection, *Poems, Chiefly in the Scottish Dialect*, to help pay for the trip. But in 1787, he was persuaded to stay in Scotland, and married Jean Armour one year later.

Burns was politically a radical, and quietly (and sometimes not-so-quietly) expressed sympathy with the revolutionary attitudes in both America and France. Literary folks now see him as one of the founders of the Romantic Movement, which would take Britain and Europe by storm in the early nineteenth century. As Burns's poetry became more popular and copies of his books sold, he was able to indulge further in his true passion, which was drinking. It made his already-weak health worse, and he died of rheumatic fever, complicated by having fallen asleep outside in the rain after a heavy bout of drinking.

His birthday, January 25, now has the honor of being known as Burns Night to his legions of fans. Devotees of his poetry will gather for a Burns Supper and read his poems, drink Scotch, and eat haggis, an unusual sausage (a sheep's stomach stuffed with pork, oatmeal, and spices) that Burns once lionized in a poem, his famous Scots-language "Address to a Haggis." It begins:

> **Fair fa your honest, sonsie face,**
>
> **Great chieftain o' the puddin' race!**
>
> **Aboon them a' ye tak yer place,**
>
> **Painch, tripe, or thairm:**
>
> **Weel are ye wordy o' a grace**
>
> **As lang's my airm.**

> **(Good luck to you and your honest, plump face,**
>
> **Great chieftain of the sausage race!**
>
> **Above them all you take your place,**
>
> **Stomach, tripe, or intestines:**
>
> **Well are you worthy of a grace**
>
> **As long as my arm.)**

Happy New Year fact: You just might have heard of another one of Burns's famous works, "Auld Lange Syne," which everyone still sings at midnight on New Year's Eve. Except most people don't know the words beyond the first line and just mumble through it; it's an annual tradition. While the tune existed in Burns's time, his words have been wedded with the melody since 1799.

WILLIAM PITT THE YOUNGER

Pitt (1759-1806) was a Tory politician who became Prime Minister at the amazingly young age of 24! Though technically a conservative, he often called himself a "new Tory" or an "independent Whig," because he was against the idea of politics being highly partisan and divisive. Serving as Prime Minister from 1783 to 1801, and then again from 1804 to 1806, Pitt was Britain's leader in the aftermath of the American Revolution, and had the distinctions of being both the last Prime Minister of Great Britain and the first Prime Minister of the United Kingdom (the change was made after Ireland was incorporated into the nation in the 1800 Acts of Union). As if that wasn't enough for Pitt to keep tabs on, he was also Chancellor of the Exchequer (the official responsible for taxes and the nation's finances) for the entirety of his time as Prime Minister!

He was dubbed "the Younger" to distinguish him from his father, William Pitt the Elder (of course!), First Earl of Chatham, who had also been Prime Minister (of course!) between 1766 and 1768.

Pitt the Younger, had the distinction (perhaps he'd term it differently?) of serving under King George III during some of the most trying times Britain had seen up until then, including the challenges of the American Revolution (when he was an MP), the French

Revolution, the official union of Britain and Ireland, and the rise of Napoleon. But this young man was more than up to the task and was remembered, then and now, as a hard-working and capable leader who ushered in a new era featuring politics that were suited for these trying times. Pitt's "new Toryism" helped establish the Conservatives as the party to beat for decades. But how did he come to power at such a young age?

Obviously, family connections had a lot to do with it. Pitt, always a precocious one (he gained entry into Cambridge at the age of 14), managed to be elected as an MP at the tender age of 21, quickly overcoming his adolescent shyness to become an eloquent speaker and debater. Politics was a dirty business at the time, and bribery was common. Pitt was reform-minded, but also realistic. He turned down various positions before deciding that the Exchequer post was where he could begin to enact his reforms. It was an enormous responsibility for one so young. But he proved himself capable time and again, remaining above the fray of the political in-fighting that swirled all around him.

Pitt had the advantage of being admired by King George III, and when the time came, George appointed him Prime Minister. Of course, not everyone was happy with someone so young taking the reins of power, and Pitt had to spend several months winning over his skeptics.

In 1784, Pitt successfully pushed through the India Act, which reorganized the East India Company, with the intent of removing corruption. He was also responsible for the creation of Australia as a penal colony. After the American colonies won their independence, they refused to accept any more convicts from Britain, so Pitt decided that settlements in Australia should be made for both settlers and convicts, and the colony of New South Wales was founded in 1788. Pitt was also preoccupied with Ireland, and wanted it joined with Britain in a formal union. He was able to achieve this union in 1800, but Pitt also wanted Catholic emancipation, allowing Catholics to take seats in Parliament and have other restrictions on them lifted. He felt this would make the Irish feel more a part of the new union being forced on them, but George III was utterly opposed to this approach. Eventually, the matter came to a head, and Pitt resigned his post in 1801.

He spent less time on political affairs for the next few years, but circumstances forced him back into the corridors of power in 1804, when he found himself appointed Prime Minister yet again. But he was still tired from years of exertion, and the pressure of the job, and the ever-present threat of Napoleon, caused his already-shaky health to take a turn for the worse. While he was heartened by the victory of Nelson at Trafalgar in October 1805, Napoleon's overwhelming victory at the Battle of Austerlitz just two months later was devastating. Crushed in spirit and drinking heavily to try and cope, Pitt died less than two months later.

> Dueling fact: Pitt fought a duel in 1798 on Putney Heath against George Tierney, a rival MP. Always a cool customer, he casually wrote to his mother after the fracas: "The business concluded without anything unpleasant to either Party."

MAD KING GEORGE III?

In some important ways, King George III lived a very unfortunate life. Though he was a popular monarch and took great interest in governing Britain and its people, he is most famous now for two things: the loss of the American colonies, and the loss of his mind, so much so that for the last ten years if his life, he was unable to do anything and his son had to rule in his place. But what really afflicted poor George? Interestingly, the explanation that is usually offered might not be true after all.

Researchers have long thought that George suffered from a disease called porphyria, which is a genetic blood disorder that can cause pains and cramps, and turn one's urine blue. Yes, blue pee! Because George had these symptoms, most historians have assumed that he suffered from this disorder, which can also affect one's mental health. But a few years ago, other researchers took another look at the matter, and now they're not so sure that he had this disease at all.

In any case, something was wrong with George, and by the 1780s and 1790s, it was painfully obvious to everyone. He couldn't sleep, had frequent manic episodes, and occasionally suffered from full-on hallucinations. At Windsor Castle, he was once seen talking to an oak tree and trying to shake hands with it; he explained that he was talking to the King of Prussia. Another time, the king was seen planting a beef steak in the ground, saying that it would eventually grow into a full-sized meat tree!

Of course, the royal family was very concerned and more than a little embarrassed, so George ended up being confined away at Kew Palace for his own good. He would go through periods of feeling better and then lapse back into his episodes again. While he was experiencing them, he had to be watched closely, and was often denied the use of knives and forks, so that he couldn't hurt himself. He was given terrible treatments like putting arsenic powder on his skin in an effort to "draw out" the sickness via the blisters that would form on it. He was also put into ice-cold baths to shock the illness, but of course, like everything else they tried, this was useless.

So, what was really happening? Researchers now think that instead of porphyria, the king was indeed suffering from some kind of genuine mental illness. His behavior in these episodes was typical of bipolar disorder and some other mental health issues. And as for the blue pee? It might have been caused by the gentian plant, which is used to treat stomach ailments and bloating. Its flowers are blue, and that could have been the source of George's mysterious blue urine.

We might never know the exact cause of George's mental health issues, but they had profound consequences for Britain and the rest of the world.

> **Love of learning fact:** Whatever his mental health issues, George was always committed to education and study. He greatly valued science and amassed a personal library of tens of thousands of books, some of which were made available to scholars. About 65,000 of these books were later given to the British Museum and Library.

THE MOVEMENT FOR ABOLITION

Britain's role in the Transatlantic slave trade in the seventeenth and eighteenth centuries was shameful, and remains a dark stain on the nation's history. But the movement for abolition gained momentum earlier than it did in America, and quickly garnered support. As we've seen, Olaudah Equiano and Dido Elizabeth Belle both had roles to play in the early abolitionist movement, but they were joined by many other voices along the way. Before the American Revolution, slavery in the American southern colonies was a lucrative enterprise for the British government, so there was little incentive to remove it, despite increased calls from religious leaders to eliminate it on moral grounds. With the loss of the colonies (and far less financial incentive), calls for abolition became more emphatic.

There were several key players in the movement, including English clergyman Granville Sharp (who advocated for slaves in legal cases), Scottish naval surgeon James Ramsay (who had witnessed the appalling treatment of slaves firsthand in the Caribbean), Thomas Clarkson (a Quaker who collected evidence of brutality against slaves and co-founded the Society for Effecting the Abolition of the Slave Trade in 1787), Ignatius Sancho (a writer and composer who was a former slave), John Newton (a former slave trader who would later write the song "Amazing Grace"), and William Grenville (prime minister when the Slave Trade Act was passed in 1807).

But perhaps the best known of these abolitionists was William Wilberforce (1759-1833), an MP with considerable sympathy for underdogs of all kinds. Wilberforce was focused on the plight of the working poor when a group of abolitionists showed him the true horrors of slavery in 1787. He then began a tireless campaign to have it abolished, an effort that culminated in the passing of the Slave Trade Act, which outlawed the slave trade within the British Empire. Unfortunately, the bill did not outlaw slavery itself, only the buying and selling of slaves, but it was a huge step forward in the abolition movement.

The Slave Trade Act gave the Royal Navy authority to patrol the oceans in search of ships carrying slaves in violation of the Act. Such ships were to be treated as pirates, and it's thought that over 150,000 slaves were freed from these ships in the years after the Act became law. But the issue of slavery still remained, and Wilberforce and others rejoined the battle to outlaw the practice completely. While Wilberforce's health failed in his last years, others took up the cause and succeeded in passing the Slavery Abolition Act in July 1833, one week before Wilberforce died. The act received royal assent a month later and became law in August 1834. Abolition wasn't immediate, of course. All slaves under the age of six were immediately freed, while those who were older were now termed to be in "apprenticeships" that would end steadily, mostly between 1838 and 1840, with a few exceptions. Slave owners were compensated for their losses, which might seem like an undue reward for such horrible behavior, but it was the only realistic way the get the act passed and make it enforceable.

Important update fact: The Slavery Abolition Act was repealed in 1998, but this didn't make slavery legal again! Rather, it was replaced by the Human Rights Act that same year, which includes antislavery laws drawn from Article 4 of the European Convention on Human Rights.

LORD NELSON AND THE BATTLE OF TRAFALGAR

Occurring on October 21, 1805, the Battle of Trafalgar was immediately, and remains, one of the most important and consequential naval conflicts in British history, right up there with the defeat of the Spanish Armada back in 1588.

The prologue to Trafalgar concerns Napoleon's long-held desire to invade and conquer Britain. He intended to do so by taking control of the English Channel, understanding that this would remove any resistance to an invasion. Using forces under the command of Pierre-Charles Villeneuve, a brilliant French admiral, the strategy seemed like a foolproof plan, but Napoleon had apparently forgotten just how scrappy the British could be, and how disastrously things had gone for the Armada more than two centuries earlier. This time, the Spanish and French fleet never even made it to the English Channel. The invasion was actually postponed, given that Napoleon had to deal with Russian and Austrian aggression to the east. So, he ordered his fleet to sail to Italy under the command of French Vice-Admiral François Rosily and land troops there.

But Villeneuve departed before Rosily arrived to take command, apparently unhappy with being replaced. With no one really at the helm, the fleet sailed from Cádiz in southern Spain on October 20,

1805. Meanwhile, the British fleet, under the command of Horatio Nelson (a decorated naval officer with a history of great deeds), sailed to meet them near Cape Trafalgar, farther down the Spanish coastline.

Despite this bold strategy, the odds were against the British. Nelson was outnumbered, with his fleet having twenty-seven ships compared to thirty-three ships in the Franco-Spanish fleet, which also included the largest warship, the *Santisima Trinidad*. Nelson adopted a bold (to say the least!) strategy, which was to sail directly at the larger fleet's battle line with the goal of breaking it up. The bold gambit worked; Nelson's fleet managed to cut the allied fleet into three parts, separating Villeneuve's flagship, the *Bucentaure*, from the rear half. The British ships took heavy fire in choosing this path, but Nelson steeled them with this now-famous message: "England expects that every man will do his duty."

Unfortunately, Nelson himself was hit by a musket ball during the fray. It struck his left shoulder and passed through the left lung and spine before getting lodged below his right shoulder blade. It was a terrible, and fatal, wound. Nelson died before the battle ended, and did not get a chance to see the amazing victory his fleet was about to secure. Still, the split in Napoleon's fleet gave the British a tactical advantage, which it pursued without mercy, cutting down ships and sailors. In the end, the allied fleet lost twenty-two ships, a resounding defeat that curbed Napoleon's sea power and elevated the British navy to unchallenged masters of the seas, as expressed in the famed patriotic song "Rule Britannia," which boasts quite bluntly, "Rule Britannia, Britannia, rule the waves | Britons never, never, shall be slaves." The triumph gave many British the confidence that God was on their side, and that Britain was destined to rule the world. And today, of course, Nelson's Column still stands proudly in the appropriately named Trafalgar Square in London.

> **Previous injuries fact:** Nelson was no stranger to wartime injuries. He'd lost sight in one eye during a siege in 1794, and had to have his right arm amputated above the elbow in 1797, after it was badly damaged by

another musket ball. The amputation was performed without any anesthesia (of course), and it's said that a half-hour later, Nelson was back out giving orders to his men!

THE DUKE OF WELLINGTON AND WATERLOO

The Battle of Waterloo (June 18, 1815) was fought near the town of that name in what is now Belgium. A French army of some 72,000 troops under the command of Napoleon met two armies, one of which (a combination of British, Dutch, and German forces) was under the command of Arthur Wellesley, First Duke of Wellington (1769-1852), while the other army (Prussian) was commanded by Field Marshal von Blücher. It was to be Napoleon's last stand, and one of the most decisive battles in the history of Europe.

After being defeated in 1813 at the Battle of Leipzig, Napoleon had been forced to abdicate his emperor's throne, and take a step back from terrorizing the continent. But then, to the horror of many, Napoleon returned to power in March 1815, as much of a threat (and a pain!) as ever.

The nations that opposed him formed what was known as the Seventh Coalition, with the intention of ganging up on Napoleon and his forces. By June 1815, Wellington and von Blücher both had armies stationed near the northeastern border of France. Napoleon's plan was to attack them separately and eliminate each one before they could join up with each other to invade France. On June 16, at the Battle of Ligny, Napoleon attacked the Prussian army and forced it to withdraw to the north. Pressing the attack, he sent one-third of his army to pursue the fleeing Prussian rear guard, where they would fight again at the Battle of Wavre on June 18 and 19. But, crucially, this prevented this segment of Napoleon's troops from returning to the main fight.

After a small-scale skirmish with French forces on June 16, Wellington learned of the Prussian army's retreat, and shifted the troops under his command to a more northerly location on June 17. He also learned that portions of the Prussian army would be able to join his own army at the new location, so he decided to make his stand. And it was here that Napoleon made a critical error. There had been heavy rains overnight, and he wanted the ground to dry out a bit before giving the command to attack at around noon. This might seem a sensible precaution, but it allowed time for additional Prussian forces to arrive.

When the order finally came, the Prussians were able to attack the French flank and cause heavy amounts of damage. Furthermore, Wellington was an expert in defensive strategies, and held his line against all French onslaughts. Napoleon tried a last desperate attack in the evening with his Imperial Guard, but again, both the Anglo-allied army and the Prussians didn't budge, and inflicted more heavy damage on Napoleon's troops. The French suffered a terrible defeat, and Napoleon is said to have wept as he left the area. He abdicated the throne again four days later, and the Coalition forces entered Paris on July 7, putting an end to Napoleon's reign and Imperial French ambitions to rule Europe forever. Britain would now become one of the most powerful nations in Europe, if not the most powerful.

But the human cost had been high, with 40,000 French casualties and about 22,000 allied casualties. Wellington mourned the deaths of so many: "My heart is broken by the terrible loss I have sustained in my old friends and companions and my poor soldiers. Believe me, nothing except a battle lost can be half so melancholy as a battle won." He was celebrated as a war hero and eventually he became Leader of the House of Lords, Britain's Prime Minister in the 1820s and '30s, and later, commander of the British Army.

Wrong location fact: Though he is the reason its name rings out across the world, Napoleon never set foot in Waterloo itself, as the battle was fought near the villages of Braine-l'Alleud and Plancenoit. Wellington made his headquarters in Waterloo and sent back his report of the victory from there, which is why the battle is now remembered by that name.

THE REGENCY AND ITS LEGACY

Poor George III only got worse as the nineteenth century dawned, and by 1811, he was completely incapable of thinking rationally, much less serving as king. It was decided that his son, also named George, would rule as the Prince Regent. This decision was not made lightly; it took more than two months of political debate to reach that conclusion. And Parliament agreed that George would rule as Regent only until his father recovered, but alas, the older George never did. King George III died in 1820, and his son ascended to the throne as King George IV; he would rule until his own death in 1830.

While the younger George wasn't mentally incapacitated like his father, he had more than his share of problems, being overly fond of food and drink, and probably being addicted to laudanum, a form of opium used at the time as a pain reliever and relaxant. This George was often at odds with Parliament, too, but at least he was mentally sound enough to understand what he was disputing!

While George's story is interesting on its own, it's the culture in England in the years surrounding his Regency that has fascinated so many ever since. In a very short time, there was an explosion of literary, scientific, and artistic changes that are still shaping the world today. The Prince Regent actively encouraged this outpouring of innovation in the arts and sciences, and often became a patron to deserving geniuses.

But such pastimes were mostly only for the well-off. Those who were poor suffered just as they always had, and the expanding Industrial Revolution only made things worse. Many of the social reforms that would come about over the next few decades were a direct response to the terrible living conditions the lower classes were subjected to during this time. With the movement to abolish slavery also in full swing, it was obvious that society needed some very big changes, whether the upper classes wanted them or not. It was the Victorians that would really step up to try to right some of these wrongs.

For many, however, the Regency means a time when some of the finest poetry and literature in the English language appeared, along with new fashions, art, and cultural graces that are still treasured. The next several entries are but a small sample of the amazing people who prospered during this era.

> Random, creepy fact, just because: Joseph Grimaldi, a popular stage and theater entertainer of the time, was likely the man who invented modern clown makeup. It's also said that his ghostly, decapitated head still haunts a theater in London, floating about in full clown makeup. Thanks for the nightmares, Joe!

BEAU BRUMMELL, MASTER OF FASHION

George "Beau" Brummell (1778-1840) was a leader in fashion in early nineteenth-century Britain. It was largely due to his influence that men's fashions shifted from the opulent and over-the-top eighteenth-century approach to looks that were more sedate and practical, yet still allowed for personal style. The look of well-off men in the

Regency and Victorian periods owes much to his influence, and for a time Brummel's aesthetic was the last word in men's fashions.

Brummell was born into a wealthy family and attended Eton College as a boy, where he rubbed shoulders with members of the nobility. After his father's death in 1794, he went to Oxford to study, armed with the knowledge that he would inherit a fortune when he came of age. But Beau soon grew restless, and decided to enter the army. He was able to join the Tenth Light Dragoons, which was the Prince of Wales' regiment (the future King George IV). The company enjoyed fine uniforms and had a taste for alcohol, both of which suited Brummell just fine. He soon became friends with the young Prince George, a connection that would only bolster Brummell's reputation and influence later on.

In 1796, Brummell was promoted to the rank of captain, but he left the service two years later and came into his vast inheritance. He set himself up in London in 1799 and determined to become the most stylish man in the city, confident in both his own taste and the support of his good friend George. And he was right to be confident. Brummell began making a splash in fashion quarters and soon, he was advising men from all walks of aristocratic and wealthy life on their sartorial decisions. He greatly toned down the excesses of previous decades, both in color and in fabric, favoring fine tailoring and good cuts. He delighted in his role as a dandy, and would sit in the window at White's gentleman's club in London and make snarky remarks about the men who walked by if he didn't like their look. His remarks and witticisms became known as "Brummellisms." But he was also sarcastic and acerbic, and it rubbed some the wrong way, including his powerful friend— Brummell had a falling out with George in 1812, after calling the Prince Regent "fat" at one reception.

Owing to his fondness for gambling, Brummell managed to run up a considerable amount of debt (even with his considerable fortune), and this precipitated his fall from grace. Eventually, he became heavily indebted to Richard Meyler, and planned to get out of paying what he owed. Meyler decided to tell everyone about Brummell's behavior and soon news spread that not only did Brummel have serious debts, he was also a bit of a scoundrel. For his part, Meyler would later be known as "Dick the Dandy-killer." Make of that what you will.

Brummell left England for France in 1816 to escape his debts, but managed to run up more debt in Calais. Eventually, in 1830, he regained now-King George IV's favor and took up a position as consul in Caen, but he was suffering from syphilis, contracted during his decadent years. He eventually died in 1840, in an asylum, having gone insane from the disease.

> Good luck fact: Brummell carried a good luck talisman for gambling. It was an old coin he found in Mayfair and had it fastened to his watch chain. He lost it in 1815, and had to flee Britain the following year because of his debts. Coincidence?

ANNE LISTER: A REMARKABLE SECRET LIFE

Lister (1791-1840) was an English writer and diarist who lived in Yorkshire. She was a reasonably wealthy landowner who inherited her family's medieval home, Shibden Hall, near Halifax in West Yorkshire. Her observations provide many insights into life at the time, including practical topics like mining and transportation via railway and canal. Lister was also a successful businesswoman, much to the surprise of many of the men around her. But, of course, what makes Lister so intriguing to modern readers is the coded entries in some of her diaries, wherein she revealed secrets that would have scandalized British society had they been wider known.

Lister wrote extensively, something like five million words, and about one-sixth of her diary entries were written in a code that combined Greek letters and algebra into what she termed a "crypthand." She was quite convinced that no one would ever break the code, so she felt emboldened to write about her life freely.

And what did she record?

Well, Lister is sometimes referred to as the "first modern lesbian." Her coded entries go into great detail about her amorous pursuits of various ladies (single and married), and her often-successful seductions. Anne preferred to dress in all black (a much more common choice for men at the time) and had no interest in lace or the feminine fashions of women. Because of her unique approach, some of the unenlightened men around Lister branded her with the derogatory nickname "Gentleman Jack," as she was not ladylike enough for their liking.

But Lister didn't care. She pursued her life with passion and vigor. She loved walking, she loved traveling, and she loved several women in her social circle. One woman in particular, the wealthy heiress Ann Walker, caught her eye. The feeling was mutual and the two began a secret relationship. Only, it ended up not being that secret. They took part in a marriage ceremony and took Anglican Communion with each other at Holy Trinity Church in York in 1834, and thereafter Anne and Ann lived basically as a married couple in Shibden Hall until Lister's death in 1840. Although the marriage was, of course, not "official" in the eyes of the law or the church, it is now recognized as the first gay marriage in Britain, and a blue plaque on an outside wall at Holy Trinity Church reads:

"Anne Lister 1791-1840 of Shibden Hall, Halifax

**Lesbian and Diarist; took sacrament here to
seal her union with Ann Walker**

Easter 1834."

Unfortunately, Lister was not destined to live a long life. While traveling in the Republic of Georgia with Walker in 1840, she contracted a fever (possibly due to a tick bite) and died. Walker had Anne's body brought back and buried at Halifax Minster, though the exact location is no longer known.

Lister's secret life might have died with her, but in the 1890s, one of her descendants, John Lister, discovered her diaries and broke the code. He was shocked by what he read and decided not to reveal it, since he was also gay and didn't want to bring attention to himself or the family. In the 1980s, scholar Helena Whitbread rediscovered Lister's diaries and deciphered them. The contents were so detailed and outrageous that she first assumed they were a hoax, but more research proved that they were authentic. Lister's diaries are now available to the public, and a popular television series has been made about her life.

> **Saved from the fire fact:** John Lister deciphered the diaries with the help of his friend, Arthur Burrell, who recommended that John burn them. Thankfully, John ignored him, and hid them behind a wooden wall panel in Shibden Hall, saving them for posterity.

LORD BYRON

The original bad boy, the primordial pop star, Byron was a sensation, enjoying legions of admirers, and sending young women swooning with his every move. These women would write Byron fan letters, ask for his autograph or a lock of his hair, cry when they heard his writings, and even faint when they saw him. His future wife, Annabella Milbanke, coined the phrase "Byromania," long before the Beatles were even a possibility. Another fan summed the phenomenon up as saying that Byron was "mad, bad, and dangerous to know." So, who was this charmer and rogue that outraged society and left many ladies (and a few lads) swooning?

George Gordon Byron, Sixth Baron Byron (1788-1824) was born in London, though he spent his childhood in Aberdeenshire in Scotland. These were not happy years; his mother experienced mood swings (she might have suffered from mental health issues) and drank too much, the family maid abused young George, and his father separated from his mother and abandoned the boy (Byron's father then died in France in 1791). George himself was born with a slightly deformed right foot, and felt self-conscious about it. He had a mild limp all his life, though he would later overcome it to become skilled at boxing, horse riding, and swimming.

Fortune finally smiled upon Byron in 1798, when his "wicked uncle" died, and he inherited the title of Lord Byron and all of the perks that came with it. He was educated at Harrow in London and then at Trinity College in Cambridge (from 1805 to 1808), where he experimented and indulged in affairs with both women and men. Ever the rebel, he protested the college's prohibition on keeping a pet dog by having a pet bear! Since there was no college rule against this and he was a nobleman, the Trinity authorities couldn't stop Byron, and he walked through the street with the animal on a leash. Must have been quite a sight!

Byron was not just a provocateur, however. He was also a writer and a poet, and his output was prolific. His masterpiece is arguably the unfinished *Don Juan*, a long poem that his admirers see as comparable to *Paradise Lost*, the *Canterbury Tales*, and Shakespeare's works. He wrote all his life, and in his own time, his fame was widespread, not only because of his skill, but because of the growing scandals caused by his numerous affairs with high-ranking ladies. In 1816, he left Britain to flee from his debts and notorious reputation, and he never returned. Making his way to Switzerland with his personal doctor, John William Polidori, he settled near Lake Geneva, and soon made friends with the poet Percy Bysshe Shelley and Mary Godwin (later Mary Shelley). During a rainy series of days in June, the friends were compelled to stay indoors because of incessantly wet weather, and turned to telling Gothic stories for amusement. This rainout would prove highly influential, as Mary would end up writing *Frankenstein*, while Polidori penned *The Vampyre*, a book that became a model for vampire stories throughout the nineteenth century.

Byron then made his way to Italy, where he continued his licentious ways. In fact, the sale of some property back in England cleared up his debts, and permitted him to live an even more debauched life while abroad, and indulge his lifelong fondness for animals by assembling his own private zoo.

In 1823, Byron sailed for Greece, being very fond of its people and their desire for independence from Ottoman Turkish rule. He donated money to the resistance, and even commanded a troop of fighters. But his wild life was catching up with him, and he became ill in early 1824, finally dying of a fever in April. It might have been complications of venereal disease, or perhaps malaria. Despite his best efforts, Byron's reputation as a poet outlived him, and it wasn't long before societies of admirers were forming to read and discuss his works; they continue to do so today—though these meetings probably feature less swooning than they once did.

> **Thanks, but no thanks fact:** Byron was originally meant to be buried in Westminster Abbey, alongside so many other greats, but this request was refused on account of his "questionable morality." It's possible that his heart was kept in Greece, while the rest of his body was sent to Nottinghamshire for burial.

MARY SHELLEY

A friend of Byron's, Shelley was a talented writer in her own right. While she and her future husband, the poet Percy Shelley, were visiting with Byron in Switzerland, she was moved to write what would become one of the most famous books of all time, *Frankenstein*. Many people see this work as the first true science fiction novel, and its warnings about the terrible consequences that come from man's attempts to control nature are still important to readers today.

She (1797-1851) was the daughter of philosopher and writer William Godwin and the legendary feminist Mary Wollstonecraft (whom we've already met, see page 253). Sadly, Mary's mother died only days after her birth. Her father remarried, to a woman named Mary Jane Clairmont (that's a lot of Marys!), but stepmother and stepdaughter never really got along. Although young Mary received no formal education, she knew how to read, and would spend hours in the family library perusing the books. From a young age, she was known for her vivid imagination. She later explained: "As a child, I scribbled; and my favourite pastime, during the hours given me for recreation, was to write stories."

In 1814, she met Percy, and the two became enamored of each other, even though he was already married at the time. But they weren't going to let that little inconvenience get in the way, and they ended up fleeing England that year. Needless to say, no one else was thrilled by this move. The couple traveled Europe for a while, and eventually found themselves in Switzerland, in the company of Lord Byron and his entourage. As noted earlier, on a particularly dreary series of rainy days in June 1816, Mary developed the idea for the book that would make her immortal: *Frankenstein, or The Modern Prometheus*. It was published in 1818, and listed "Anonymous" as the author, since publishing was a profession seen as unfit for ladies (as you'll see in the next entry, Jane Austen had the same problem). As Percy wrote the introduction, many just assumed he had written the entire thing.

In the book, Mary details a young doctor's search for the secrets of life, producing a shocking, provocative, and utterly new text. It was a cautionary tale about hubris and presumption in the ever-expanding scientific community, a warning not to mess with forces that humanity has no business meddling in. In the contemporary age, where cloning, genetic engineering, artificial intelligence, and other scientific advances are causing a quagmire of ethical issues, the book remains as pertinent as ever. Frankenstein, of course, is the name of the doctor, not the monster, who had no name. The tale has been loved since it first appeared, inspiring countless adaptations for film, television, and other mediums, with Frankenstein's monster becoming as big of an icon in the horrorsphere as Dracula or the Wolf Man.

Percy and Mary had wed in 1816, after Percy's wife committed suicide. But tragedy was soon to visit the happy couple, as Percy himself died in 1822. This left Mary a widow at 24 with a young son to care for. The couple had been living in Italy, but after the death of her true love Mary returned to London and resumed writing, producing more novels and travel accounts. She lived until 1851, when she died of brain cancer.

> **Stony heart fact:** Mary kept Percy's heart with her for the rest of her life, unwilling to part with all of him. Percy had been cremated, but his heart had calcified and didn't burn, so perhaps Mary saw it as a sign of their undying love and retrieved it. After she died, it was found in her desk, wrapped in a piece of paper upon which one of Percy's poems was written.

JANE AUSTEN

Jane Austen is one the most beloved English authors, standing comfortably alongside Shakespeare and Charles Dickens. Honestly,

how many adaptations of her novels have you seen over the years? Come on, confess!

Best known for *Pride and Prejudice*, all her novels explore the lives and manners of middle- and upper-class folk during the Regency, providing a fly-on-the-wall view of a world that is long gone, but still vividly with us through her works.

Austen (1775-1817) wrote six major novels, all of which are classics and widely beloved: *Sense and Sensibility* (1811), *Pride and Prejudice* (1813), *Mansfield Park* (1814), *Emma* (1815), *Northanger Abbey* (1818, posthumously published), and *Persuasion* (1818, posthumously published), as well as a short work, *Lady Susan*, which was not published until 1871. Again, since writing was an "unsuitable" occupation for ladies at this time, Austen was compelled to release her works anonymously, though the Prince Regent himself became fond of her work—perhaps too fond of it, as you'll see in a bit.

Austen was born into a comfortable family and enjoyed a happy childhood where her education was encouraged. She and her sisters wrote plays and staged them with their parents' encouragement. She and her sister Cassandra went to school, but both of them came down with typhus, which nearly killed young Jane. Afterward, she remained home, but continued to read and to learn. She began to write, and some of this teenage material would find its way into her immortal novels.

The Austen family moved to Bath, but her father's death in 1805 and a series of financial issues put the family's life in a state of upheaval for a while. In 1809, Jane settled in Chawton, north and east of the city of Southampton. Over the next several years, she would publish her books anonymously, though in November 1815, she received a communication from James Stanier Clarke, the royal librarian, saying that the Prince Regent himself was fond of her work, and kept copies of her books in all of his residences. It turns out that Austen's brother had been treated by a doctor who also attended to the prince, and he informed the Prince Regent that Jane was the author of those books he greatly enjoyed.

The prince had Clarke invite Austen to meet with him at one of the royal homes in London. Clarke also told her that the prince graciously gave her "permission" to dedicate her next book, *Emma*, to him, should she wish to do so—which, of course, was an instruction, not a suggestion. Austen detested the Prince for his debauched lifestyle, but she could hardly refuse such a "royal invitation," even if she thought hard of a way to get out of it. She eventually contacted her publisher to let him know that the book would need to include said dedication.

By 1816, Austen was beginning to feel unwell, but she pushed through and ignored the problem. Eventually, in 1817, she had no more energy and could barely walk. By April, she was confined to bed in severe pain, and after being ushered to Winchester for treatment, she died in July 1817. She might have been suffering for Addison's Disease (an adrenal disorder), Hodgkin's Lymphoma, or perhaps tuberculosis contracted from consuming unpasteurized milk. After her death, her family arranged for *Persuasion* and *Northanger Abbey* to be published as a set, and her brother finally unveiled her as the great anonymous author. In 1832, a publisher named Richard Bentley bought the rights to all of her books to reprint them, and they've been in print ever since, though it would not be until the 1920s that readers truly began to recognize her genius. That deep appreciation has not flagged for a moment since.

> Fan fic fact: In 1823, a letter to *The Lady's Magazine* asked how one could become a better writer, and the magazine's editors elected to use the character of Austen's ghost to give helpful answers, making this the first piece of fan fiction to feature Jane Austen!

THE BRONTË SISTERS

This trio—Charlotte, Emily, and Anne Brontë—lived short lives and wrote relatively few novels, but their works are among the best loved in all of English literature.

Their seemingly un-English surname was adopted by their father, Patrick Brunty or Prunty, who came from Irish ancestry. Knowing the prejudices against the Irish at the time, and wanting to better himself, he changed his last name to Brontë; the umlaut over the "e" was to let people know that the name had two syllables, so that they wouldn't say "Bront." Some have thought that since his brother, William Prunty, was in hiding from the British for his pro-Irish political activism, Patrick wanted to distance himself from the family name. In any case, the strategy worked—Patrick was educated at Cambridge, ordained, and installed as the rector of Haworth, a village on the Yorkshire moors, a bleak landscape that would heavily influence the sisters' imaginations and storytelling.

The sisters also had a brother, Branwell, a gifted painter who would ultimately become addicted to alcohol and opium and die at the age of 31. In fact, all of the Brontë offspring were destined for short lives. Two other daughters had died as children, and Charlotte, Emily, and Anne all died before reaching the age of 40.

As children, the three sisters enjoyed writing poetry and making up stories. They created their own fictitious worlds, one of which was Gondal, an island kingdom in the northern Pacific Ocean. The girls wrote poems and short entries about this exotic land, and some see these tales as a fine early example of speculative fiction and fantasy, created not long after Mary Shelley's pioneering science fiction work, *Frankenstein*.

But of course, their towering novels are what the sisters are best known for: Charlotte's *Jane Eyre*, Emily's *Wuthering Heights* (her only novel), and Anne's *The Tenant of Wildfell Hall*. Each of these works is a masterpiece in its own way, employing Gothic themes and unforgettable characters to evoke the moody landscapes of their home on the moors. Generations of readers have thrilled to these books, which, like the works of Jane Austen, have never gone out of style or popularity.

Like so many women writers of the time, they did not publish their books under their own names, but instead, went by pennames, all using the last name of "Bell": Currer (Charlotte), Ellis (Emily) and Acton (Anne). At the time, some readers even thought that their works were all composed by the same person!

Due to their unique subject matters, the Brontë sisters' books aroused some controversy during their lives. *Wildfell Hall,* with its themes of alcoholism and marital abuse, was popular but divided readers. Charlotte herself considered the subjects inappropriate, and after Anne's death in 1849, Charlotte prevented the book from being published again, which for a while, left Anne in obscurity. *Wuthering Heights* was both praised and condemned, for its unusual storyline and bleak themes. One memorable review in *Graham's Lady Magazine* exclaimed: "How a human being could have attempted such a book as the present without committing suicide before he had finished a dozen chapters, is a mystery. It is a compound of vulgar depravity and unnatural horrors." Gotta love critics! But Emily had the last laugh, as the work is now considered an all-time classic.

Despite their successes, the Brontë Sisters were destined to die young: Charlotte from complications of pregnancy at the age of 38, Emily from tuberculosis at the age of 30, and Anne also of tuberculosis at the tender age of 29. One wonders what other magnificent tales they might have told had fate permitted them longer lives!

> **Antisocial fact:** Of the three sisters, Emily was the most reclusive and uneasy around other people, much preferring the company of animals. At one point when she was a teacher, she told her students that she preferred the school dog to any of them! At least the warm feelings were

mutual—it was said that after her death, that dog, Keeper, followed Emily's coffin as it was transported to its grave, and howled outside of her bedroom door for a week afterward. How sad!

THE ROMANTIC POETS: BLAKE, WORDSWORTH, COLERIDGE, AND KEATS

Within the span of a few decades in the late eighteenth and early nineteenth centuries, the English language was gifted with an outpouring of astonishing works by a group of poets whose names continue to ring out. The stories of the four most important from this era follow.

William Blake (1757-1827) was a gifted visual artist in addition to a brilliant poet. His artwork was wildly different from anything seen at the time, and many thought that he had mental issues because of it and his unorthodox views. Though largely unrecognized in his own time, Blake would later take his place among the top ranks of British artists thanks to his poems and books such as *Jerusalem: The Emanation of the Giant Albion*, where Blake's stunning personal mythology is accompanied by his remarkable illustrations. Blake was ahead of his time in almost every regard, as he hated slavery and was a strong advocate for racial and gender equality long before those ideas took hold in the mainstream.

William Wordsworth (1770-1850) was destined to be the longest-lived of these poets, and, along with Samuel Taylor Coleridge, he is credited with launching the Romantic Movement for literature

in Britain. He made the "required" poetic tour of Europe in the early 1790s and came into contact with the French Revolution, with all of its invigorating ideas and objective horrors. In 1795, he met Coleridge and they published their *Lyrical Ballads*, which are considered some of the most important and influential poems in all of English literature. Wordsworth lived well into the Victorian era, and his final work, *The Prelude*, published the year he died, is possibly the greatest achievement of English Romanticism.

Samuel Taylor Coleridge (1772-1834) essentially co-founded the Romantic Movement in Britain with Wordsworth, and was a member of a group known as the Lake Poets, those who visited or even moved to the Lake District in northwest England for inspiration, establishing the region as a popular tourist's site ever since. While his most famous works are the poems "The Rime of the Ancient Mariner" and "Kubla Khan," Coleridge was also a fabulous literary critic, and is believed to be the last writer who had read every single entry in the canon before embarking on his career.

John Keats (1795-1821) died from tuberculosis at only 25, which means he truly embodied the Romantic idea of the genius artist whose life is cut tragically short. Keats didn't make that much of a splash in his short lifetime, but, as is often the case, his fame grew after his death, and he was soon to become a major influence on the Pre-Raphaelite poets and artists (see page 309) thanks to poems such as "Ode to a Nightingale" and "Ode on a Grecian Urn."

> Dreamy fact: Coleridge's "Kubla Khan" is only a fragment of what it was meant to be. It was inspired by a vivid dream he had that might or might not have been influenced by opium, depending on whose version of the story you read. When Coleridge woke up, he started work on the poem at once, thinking it would be several hundred lines long. But his inspiration was interrupted by a businessman from the nearby village of Porlock at the door. When Coleridge was finally able to return to his poem, he was horrified to find that everything he had wanted to write down was gone from his mind. He had composed fifty-four lines, but

there would be no more, and he didn't even bother to publish what he'd gotten down for almost twenty years. One scholar would later say, "If there is any man in the history of literature who should be hanged, drawn, and quartered, it is the man on business from Porlock."

BURKE AND HARE: GRAVE ROBBERS FOR HIRE

Let's move along from Regency Romanticism to one of the other great nineteenth-century pastimes: grave robbing! It's the stuff of horror stories (*Frankenstein*, anyone?), but what was the purpose of digging up dead people, other than to rob corpses of any wealth buried with them?

Well, believe it or not, the issue actually has to do with an act of mercy. In 1823, the British government passed the Judgement of Death Act, which greatly reduced the number of crimes for which a person could be executed. This was a kind and enlightened idea, since before then, executions could be carried out for a number of minor crimes, even petty theft.

But for medical doctors and researchers, this new law created a big problem. They had previously been allowed to dissect the corpses of the condemned for medical and educational purposes. But with far fewer people now being executed, that steady supply of bodies started to dry up.

So, some doctors began paying some pretty shady fellows to go into cemeteries in the middle of the night and dig up the bodies of recently deceased people in order to continue their research. Known as "resurrectionists," these grave robbers were often paid a pretty penny to provide corpses, the fresher the better. It got so bad that some wealthy families installed watchtowers over cemeteries, where paid guards could keep an eye out for nocturnal invaders!

And, as you might have anticipated, it wasn't long before these resurrectionists gave up on digging up bodies and went straight to the source: killing people and bringing their bodies to their doctor clients, who accepted them without question.

Two of the most infamous of these murderers committed their crimes in Scotland in the 1820s. William Burke and William Hare were both from Ireland, but had moved to Edinburgh for work. Hare helped run a boarding house, and in December 1827, when one of the older tenants died, he hit on an idea for making some extra money. Burke and Hare took the body to Professor Robert Knox, an anatomy teacher at Edinburgh University. Knox was only too happy to have a fresh corpse to work on, and promised money for any others they could provide. The pair quickly got tired of waiting for people to die, and simply started to help nature along! In 1828, they began suffocating victims, which left the bodies unmarked, and more suitable for medical study. They preyed on poor neighborhoods, where the victims, unfortunately, would not be as noticed or cared about by "polite society." In all, they are known to have murdered sixteen people, but the number of actual victims is probably much higher.

Eventually, they got greedy and sloppy, and a body Burke had hidden under a bed was discovered by a couple that had been lodging in his home. They reported the murder to the police, but it was difficult to find hard evidence of Burke and Hare's crimes. Eventually, Hare was offered immunity to testify against Burke, which he was quite happy to do! Burke was found guilty and hanged in January 1829, while Hare and Knox walked free. Burke had claimed that Knox didn't know where the bodies came from—an obvious lie that outraged many. But without proof, there wasn't much that the police or courts could do.

In 1832, the new Anatomy Act allowed for bodies to be donated for medical research, which cut down on the amount of grave robbing, though it undoubtedly continued well into the Victorian era.

Murderous fact: The practice of suffocating a victim so that there were no marks on the body came to be known as "Burking."

CHAPTER 7

THE VICTORIANS AND EDWARDIANS

(1837-1914)

VICTORIA: THE TEENAGE QUEEN

Young Victoria's path to the throne was not easy, or even likely. She was the daughter of Prince Edward, the fourth son of King George III, which meant that she had a whole lot of heirs ahead of her in line for the throne, enough that she likely never thought the crown was a possibility for her. But fate has a way of bringing about unexpected conclusions, and by the 1830s, events were in motion that would change the course of not only Britain, but the whole world. One by one, the sons of George III died off, and they had no legitimate heirs of their own (all of them having died as children). Victoria's own father died in 1820, when she was less than a year old. All of a sudden, the royal line consisted only of George's son William, who was ruling as King William IV, and the child Victoria. What a burden and responsibility she must have faced!

Victoria's mother, Princess Victoria of Saxe-Coburg-Saalfeld (great title!), was not on the best of terms with William. As his health faded in the 1830s, it was suggested that the Princess serve as Princess Regent for Victoria until her daughter turned 18. But old William wouldn't dream of it. In August 1836, at a banquet for the well-to-do, William, who knew he wasn't long for the world, declared that he hoped to live for nine more months, "I should then have the satisfaction of leaving the exercise of the Royal authority to the personal authority of that young lady, heiress presumptive to the Crown [Victoria], and not in the hands of a person now near me [her mother], who is surrounded by evil advisers and is herself incompetent to act ... in the situation in which she would be placed."

Quite the burn! Mother Victoria was tempted to get up and leave right then and there, but was somehow persuaded to stay for the dinner, though she and her daughter left the next day. And the amazing thing is that William did as he said! He hung on until just after

Victoria's 18th birthday, ensuring that her mother never got the chance to be Regent, not even for a few weeks!

Being a new, and extremely young, queen, not a lot was expected of Victoria. Certainly, no one expected her to be a woman who would rule Britain until the dawn of the twentieth century and lend her name to a golden age, as Elizabeth before her had done. And while Victoria didn't have Elizabeth's brilliance for governing, she was plenty shrewd and smart, and in time, proved herself to be more than up to the task of ruling Great Britain.

The Prime Minister, William Lamb, Second Viscount Melbourne, became Victoria's advisor and close friend in her early years—a little too close for some. While most insisted that they had a father-daughter kind of relationship, some suspected that it was more than that, and that the queen was actually infatuated with Lamb, even though he was 30 years older than her. Indeed, some snarky subjects took to calling Victoria "Mrs. Melbourne." Although it's possible that Victoria had a huge crush on the prime minister, she must have known that the relationship could never really go anywhere. In any case, when the young Prince Albert of Saxe-Coburg came into her life, Victoria saw that he was the man for her. They married in 1840, and went on to have nine children together.

> **Gunfire fact:** Victoria survived several assassination attempts early in her reign. On May 29, 1842, a man named John Francis tried to shoot her as she rode by in her carriage, but the gun didn't fire, and Francis was able to get away. Victoria decided to ride by the same place the following day, in hopes of luring Francis out. It worked, and he was arrested after trying to shoot her again!

ADA LOVELACE, CHARLES BABBAGE, AND THE FIRST COMPUTER

Lovelace (1815-52) and Babbage (1791-1871) are rightly seen as the "mother and father" of the computer. We take computers so much for granted these days that it's hard to imagine a time when we didn't have them, never mind envision the mental leaps someone would have to make to come up with the idea more than two centuries ago. And while these two weren't exactly the Steve Jobs or Bill Gates of their time, both made important contributions to the development of these revolutionary machines.

Babbage was born in London and educated at Cambridge, but struggled to secure a permanent teaching position or other appointment once out of school, and often relied on family money for support. But his father died in 1827, leaving him the sum of about £100,000, which is nearly $12 million in modern money! As such, Babbage was now independently wealthy and could pursue his interests to his heart's content. And one of his main interests was designing a calculating machine.

Lovelace was Lord Byron's only legitimate child, the daughter of him and Anne Isabella Milbanke, better known as Lady Byron. Lady Byron was a mathematician herself, and Lovelace would develop her own interest in the subject with her mother's encouragement. Lovelace never saw her father; her mother separated from Lord Byron right after Ada was born and kept her away from him, fearing that his "insanity" would affect her. Left to her own devices, Ada fully engaged with her curiosity—at one point, she looked into the possibility of designing a flying machine in the shape of a horse!

In 1833, Ada's path crossed Babbage's, when she was introduced to him by her mentor, Mary Somerville. At the time, Babbage was working on a mechanical calculator that he called the Difference Engine. Babbage was impressed with Lovelace, whom he called the

"Enchantress of Numbers." The two began a series of correspondences, as she was most interested in his work on the Difference Engine, and later, another device that he called the Analytical Engine, which contained many of the properties of the modern computer.

Ada is sometimes credited with writing the world's first computer program, but this isn't actually true. In 1840, Babbage traveled to Italy to give a lecture on the Analytical Engine. Lovelace was tasked with translating notes on the conference from French, and she expanded the appendix to include more material; her work was published in 1843. One section contained what was clearly an algorithm for the machine—essentially, a computer program. This discovery caused many to credit Lovelace with the invention of computer programming, but recent research has proven that Babbage was writing algorithms for the machine as early as 1836.

Where Lovelace went beyond Babbage was in seeing the possibilities of his primordial computer. She saw it as having applications in all sorts of areas, including composing music, whereas Babbage was fine with it being confined to basic arithmetic. So, she was a visionary who manage to see how important and multifaceted computers would one day become. Lovelace offered to help Babbage implement this vision and secure funding to have such a machine built, but he foolishly declined. Would there have been a computer revolution in the 1840s if he'd listened? Would Silicon Valley have arisen in Victorian London? Might Britain in the later nineteenth century have become a Steampunk wonderland? Unfortunately, we'll never know.

> Gambling fact: For all of her genius, Lovelace had a gambling habit that slowly drained her family's finances. She seemed to be interested in trying to use mathematics to predict the outcome of horse races, but it doesn't seem to have done her much good.

MICHAEL FARADAY

F araday (1791-1867) was an English scientist whose electricity-related discoveries (especially electrochemistry and electromagnetism) changed the course of human history. His greatest work was the discovery of electromagnetic induction, which is the idea that powers the electric generator and transformer. This discovery allowed electricity to move from being a curiosity that some fringe scientists liked to work with to become a practical tool. To say that this had a huge impact on the Industrial Revolution would be a massive understatement! Faraday also discovered that the field surrounding the conductor carried a direct current, which is the foundation of the electromagnetic field as physics now understands it. If this is all a little too scientific and confusing, just know that without his discoveries, we wouldn't have electricity (or lights, televisions, computers, etc.) as we know it.

Faraday came from humble beginnings in London and as such did not have a proper education. As a teenager, he became apprenticed to a bookbinder, which might seem very far away from being a scientist, but he used his connection to books to read deeply about scientific topics. As a young man, Faraday went to a series of lectures given by Humphry Davy, a chemist from the Royal Institution (which was dedicated to scientific research). Faraday was so impressed that he wrote a letter to Davy, asking if he could become his assistant. And Davy said no. But a year later, in 1813, Davy did appoint Faraday to the position of chemical assistant at the Royal Institution, a big opportunity for the eager young scientist. Faraday would soon accompany Davy and his wife on an eighteen-month grand tour of Europe (France, Belgium, Switzerland, and Italy), and he met many important scientists along the way. After returning to England, Faraday was well on his way to conducting research and making discoveries of his own.

In addition to his work on electricity, Faraday also excelled at chemistry, inventing a prototype of the Bunsen burner and discovering the chemical benzene (which is used in everything from rubber and detergent to dyes and gasoline). In addition to his other titles, he became the Fullerian Professor of Chemistry at the Royal Institution. Not bad for a guy who never had a formal education!

Faraday was also an exemplary human. Far ahead of any large-scale environmental movement, he became an advocate for repairing and stopping the damage the Industrial Revolution was already causing. When he was approached about helping to manufacture chemical weapons for Britain to use in the Crimean War in the 1850s, he refused on ethical grounds. He was offered a knighthood, but also refused it, preferring to remain humble "Mr. Faraday." In later life, he was given a home, free of charge, at Hampton Court, and lived out his last nine years there. In a last act of humility, he even refused an offer to be buried in Westminster Abbey.

Homage fact: Albert Einstein had a picture of Faraday on a wall in his study. There might be no greater praise of a scientist than that!

GEORGE STEPHENSON: FATHER OF THE BRITISH RAILWAY

Stephenson (1781-1848) was born in the north of England, near the city of Newcastle upon Tyne to a working-class, illiterate family. Stephenson himself would not be able to read or write until his later teenage years, but once exposed to writing and mathematics, he excelled at both. As a young man, he worked on various machines and at coal mines, which were starting to show up in more and more places (it was the early years of the Industrial Revolution, after all).

After a series of hardships and tragedies, including the death of his wife in 1806, Stephenson set about working on his own version of a steam engine, designed for hauling coal at the Killingworth colliery. He named it *Blücher* (after the Prussian general at Waterloo) and it could haul thirty tons of coal up a hill at the dizzying speed of 4 miles per hour. It was slow, but that was work that men didn't have to do, which saved time and effort. It was the first of sixteen engines Stephen would design for the company.

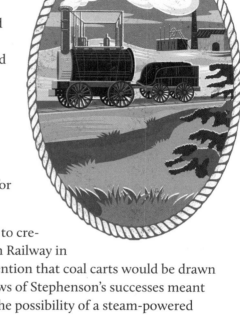

In 1821, Parliament passed a bill to create the Stockton and Darlington Railway in northern England, with the intention that coal carts would be drawn by horses on metal rails. But news of Stephenson's successes meant that people became excited by the possibility of a steam-powered engine. Stephenson and his son surveyed the landscape and then assembled a company to manufacture the engine. Rail lines were laid and the engine, named *Locomotion*, was built (it was the first of several). The line opened on September 27, 1825; the journey from one point to the other took two hours, but Stephenson's engine reached speeds of almost 25 miles per hour.

It wasn't long before there was a great interest in using the line for passengers, and the first passenger engine, *Experiment*, was soon chugging people back and forth. It also wasn't long before there was talk of a Liverpool and Manchester Railway for passengers, and Stephenson was brought in to design it. It opened on September 15, 1830, and drew large crowds, among them the prime minister and the Duke of Wellington. Eight trains set out, including one, the *Northumbrian*, driven by Stephenson himself. Tragedy struck, however, when another train, *Rocket*, struck and killed William Huskisson, the MP for Liverpool. Stephenson wasn't blamed for the tragedy, and in fact, the day cemented his reputation. He was soon being asked to work on railway projects all over the northern part of the country, as everyone wanted in on fast, reliable transportation that could replace horse-drawn carts.

Stephenson also realized that eventually, these railways would want to be linked up to each other, and so he devised a standard gauge (size) for the rail lines that became universal. That way, any line could connect to any other with ease.

In the 1840s, he stepped away from railway design something of a celebrity, attracting interested builders from as far away as America. Stephenson's railways further stimulated the Industrial Revolution by moving freight, cargo, and people much farther and faster than ever before.

> **Deathly fact:** Despite its murderous beginnings, the *Rocket* engine would become the model for future steam engines, breaking numerous records for speed.

ISAMBARD KINGDOM BRUNEL: ENGINEER EXTRAORDINAIRE

B runel (1806-59) was the son of a French engineer, Marc Isambard Brunel, who had fled the French Revolution, first for America, then Britain. His father's choice was a provident one, as Isambard went on to become one of the most highly regarded engineers of the Victorian era, responsible for innovative designs for railways and steamships.

Brunel received most of his education in France (long after the dangerous days of the Revolution had ended), before returning to England to work under his father. One of their chief projects, beginning in 1825, was the construction of a tunnel under the Thames that would connect the north and south banks. But such work was highly dangerous, with leaks and collapses an ever-present risk. Brunel himself was injured in a flooding accident in 1828, which halted the project for a few years. He spent almost six months recovering.

Deciding that his talents could best be used elsewhere, Brunel turned his attention to other projects. One of the most famous was the Clifton Suspension Bridge in Bristol. Work on it started in 1831, but Brunel almost didn't create the design. He submitted four different possible plans, but each of them was rejected, while the committee head, an engineer named Thomas Telford, conveniently was able to advance his own design as the winner. The problem was that the public hated it! A new competition was scheduled, and Brunel ultimately won. Sadly, the bridge construction suffered many delays and Brunel would not live to see it finished. Maybe that was for the best, though—when the bridge was completed in 1864, there had been many changes to the original design.

One of the other great achievements of his life was the Great Western Railway, of which he was appointed chief engineer in 1833. This line ran from London to Bristol, and eventually on to Exeter, a true marvel of Victorian engineering. Though the way was largely flat (as was his intention), there were still rivers, valleys, and other natural obstacles to a smooth line. Brunel's design allowed for these, using bridges and viaducts, stations at certain points, and tunnels where necessary. The line began at a London station, Paddington, which itself was a marvel of engineering and is still in use today.

When the Crimean War began in 1854, the British government asked Brunel to design a ready-made hospital that could be shipped to Turkey. The seemingly Herculean task took him just six days, and won the admiration of Florence Nightingale (more on her in a bit), who referred to Brunel's structures as "those magnificent huts."

Brunel's other passion was steamships, and he designed several memorable ones, including the SS *Great Western*, which made many trans-Atlantic trips in the 1830s and '40s; the SS *Great Britain*, which is now seen as the first truly modern steamship; and the enormous SS *Great Eastern*, which was designed to sail between London and Sydney nonstop. Unfortunately, an explosion on board during the latter's first test run in September 1859 ruined any chances of it ever doing this. The news of this failure never reached Brunel, as he had suffered a stroke only days before the incident, and died a few days afterward.

> Short fact: For all of his amazing and towering engineering feats, Brunel was only five feet, and took to wearing tall hats and standing as straight as possible. He was undoubtedly self-conscious about his height, and this might have contributed to his ambitious engineering works. He even admitted: "As I pass some unknown person who perhaps does not even look at me, I catch myself trying to look big on my little pony." He also wrote: "I often do the most silly useless things to appear to advantage before or attract the attention of those I shall never see again or whom I care nothing about."

THE URBAN POPULATION BOOM DURING THE INDUSTRIAL REVOLUTION

For most of its history, Britain's economy and everyday life were primarily agrarian. Cities, while they often housed a lot of people, were nowhere near the population levels that the surrounding areas were. This rural-leaning economy and society were in many ways at the heart of Britishness, extending all the way back to Roman times. But by the eighteenth century, this way of life began to wane, and by the late nineteenth century, the landscape of Britain had been altered forever.

Exact population numbers are difficult to know, of course, since there was no census, but Britain's population probably sat between five and six million people in the eighteenth century.

With the beginnings of industrialization, the population, especially in the cities, began to grow at an amazing rate. The new factories needed workers and the promise of more money and a more reliable income was enough to draw hundreds of thousands of people away from the hardships of their rural lives to work in the increasingly bleak and smoke-filled urban developments, many of which were quickly becoming hells on earth. Foreign workers were also attracted to Britain's cities, and it's thought that between 1750 and 1850, Britain's population at least doubled.

One of the big problems with this rapid expansion was that cities didn't have any way to accommodate all of these new people. It wasn't long before new houses were being tossed up, developments motivated more by considerations of profit than safety, quality, sanitation, or anything, really. The joined terrace houses that are so common in Britain now first came about during this time. People who had once enjoyed the fresh air and limitless spaces of the country were now living as large families in a single room, stacked on top of one another in crowded, dirty slums. Disease was rampant, and in some cases, dozens of homes shared just a few toilets. It was a health disaster waiting to happen, and happen it did, as epidemics spread through cities. Overall, though, death rates dropped nationwide, thanks to increased food production and better wages (even though such wages were paltry compared to those of the well-off).

Urban life was here to stay, and the landscape of Britain (both real and in the mind) was changed forever, for better and worse. Despite the all-too-common terrible living conditions, there remained a confidence among many (especially young people) that moving to a city would improve their prospects in life and increase their chances of success, meeting someone to marry, and more. And for the most part, they were right. This hopeful belief still lingers around the world, as we witness the rise of metropolises with tens of millions of people living in them. The reality is that conditions are worse than ever, but the lure of the city, ignited by the Industrial Revolution, retains its strength.

> **Totally gross fact:** The sewage from so many people was almost impossible to get rid of, and often, the more evil of landlords and property owners didn't even try, which meant that sewer water and waste often backed up into people's homes. Ew!

CHARLES DICKENS AND THE SOCIAL REFORMERS

J ust about everyone knows Charles Dickens for *A Christmas Carol*, as well as his other great works, including *David Copperfield*, *Oliver Twist*, *A Tale of Two Cities*, and many more. Often his stories addressed issues such as poverty, inequality, cruelty, child abuse, and other problems that confronted the early Victorians in their rapidly expanding industrial economy. There was no shortage of greedy people who sought to profit off of the work and misery of others, and Dickens was among those who were fiercely critical of these callous individuals. But, although his writings helped to bring these people and the problems they created to more people's attention, Dickens didn't really have too many ideas about how to take care of them.

What were some of the problems that England faced at the time? Sadly, there were many.

Poverty: As more and more people moved from the countryside into cities to find better pay, slums filled with the poor grew quickly. These were often terribly depressing and dangerous places; whole families were crammed into small, dirty houses, and disease, crime, and desperation were everywhere.

Exploitative Factory Work: Many of those who did find work were now toiling away in factories or other places that were dangerous, and had no regard for safety or welfare. People might work twelve to sixteen hours a day for greedy business owners who barely paid them anything considering the time and effort they spent. Injuries were common, and the attitude of such owners and bosses was that if you couldn't do the job, they were happy to replace you with someone who could.

Workhouses: These were places that offered some charity, at least in theory. But in reality, they were pretty horrible. They offered the very poor food and shelter, but in exchange they were expected to work in terrible and dangerous conditions, and in Dickens' own words, many people would rather have died than go to one of these institutions.

Debtors' Prisons: If you were in debt to a bank or anyone else and couldn't pay on the loan, it was very possible that you would end up in a debtor's prison, where you would serve a sentence until it was decided that you had been there for long enough. Dickens's own father was sent to debtor's prison for a while. They were humiliating, soul-crushing, and did nothing to rehabilitate the "offender."

Child Labor: Children were not immune from working, and could be pushed just as hard as adults. Children as young as 5 or 6 were often put to work in dangerous jobs, such as the climbing boys for chimney sweeps (cleaners), who were small enough to get up into the dirty, ash-filled chimney itself and clean it.

> **Clean up your act fact:** Reformers saw all of these terrible conditions and were outraged. They worked constantly to try to get the government to pass new laws that would ease the suffering of the very poor and make working conditions safer. But it took them a long time, since many of those in power were quite happy with the system as it was. Over time, things did begin to shift, as Dickens and other writers forced these unpleasant topics into daily conversation, and helped to get some reforms made into reality.

VICTORIAN CHRISTMAS

There is much about Christmas celebrations that we now accept as having always been a part of the holiday: the tree decorated with ornaments, presents, stockings by the chimney, wreaths and other greenery, Christmas cards, feasts, and so much more. But a look back reveals that Christmas has been very different in various times and places. Christmas was rarely celebrated (if at all) in colonial North America, and remained a lightly regarded day well into the nineteenth century.

So, what did the Victorian age bring to Christmas? Well, plenty! Victoria's husband, Prince Albert, was a big fan of the holiday, and brought some of his German traditions along. In 1848, a newspaper called the *Illustrated London News* published a drawing of the royal family posed by a fully decorated Christmas tree. The image wowed everyday folks. Once the English started seeing the royal couple having festive fun, they wanted to join in, too! Below are just a few of the traditions that were established during this time:

Christmas Trees: Decorated trees had already been a tradition in Germany, especially among the wealthy. In 1800, King George III's German wife, Charlotte, brought the idea of the tree with trimmings to Windsor, but the concept didn't quite catch on and spread throughout English society. Albert, however, was a big fan of the Christmas tree, and his fondness for decorating palace trees with ornaments and candles (they had to be careful with flames, though!) proved to be a hit. The English loved the idea, and a Christmas tree soon became a must-have.

Gift-giving: Giving gifts at the holidays was already pretty common among the upper classes (monarchs had long expected gifts during the season), though presents tended to be given either at the New Year, or on Christmas Eve, rather than on the day itself.

Christmas Cards: In 1843, arts patron Henry Cole (who also founded the Victoria and Albert Museum in London) had an idea. He wanted to send responses to letters and Christmas greetings to friends without having to write long messages to each. So he came up with the idea of paying an artist to draw an image of holiday celebrations with a simple message: "A Merry Christmas and a Happy New Year to You." These were printed up as cards, which allowed Cole to personalize each one with a short note. And so, the first Christmas card was born! Even the queen was impressed with this idea, and many people were inspired to create their own cards. Within a few decades, Victorians were sending Christmas cards like crazy to all their friends!

The Christmas Cracker: Confectioner Tom Smith invented these crackers in 1848. At first, they were a way of simply holding sweets,

and they snapped when the wrappers were pulled open. Eventually, these candies were replaced by small toys and paper hats. For the record, candies might have been a better option.

The Christmas Turkey: Meats of all kinds had been featured in Christmas feasts over the centuries, but the Victorians established the turkey as the centerpiece of the traditional Christmas meal. Of course, not everyone could afford such a big bird, like poor Bob Cratchit, and the less well-off would often have to settle for something smaller, like a goose.

> **Bizarre Christmas card fact:** After the craze for Christmas cards took off, the Victorians came up with some really weird ones, featuring paintings of everything from a frog and a beetle dancing together to a mouse riding a lobster, from a dead bird to a child boiling in a huge teapot, from evil and animate Christmas puddings to a sinister clown about to attack a policeman. Why all this non-Christmassy strangeness? The holidays were a time of humor and blowing off steam, and for the Victorians, part of the celebration was sending some truly surreal holiday cards to amuse each other. The weirder the better!

THE PRE-RAPHAELITES

Founded in 1848, the Pre-Raphaelite Brotherhood (later called the Pre-Raphaelites) was an organization made up of seven artists, poets, and critics, the most important of which were William Holman Hunt, John Everett Millais, and Dante Gabriel Rossetti. They were inspired by the work of writer, critic, and philosopher John Ruskin, who wrote that artists must be "true to nature" (he would later become a champion of the Pre-Raphaelite Movement). These men wanted to portray serious subjects in their art, with a great amount of detail and realism, and they opposed the neo-Classical style being promoted by the Royal Academy at the time, which held up the Renaissance artists Raphael (1483-1520) and Michelangelo (among others) as the ideals of how paintings should look. They saw the art of this era as too idealistic, and wanted to inject more realism into their work. Hence, the group's name—they wanted to go back to some of the styles that prevailed prior to Raphael.

They saw themselves as a reform movement for art, standing opposed to what the institutions of the day were telling artists they were "supposed" to paint. While many of their subjects were religious, others drew inspiration from literature and poetry, and explored ideas about love, life, and death, with an eye for detail and a passion for color. They wanted to remain faithful to showing the natural world, even if that image was not as beautiful as some preferred. And there was a preference for nature and its irregular lines over the mechanical, a sharp contrast to visions of the Industrial Revolution happening all around them. This was one reason for the return to a kind of neo-medieval style, a style that would also find a home in the Arts and Crafts Movement (see page 346). There was a romantic belief that preindustrial, medieval society offered something better than the machinery that seemed to be taking over the world (and continues to!).

In addition to rejecting what they saw as the Academy's stuffy and limiting perspective, they also objected to its rigid teaching methods. The Pre-Raphaelites believed that experience was just as important as simply repeating technical exercises over and over again, if not more. Of course, the art establishment was not happy with these upstarts coming in and basically telling them that they were outdated and misguided! And, although there was a lot of resistance initially, eventually art fans and critics started to come around to this new way of thinking.

The initial group itself disbanded after only five years, but by then they had taken the art world by storm and launched a movement that would last for decades. A second Pre-Raphaelite movement started in the 1860s, with the same kinds of goals and an ever-growing dislike of industrialism.

Critical fact: Needless to say, many people hated the Pre-Raphaelites. In one especially awful review of a painting of the Virgin Mary and the Christ child by Millais, no less than Charles Dickens said, of Jesus, that he was "a hideous, wry-necked, blubbering, red-haired boy in a night-gown." He said that Mary was "so horrible in her ugliness that (supposing it were possible for any human creature to exist for a moment with that dislocated throat) she would stand out from the rest of the company as a monster in the vilest cabaret in France or in the lowest gin shop in England." Dickens's spicy take didn't quite have the intended effect, as a number of people, even Queen Victoria, then felt that they had to see this painting themselves.

THE GREAT EXHIBITION OF 1851

This international exhibition ran at London's Hyde Park from May 1, 1851 to October 15, 1851, and was the talk of the nation and beyond. As its name implies, it was a collection of exhibitions of culture and industrial achievement from nations around the world. In total, there were something like 17,000 exhibits, showcasing the richness of different countries, though, naturally, the hosts wanted to outshine them all. Everything from new inventions and textiles to farm equipment and more was available for visitors to view. Unfortunately, the French exhibitors won more awards, which obviously didn't sit too well with the Brits.

Prince Albert was the biggest supporter of the exhibition, believing that it would help Britain keep up with France, where similar events had already been staged. Albert and other enthusiasts persuaded a

somewhat reluctant British government that the whole business would be self-funding, and they were right. So many tickets were sold ahead of time that the exhibition was paid for by the time it opened!

The crowning achievement of the exhibition was the amazing Crystal Palace, which is pretty much exactly what it sounds like. Architect Joseph Paxton proposed the idea of a building made mostly of glass. The planners rejected the idea at first, but Paxton was so convinced of his design that he took out ads in newspapers to drum up support. It worked; the public loved the idea and the commission set up to study the project eventually gave in and let Paxton realize his marvellous vision. The main building was 1,848 feet long and 408 feet wide. It was basically a giant greenhouse (and must have gotten pretty hot inside during the summer!). Schweppes (yes, the sparkling water and soda company) was the official sponsor, which goes to show that corporate sponsorships have been happening for a long time.

Queen Victoria was an active supporter as well, visiting the exhibition thirty-four times during the six months it was open. But real success came via the public, who couldn't wait to go and see wonders from all over the world. At least six million visited during the run, an average of over 42,000 people a day! Among the famous and notable individuals who attended were Charles Darwin, Lewis Carroll, Charles Dickens, Charlotte Brontë, and Karl Marx. So many people showed up that some in the aristocracy and in government worried they might form mobs and cause terrible damage. Happily, nothing of the sort happened, and people simply came to be amazed, gawk, and have a great time.

People who live in glass houses fact: Many other architects ridiculed Paxton's design, saying that it would collapse under its own weight, or from the vibrations caused by so many people walking inside it. So Paxton set up a test building and asked people to walk inside and around it, both randomly and in unison, and to jump up and down all together. Nothing happened. They even called in the British military to march in step. Again, all was fine. So, the Crystal Palace was built as planned, and it stayed up just fine. It later was moved to south London and lasted until 1936, when it was destroyed in a fire.

CHARLES DARWIN

D arwin (1809-82) and his work changed natural science and biology forever, upending a centuries-old belief system and offering an entirely new way of thinking about how life emerged on planet Earth. His work was highly controversial then, and for some, remains so, as there are many devoutly religious folks who still refuse to accept his theories and findings. Despite their protestations, however, Darwin's theories on evolution and how species originate remain at the heart of modern science.

Darwin was born into an open-minded family consisting of a father who was a successful physician, and a mother who came from the Wedgwood family that was famed for its pottery. While Darwin eventually went to the university in Edinburgh to study medicine, he was far more interested in the natural world, and as such, his father arranged for him to be sent to Cambridge—not to study science, but rather to train to join the Anglican clergy (churchmen were often naturalists at the time, so it made some sense, given young Charles's interests). Upon leaving Cambridge in 1831, Darwin was offered the opportunity to sail as a naturalist on the HMS *Beagle*, a ship bound for South America, where it intended to map the continent. Darwin eagerly accepted and spent the next three years exploring South America and collecting animal specimens. In 1835, he sailed around the tip of the continent and made a stop that would change his life, and human thought forever.

On the Galapagos Islands, Darwin began to notice subtle differences between the same species on each island. Each island seemed to have a different species of finch, for example, and locals could tell which island a tortoise came from just by looking at it. Darwin began to formulate an idea that these animals had once had common ancestors, but had diverged at some point in the past. He continued observing and making notes until 1836, when he returned to Britain. Once home, he set to writing several books about his travels and observations he'd made.

Darwin was also keenly interested in geology, and had been influenced by the work of Charles Lyell, who had proposed what he called uniformitarianism, a theory that geological formations developed very slowly over vast amounts of time. Darwin began to think that animals might also change and develop new characteristics over long stretches of time, and in 1837 he began work on a book that would express this theory. Over the next few years, Darwin observed how animals varied from each other, even within their own species. They adapted to their environments, such that if certain characteristics proved more beneficial within a particular space, those members of the species that didn't have it would die out sooner, allowing the survivors to pass on their genes. An herbivore that could run faster than a predator, for example, would be much more likely to survive and reproduce. Over time, the whole species would slowly change, with speed becoming pervasive.

In 1857, Darwin received a paper from a naturalist named Alfred Russel Wallace. It turned out that Wallace was working on a similar theory about how species evolve over time. Wallace had presented this paper to the respected Linnean Society, and while that group didn't think much of it, Darwin recognized that his grand theory was in danger of being scooped up by another. As such, he revised his work and published *On the Origin of Species* in 1859. The book laid out his views of how species change in relation to their environment, and became an immediate best seller. It also, of course, was very controversial, which only made Darwin and his ideas all the more famous. The book was heavily criticized by the devoutly religious, because it suggested that not only had animal species not always been the way they were at present—and thus not the flawless result of God's handiwork—but also that vast spans of time were necessary (and had occurred) to power this evolution, which contradicted the Biblical creation stories.

Darwin wrote several more books about evolution, including *The Descent of Man* in 1871, which outlined how evolution would have worked in the human species. Surprisingly, this text was not as controversial as one might expect, because the main theories of evolution had already been set down more than a decade earlier. Over time, and with the advances in genetics, DNA, and biology, study after study has shown Darwin to have been correct. His bold theories opened the door for whole new branches of biological study, and revealed just how rich and miraculous is the tapestry of life on Earth.

> **Squeamish fact:** Darwin might have gone on to be a doctor like his father were it not for one small issue: he couldn't stand the sight of blood, and the horrors of nineteenth-century surgery would no doubt have made his stomach turn! So, he turned to divinity and naturalism, and the rest is history.

THE DEATH OF PRINCE ALBERT

The royal family had become familiar to much of the British public, so when Prince Albert died on December 14, 1861, it was almost as much of a shock to the nation as it was to Victoria and her family.

Many historians have said that Albert's death (at just 42) was probably due to typhoid fever, a common enough killer at the time. But recent investigations into the matter have brought new possibilities to light.

Albert was not in the best health for most of his life. He had an ongoing stomach problem, and he tended to push himself far too hard between work and royal duties, trying to keep up with the enviable energy of his wife, Victoria. He would get head colds easily, and suffer badly from them. To make matters worse, Victoria hated heat and insisted on keeping everything cool, if not cold, in their homes, even during the winter. This stance forced poor Albert to wear a fur coat and a wig to keep his balding head warm while indoors!

In short, Albert's sense of duty would not allow him to relax, even when he should have. He would often eat in a hurry to return to his work, which made his already-sensitive stomach even worse. He also made great efforts to hide his bad health from Victoria, so as not to upset and worry her, which again exacerbated his issues. She tended to think her husband was exaggerating his health problems, but that might have been because she didn't want to have to think about them. In 1853, Albert caught measles from one of his children, and took a long time to recover, a respite that started up the rumor mill, including accusations that he was a Russian spy.

All of these problems took their toll, and his health declined until he suffered from constant stomach pain. By late 1861, Albert was in very bad shape, and it is now thought that he might have died from a particularly bad flareup of Crohn's Disease (an inflammation of the intestines), combined with pneumonia.

Whatever the cause, his death on December 14, 1861, was a shock to Victoria and the whole royal family. The queen plunged into a deep depression, clueless as to how she would go on without her husband. She withdrew from public life and was rarely seen in public for long stretches at a time, and his death marked a turning point in England's direction and future.

Mournful fact: While mourning, Victoria took to wearing black clothing, and did so for the rest of her life—about 40 years. She left the happy days of color, plaids, and spectacle behind, and never considered remarrying.

THE LONDON UNDERGROUND

The Underground (also widely known as "The Tube") is a marvel of Victorian (and later) engineering, the world's first true subway system. It handles up to five million passengers every day and is still used for the main reason it was built: to relieve traffic congestion "overground."

Though the idea had been proposed in the 1830s, The Underground began its life as a project of the Metropolitan Railway in March 1860, when a tunnel stretching about 3.75 miles was dug between what is now Paddington and King's Cross. On January 10, 1863, it was opened to much fanfare, featuring a set of wooden carriages pulled by a steam engine. The underground rail was a huge hit, with something like 38,000 people giving it a go on opening day alone. Within a year, over nine million passengers had boarded the train, and the numbers only grew from there.

Of course, such a smashing success meant that more people wanted to get in on the action, and soon other companies and investors were putting up proposals for expanding The Underground to various areas of the city. By 1869, a rail line had been built through the Brunels' tunnel (see page 301), connecting the north and south banks of London. It wasn't always easy going, and rivalries broke out among engineers, investors, and companies. There was also the issue of poor ventilation down in the tunnels, with steam power leaving behind considerable pollution.

But by 1870, technology had improved enough so that deeper tunnels could be dug safely and without fear of collapse. By the end of the 1880s, electricity was all the rage, and in 1890, it was employed to power the railways, a development that made them both cleaner and safer. More routes and tunnels were then proposed, and, with the help of American investment, The Underground began to expand and take on its modern form in the early 1900s. By 1906 and 1907, much of this work was complete, and the following year, the system operators started promoting The Underground as one big, unified network.

That year, 1908, was also when a version of the famous red and blue circular Underground sign first appeared, and when electronic ticket machines began to be used in stations. The first escalators were introduced to Earl's Court in 1911; it had been all elevators and steps before that. The London Underground had truly arrived, and just in time to accommodate another boom in London's population. And while the first version of the famed Underground map wouldn't show up until 1933, by the Edwardian years, it was established as an institution.

> **Late to the party fact:** While The Underground dates back to 1863, the first royal didn't board a train until 1969, when Queen Elizabeth II officially opened the Victoria Line, and rode on it. Perhaps the royals before her saw it as beneath them (literally!). That wasn't to be Elizabeth's last trip on the Tube, as she rode it again for special occasions in 1987 and 2013 (the 150th anniversary of The Underground, in fact).

INVENTIONS GALORE

f there's one thing that the Victorian era is known for, it's the inventions sparked by the Industrial Revolution. An astonishing variety of gadgets, machines, and improvements (some useful, some not so much) came to inventors' minds and quickly found their way to the public, both in Britain and beyond. This short list of some very important inventions shows just how radically different the end of the nineteenth century in Britain was from the beginning of it. And this list is nowhere near complete.

The lawn mower (1830): The humble but very useful lawn mower was developed by inventor Edwin Beard Budding, originally to trim sports grounds and large lawns. It was much more effective than a scythe; can you imagine having to mow your entire lawn with a scythe?

The first commercial telegraph (1837): Sir Charles Wheatstone and Sir William Fothergill Cooke brought out the Cooke-Wheatstone electrical telegraph, which opened the way to communication over long distances. We wouldn't have cell phones without it!

The first chocolate bar (1847): Perhaps the most important invention of all! J. S. Fry & Sons was at the time the largest producer of chocolate in Britain, and when they hit on this idea, they changed snacks and desserts forever!

The hypodermic needle (1853): You might squirm at the idea of needles, but this truly was a game-changer and a lifesaver. Scottish doctor Alexander Wood's invention allowed for medicines and vaccines to be directly injected beneath the skin and into the blood stream, a revolutionary innovation that would save millions of lives.

Traffic lights (1868): Yes, there were traffic lights before there were cars! The first were installed outside the Houses of Parliament on December 9 to direct horse-drawn carriages, but, being gas-powered, they blew up less than a month later! It would be a while before anyone tried to revive the idea in a different design.

The light bulb (1879): Okay, you've probably heard that Thomas Edison invented the light bulb, and that's not wrong, but English inventor Joseph Swan was working on his own version at the exact same time. Edison and Swan patented their different designs in 1879. After suing each other, their companies eventually combined to create the Edison & Swan United Electric Light Company, often known as "Ediswan."

Foul fact: There were no public toilets in Britain until they were invented in 1851.

ALEXANDER GRAHAM BELL

Most people probably know that Scottish inventor Alexander Graham Bell (1847-1922) invented the telephone, but it turns out the matter's a little more complicated. The idea of being able to talk over longer distances was something that people had wanted to do for some time. As early as the seventeenth century, British scientist Robert Hooke experimented with ways of speaking over a vibrating wire. The "tin can" phone, where two cans are connected by a length of string, allowing people to talk to each other, is basically a rudimentary version of Hooke's idea.

Bell was born in Scotland, but spent time in London and then moved on to Canada and the United States; he would pop back and forth between the countries while teaching and continuing his scientific experiments. He recorded in his journal how on March 10, 1876, he uttered his famous words into his prototype: "Mr. Watson—Come here—I want to see you." He went on to note: "To my delight he came and declared that he had heard and understood what I said." So, Bell invented the device that we all now take for granted (and rarely talk on), right?

Yes. Sort of. Again, it's complicated.

From the 1850s to the 1870s, a number of inventors laid claim to creating the telephone, including Bell, Antonio Meucci, Elisha Gray, and Thomas Edison. Each invention was a variation on the same idea, so it's difficult to say exactly who "invented" the telephone. Bell's iteration was basically the one that came along at the right time, though there were accusations of theft (many thought Bell stole Gray's idea, for example). And while Bell was the first person to patent a telephone, debate about the issue continued right into the early 2000s, with both the American and Canadian governments weighing in. The United States recognized Meucci's contributions, while Canada overwhelmingly endorsed Bell, the Canadian immigrant. The controversy still hasn't completely died off.

Interestingly, Bell even invented a kind of early wireless phone, the "photophone," in 1880. It could transmit sound via light waves, but the technology just wasn't there for it to have much use, at least not until the invention of fiber optics in the twentieth century. Suffice to say that Bell would be utterly astonished (and probably a bit worried) by everything his invention can do today!

> **Hearing fact:** Bell's mother and wife were deaf. As a child, he would speak next to his mother's forehead so that she could feel the vibrations and gain some understanding of what was being said. The experience was one of the main reasons that he became interested in sound waves and how they are transmitted and interpreted.

BENJAMIN DISRAELI

D israeli (1804-81), was a famed statesman who served twice as prime minister under Queen Victoria, first in 1868 and then again from 1874 to 1880. He was born in West London to a Sephardic Jewish family, but when his father, Isaac D'Israeli, had a falling out with the local synagogue, the family left Judaism altogether, and young Benjamin was baptized as an Anglican. This, although Britain was not virulently antisemitic at the time, allowed Benjamin more opportunities than he might have otherwise had (Jews were not allowed to run for Parliament until 1858, for instance). And he was apparently very grateful for this spiritual shift—much later, he would describe himself as "on the side of angels" in response to Darwin's theories about evolution and natural selection, championing his adopted faith.

As a young man, Disraeli tried training as a barrister, but failed to find his footing. He also made some bad mining investments and got himself into some real financial trouble. It was all looking rather bad for poor Benjamin, but he did have one significant talent: writing. He anonymously produced his first novel, *Vivian Grey*, serialized in 1826 and 1827, and while it sold well, the critics were pretty unkind, especially when they found out that Disraeli wrote it. They accused him of writing a satire beyond his class and unfairly caricaturing certain people. They also accused him of making grammatical errors that showed his impoverished education. While Disraeli was undoubtedly upset, he continued to write and brought out several more novels, including *The Young Duke* in 1831, where he coined the phrase "dark horse" while describing a black horse unexpectedly surging to win a race. The book sold well enough for him to finance a trip to southern Europe and Egypt in 1830, a journey that had a profound impact on his worldview.

Disraeli might have remained a Victorian novelist, remembered along with Dickens, Trollope, and others, but his life forever changed when he ran as a Conservative for MP of Maidstone in 1837 and won. From then on, his life would be defined by politics as much as writing, though he did continue to author novels until the end of his life. He then was elected MP for Shrewsbury in 1841, and while the new Conservative prime minister, Sir Robert Peel, had been supportive, he did not offer Disraeli a place in the cabinet. This led to a rivalry between the two that only intensified over the next few years. Eventually, Disraeli was able to assemble an effective opposition to Peel over a series of unpopular policies, and Peel resigned in 1846. This development put Disraeli in prominent position within the party, but his fortunes shifted as voters soon took back the government from Conservative rule.

His real opportunity came in 1868, when he became prime minister after the retirement of Lord Derby. He famously said of his rise, "I have climbed to the top of a greasy pole," as good a description of political power as there ever has been! But he proceeded to lose in the election just one year later, and would have to wait until 1874 to again be elected to the land's top political office. This second run lasted several years, and saw Disraeli forge a legendary rivalry with the liberal William Gladstone. He also became a good friend to Queen Victoria during his time in office, and the queen declared that Disraeli was her favorite of the prime ministers—perhaps because he was the one who proposed that she be declared "Empress of India" in 1876. He was also successful in purchasing shares of the Suez Canal from the Ottoman viceroy of Egypt, Ismā'īl Pasha, giving Britain more control of this all-important passage.

As the election of 1880 neared, Disraeli's health was in decline. After the Conservatives lost, he resigned, but continued writing, and thinking about a possible political future. Alas, Disraeli's health continued to falter and he died in April 1881.

> **One last visit fact:** Queen Victoria offered to visit him in his last weeks, but he declined, saying to his friends, "She would only ask me to take a message to Albert."

LEWIS CARROLL

Charles Lutwidge Dodgson (1832-98), better known to readers by his penname Lewis Carroll, is the author of the whimsical and delightfully oddball children's classics *Alice's Adventures in Wonderland* and *Through the Looking Glass*. A gifted author and scholar, he was also interested in mathematics and puzzles, and his various unique observations found their way into his writings.

Carroll was something of a sickly child, and suffered a number of health problems in his youth, including a fever that left him deaf in

one ear. He also developed a stutter, which would stay with him for good. Nevertheless, as an adult, he was ordained as a deacon in the Anglican Church and settled into teaching at Christ Church, Oxford, a position he would hold for the rest of his professional life.

But of course, it's his books that have made him a household name the world over. The weird and surreal world of Wonderland, where Alice has her many adventures, seems at first to be just a string of nonsensical stories, but underneath these wacky vignettes Carroll inserted wordplay, puns, social and political commentary, math and logic concepts, and much more. Both books examine Victorian ideas of childhood and what was expected of children, and turn them upside down. Some say that the misfortunes that Alice must deal with mirror Carroll's own misfortunes as a child. The books were published in 1865 and 1871, featuring illustrations by the great Victorian artist, Sir John Tenniel. *Alice's Adventures in Wonderland* was a smash hit, and brought Carroll money and fame; the fame he could do without.

Despite the books' popularity, a cloud has hung over Carroll since his own time, as many researchers have believed that he had a strong and unhealthy attraction to young girls. His friendship with Henry Liddell, Dean of Christ Church, extended to his family and Henry's young daughter, Alice. It might seem obvious that she was the inspiration for his fictional Alice, though Carroll denied this. But most scholars now think that she was. Carroll enjoyed painting and taking pictures, and a small number of both are of nude children, especially girls under the age of puberty. This has led to accusations that he was a paedophile, but suppressed his urges through photography and painting.

More recent research has suggested that this accusation was probably not true. Despite the prudish Victorian attitudes toward sex and nudity, artistic nude paintings and photographs of children were somewhat common at the time, since they were seen as a symbol of innocence. Such images even showed up on Christmas cards!

The idea that Carroll had no interest in adult women has also been debunked, as his diaries and notes show his interest in several women throughout his life. It seems likely that some biographers in the early twentieth century projected their own morality and judgement onto a man who was a bit odd and had a hobby that was common at one time before falling out of fashion.

> **Book dedication un-fact:** Rumor holds that Queen Victoria liked *Alice* so much that she asked Carroll to dedicate his next book to her (not unlike the Jane Austen situation with the Prince Regent, see page 282). According to this apocryphal text, Carroll readily agreed, and dedicated a boring mathematical text to her majesty! For his part, Carroll vehemently denied that this ever took place, saying, "It is utterly false in every particular: nothing even resembling it has occurred."

GILBERT AND SULLIVAN

By any measure, William Schwenck Gilbert (1836-1911) and Arthur Sullivan (1842–1900) were a theatrical team for the ages. Gilbert wrote librettos (the stories for operas) and Sullivan composed music. Together, they created absolute magic. In a time when "serious" British music was lagging behind what was being produced on the rest of the continent (which was dominated by Germany), and wouldn't start to find its footing again until the 1880s, Gilbert and Sullivan were delivering light, comic operas that delighted the masses and showed that Britain could indeed produce classic works, even if they were not as "serious" as those being fashioned by German composers. Over the course of their quarter-century partnership, they wrote fourteen operettas, among which are their classics, *The Pirates of Penzance*, *H.M.S. Pinafore*, and *The Mikado*.

Gilbert had both a fine sense of humor and an appreciation for the absurd, and he routinely created worlds where things were upside-down and not as they seemed. Sullivan was able to match this whimsy with his creative and tuneful music, though he would later be criticized for wasting his time and talent on such light-hearted fare.

The two men first worked on an 1871 Christmas entertainment called *Thespis*, and then didn't collaborate for the three next years, as they focused on solo projects. But they were brought back together to create *Trial by Jury*, a musical spoof of the legal profession, and it was a hit. This convinced them that they had a good thing going, and should work together again. And again.

In 1878, they brought out *H.M.S. Pinafore*, which made fun of the British navy in a good-natured way. It ran for over 500 showings, an astonishing number, and unauthorized versions were produced in the United States. The following year, they produced *The Pirates of Penzance*, which actually premiered in New York, but soon after had its first London showing. It was another hit with critics and audiences.

By 1881, Richard D'Oyly Carte, the theater manager, composer, and talent agent who had first brought Gilbert and Sullivan together, decided to open the Savoy Theater, which would be a dedicated place for the duo to premiere their works. It seated about 1,300 people and was the first public building in the world that was lit solely by electric lights. Carte was convinced that comic opera, which was huge in France, could be just as popular in Britain, and he was betting on Gilbert and Sullivan to make that dream a reality. Of course, the Savoy would be used to stage many more productions in between Gilbert and Sullivan offerings.

But in 1890, the whole dream nearly fell apart. Gilbert found out that expenses for maintaining the building were being charged to his partnership, rather than Carte taking care of them. He angrily confronted Carte, and perhaps surprisingly, Sullivan sided with Carte, rather than Gilbert. This led to heated words and the dissolution of their partnership, at least for a while. Gilbert sued Carte and won, but this only made things worse, as Gilbert also vowed never to write for the Savoy again.

That might have been the sad end of this brilliant team, but Carte and his wife quickly realized that Gilbert and Sullivan collaborations were so profitable that there was no reason, not even a lost lawsuit, to not try to reunite them. Their music publisher, Tom Chappell, was able to negotiate a truce, and they agreed to work together again. To be honest, they had never been the best of friends, but each realized that the other possessed something special. They produced two more works together, but the last one, *The Grand Duke* (in 1896), was a failure, a dramatic change from their staggering successes a decade earlier.

Gilbert and Sullivan remained apart after that—they attended the same event in 1898 and didn't even speak to each other. But when Sullivan died in 1900, Gilbert insisted that they had made amends, and had nothing but good things to say about his former partner. Their creations would influence generations of musical theater devotees, and modern musicals on both Broadway and in London's West End owe a great deal to the genius of these two.

> **Mistaken identity fact:** Once, while Sullivan staying at a hotel in Chicago, a large and dangerous-looking man came into the lobby, demanding to see him. Sullivan nervously came down to find out what was going on. The man was astonished and exclaimed, "You're not John Sullivan!" He had to explain that he was in fact, Arthur Sullivan, the British composer. His visitor had thought he was John Sullivan, a famous boxer, and had presumably come looking for a fight. Happily for Arthur, the man was not a disgruntled fan of musicals!

OSCAR WILDE

Irish writer Oscar Wilde (1854-1900) was a remarkable writer, playwright, poet, and humorist. He lived life on his own terms, frequently scandalizing conservative Victorian society and its hypocritical values. Eventually, Wilde was imprisoned for homosexuality, and the ordeal of his incarceration took a terrible toll on his health; he died shortly after his release.

While his humorous works are among his most beloved writings, he is perhaps best remembered for his horror-adjacent novel, *The Picture of Dorian Gray*, a Gothic tale that looked at the dark underside of respectable society in ways that might have made the people of the time very uncomfortable. It tells the story of a charming and handsome young man, Dorian, who makes a Faustian pact to stay young forever, while a painting of him, kept hidden in an attic, grows increasingly hideous, weighed down not only by his age, but also scarred by his many sins. One newspaper splendidly proclaimed that the book was "heavy with the mephitic odours of moral and spiritual putrefaction." So, five out of five stars, then?

Wilde was also known for his plays, which could stir up just as much controversy. His play *Salomé*, written in French, tells the story of the famed dancer who demanded the head of John the Baptist. Because Britain did not allow stage plays to portray Biblical characters (an old law), it was shown instead in Paris, in 1896.

Unlike some of his other works, Wilde's play *The Importance of Being Earnest* was well received and instantly recognized as a masterful comedy about social obligations and fake identities, and was also a hit with audiences.

But that moment of success was immediately imperiled, as Wilde had made many enemies during his time in the spotlight. The Marquess of Queensberry was scandalized and furious that his son, Lord Alfred Douglas, was having a secret affair with Wilde, something that was not only unacceptable at the time, but also illegal. The Marquess accused Wilde of homosexuality, but Wilde pushed back and wanted to press charges for libel. However, Queensbury had the money to hire detectives and prove his claims. He found the evidence he needed and succeed in getting Wilde arrested. Wilde was found guilty and sentenced to two years' hard labor, from 1895 to 1897.

After his release, Wilde went to Paris, but he didn't have long to live. He died of cerebral meningitis in 1900, his brutal prison term having permanently damaged his health. His remains were eventually buried in Paris' Père Lachaise Cemetery in 1909, and soon fans began to make pilgrimages to his grave. By 2011, his tomb was covered with so many lipstick marks from kisses that the city authorities cleaned the stone, and put a glass barrier around it, which subsequently has also been covered in lipstick kisses and love notes! One has to imagine that Wilde would be tickled by the entire thing.

> **Funny final words fact:** Wilde never lost his sense of humor. According to different stories, he might have said about the hotel room where he died: "Either these curtains go, or I do," or maybe, "This wallpaper will be the death of me—one of us will have to go." No one is quite sure if either of these quotes is authentic, but they do show Wilde's legendary wry wit.

PENNY DREADFULS

By the nineteenth century, Brits had something of a love for crime stories. At public executions, people could buy cheap broadsides, which were single-sheet newspapers that would tell all about the crimes of the person about to be hanged, and typically included a warning to others not to go down the same path. Gothic literature, ghost stories, and other lurid tales all formed a part of the popular entertainment of the time. By the 1830s, short publications called "Penny Dreadfuls" sought to capitalize on this inclination.

Hugely popular with the working classes, they were cheap (only a penny each, hence the name), and allowed the reader to escape into a world of ghosts, goblins, true crime, and horror once a week. The stories were often written in serial form, in other words, they continued from week to week, just like a TV show. The serialization of a story was how Dickens' novels first were printed, though not in Penny Dreadfuls (but some of these papers did rip off his stories and ideas). They were literature for the masses, especially boys and young men, but they introduced some characters and ideas that would become famous over time. Here are two of the most famous stories:

The String of Pearls: A Domestic Romance (1846-47). This story introduced the world to the notorious Sweeney Todd, the "Demon Barber of Fleet Street." Todd worked with a certain Mrs. Lovett, and the two did some pretty horrible things. Todd would act as a barber and choose victims as needed. After they were seated in his barber chair, he would dump them through a trapdoor attached to the chair, causing them to fall into the cellar and break their necks. If they survived, Todd would go down to them and slit their throats with his barber's razor. Mrs. Lovett would take the bodies and make them into her fresh meat pies! Of course, they are eventually found out, and it all goes badly for them.

Varney the Vampire (1845–1847). Vampire lore had been around for centuries, especially in Eastern Europe, but this Penny Dreadful story introduced some of the tropes that are now canon. Varney was cursed with vampirism and had a taste for human blood. He is the first vampire said to have sharp fangs and to bite necks. He is also super-strong and can hypnotize his victims. But he can move in daylight and doesn't fear crosses or garlic. He is presented as a vampire that the reader can sympathize with, rather than just hate, and when he finally kills himself by throwing himself into the volcano Mount Vesuvius in Italy, it is a tragic moment. A half-century later, Irish author Bram Stoker would be influenced by *Varney* and other sources while creating the greatest vampire of all time, Dracula.

Print fact: Penny Dreadfuls served a purpose by providing cheap entertainment to large numbers of people eager for novelty and distraction. One modern newspaper has even called them the video games of their time!

THE LEGEND OF SPRING-HEELED JACK

He jumped out of the night and terrorized England for decades, from the 1830s until just after 1900. People called him Spring-Heeled Jack, and he was truly worthy of the name. Witnesses who saw him said that he was a figure in pale clothing, who could leap incredible heights and distances.

The first major sightings of this strange being started in early 1838 in South London. Jack was already known from a few earlier reports, and one night, a woman named Jane Alsop answered her door. A man was standing there insisting that they had just caught Jack and he needed a light. Eager to see this strange creature, Jane brought out a candle. But as she gave it to him, he attacked her, breathing blue flame in her face and slicing at her with sharp claws. Jane managed to escape and run back to her house, but Jack bounded into the night before anyone could catch him. Later, Jane described him as having eyes that glowed like fire, and wearing a helmet and some kind of tight-fitting white clothing.

If people hoped that this monster would soon vanish, they were out of luck. Only days later, he attacked another young woman, Lucy Scales, blowing blue flames at her as well. Over the next several years and decades, Jack would be spotted throughout London and mid-England. In 1877, he attacked a military base in the town of Aldershot, and escaped, despite the soldiers' attempts to trap him. In the city of Lincoln, he was seen again, and when residents shot at him, he simply laughed and leapt away, jumping over rooftops!

There were a few serious attempts to catch Jack over the years, with one hunt even led by the Duke of Wellington. Although the police tried their best, no one ever succeeded in apprehending this mysterious monster, who seemed immune to bullets and would simply laugh and jump away whenever he was attacked. His last reported appearance was in 1904 in the city of Liverpool, far to the northeast of his usual haunts. There, some people tried to corner him, but as usual, he sprang from the street up to the rooftops and then back down again, before vanishing into the night. After that incident, he was never seen again ... until a similar creature showed up in New Mexico, of all places, in 1938, where one night, a couple claimed they saw a figure dressed in white with a cape and glowing eyes, who laughed and could jump very high. They said they had never heard of Spring-Heeled Jack before, but their description was very close to the creature that had terrorized Britain.

So, who or what was this bizarre intruder? For a while, people thought that there might be a whole gang of Jacks out there, causing

mayhem and terrorizing neighborhoods across England and over many decades. While this is certainly possible, it doesn't answer the question of why they would waste time doing this for so long, and even more importantly, how Jack—or these collection of Jacks—was able to jump to such crazy heights and land without ever seeming to be injured. Many people thought he was a demon, and more recently, theories have speculated that he was an alien, causing trouble for some unknown reason.

In the end, nobody knows. After his last disappearance, Spring-Heeled Jack never returned, taking whatever secrets he held with him into the dark one last time.

> **Similar legends fact:** Prague had its own leaping phantom during the Nazi occupation of the city from 1939-45, known as Pérák, the Spring Man. He was said to be able to jump great heights and enjoyed startling people in the dark streets.

JACK THE RIPPER

History's most famous serial killer continues to fascinate and frighten well over a hundred years after his grisly murders shook Whitechapel, in East London. Ever since, there has been an obsession with discovering the identity of the killer known as Jack the Ripper, whose gruesome murders of five women in the autumn of 1888 shocked Britain and the world. Five women, the so-called canonical victims, were found murdered and horrifically mutilated in various places in and around Whitechapel. Police were frustrated by the lack of good leads, and the public was increasingly terrified by the madman walking among them. The last murder attributed to Jack happened on November 9, 1888. After that, the killing stopped, and it seems like Jack never struck again. But who was he?

At this point, there is almost no way to definitively prove Jack's identity. There have been hundreds, if not thousands of theories and books from self-styled "Ripperologists" claiming to have solved the mystery once and for all. But none of these have offered up the conclusive proof they claim to have. And while many such books have been written by reputable researchers, many others are self-published drivel, badly written and without real substance, making the mysterious matter all the more confusing for someone trying to learn more about the case.

There are a few likely candidates, but the identity of this notorious serial killer is probably lost forever. There have been over one hundred men suggested as the killer, but the evidence to prove it is now circumstantial at best. Some of the more outlandish theories include Prince Albert Victor (son of the future King Edward VII), Sir John Williams (doctor to Queen Victoria's daughter, Princess Beatrice), and Lewis Carroll (author of *Alice's Adventures in Wonderland* and *Through the Looking-Glass*). All of these are as ridiculous as they seem, and have been thoroughly debunked.

More recently, some scholars have suggested that this constant fixation on these gruesome murders (in the form of books, movies, Ripper tours of Whitechapel, etc.) is unhealthy and even offensive. One recent study (*The Five* by Hallie Rubenhold) was devoted instead to the killer's victims: Mary Ann Nichols, Annie Chapman, Elizabeth Stride, Catherine (Kate) Eddowes, and Mary Jane Kelly, an attempt to humanize them and bring their stories to the public. People sometimes forget that behind these sensational crimes and murder mysteries, there are real people who experienced appalling pain and loss. This same study showed that at least three of the victims (Nichols, Chapman, and Eddowes) were probably not prostitutes at all, despite all five women being portrayed as such in most history books. This discovery further challenged the long-standing but unspoken misogynistic assumption that these victims somehow "deserved" their fates.

Jack the Ripper is a horrific cultural icon, and the fact that his identity remains a mystery is why his story, rightly or wrongly, has endured for so long.

> **Psychic fact:** Perhaps in desperation, some started looking for answers about Jack's identity from the beyond, turning to mediums for clues. One such medium claimed to have summoned the spirit of Elizabeth Stride, who revealed that Jack was part of a gang of twelve men that had committed many other murders, but no links to gang activity were uncovered. Another medium claimed that a Thomas Totson of 20 Wurt Street in London was the killer, but that address doesn't exist, and no man by that name was found. So, police had no luck with these answers obtained (allegedly) from the metaphysical world.

FLORENCE NIGHTINGALE

One of history's best-named notables, Nightingale (1820-1910) was an English statistician, reformer, and nurse, whose practices made her the founder of modern nursing. She was best known in her own lifetime for her heroic work during the Crimean War (1854-56, in what is now Ukraine), where she trained nurses and set up care facilities for wounded British soldiers in a hospital in Scutari (now known as Üsküdar), outside of the Turkish city of Constantinople (now Istanbul). While there, her tireless efforts and hygienic innovations helped to greatly reduce the number of soldiers dying from infection.

She was born in Florence, Italy, while her British parents were traveling, which by the way, is why her parents named her as they did. (It's a good thing she wasn't born in Bra, a town in Piedmont, or Bastardo, which is in Umbria!) Her family was wealthy and traveled widely; when she was young, Nightingale visited places throughout Europe and Egypt. As was often the case for young women in the upper classes, though, she was expected to do her duty and marry young. But from a young age Nightingale had a calling to help the sick and needy. She informed her father that she wanted to study to become a nurse, and he wasn't at all happy about it, but he eventually gave in and let her go to Germany and then Paris to receive training. Upon returning to England, she took up the position of superintendent of the Institute for the Care of Sick Gentlewomen.

At the outbreak of the Crimean War, she heard about the appalling conditions in the camps and was determined to help. She made the journey to Turkey and immediately got to work. She informed the British government of her needs, and as we've seen on page 302, officials commissioned Isambard Kingdom Brunel to design "pop-up" hospitals and have them shipped over. Simple activities like hand-washing and flushing the sewers drastically reduced the death rates of soldiers, who had been dying more often from infections than wounds. Nightingale's attention to injured soldiers at all hours of the day became legendary, and she was known as the "Lady with the Lamp," since she would often visit them in the dark, to offer comfort and support. Stories of her deeds became known back in Britain, though some have since suggested that these accounts were exagger-ated by the media as part of an overall patriotic push for the war effort.

After the war ended, Nightingale returned to Britain, and helped set up a nursing school at St Thomas' Hospital in London. Though she was devoutly religious, the school itself was the first nursing school in the world with no religious affiliation, and still exists as part of King's College, London, where it is known as the Florence Nightingale Faculty of Nursing and Midwifery. She also became a prolific writer, using statistics and straightforward language in her works, which include the all-important book, *Notes on Nursing*, written in 1859, which became a required textbook for all students.

Her influence extended abroad as well, as Lincoln's Union govern-ment approached Nightingale for medical advice and adopted her sanitation practices during the American Civil War to help reduce infections and deaths in the field. Several of the women Nightingale mentored and trained would take their skills around the world, including back to the United States, Australia, and Japan. Though health problems plagued Nightingale in her last decades, she still tried to keep up with developments in medicine, and advocated for improving sanitary conditions in India and at home, as well as championing women's causes.

Legacy fact: Graduating nurses in the United States still recite the Nightingale Pledge, a form of the Hippocratic Oath that was created in 1893 in her honor, and the Florence Nightingale Medal is an award given by the International Red Cross for outstanding work in nursing.

MARY SEACOLE, THE OTHER CRIMEAN WAR NURSE

Mary Jane Seacole (1805-81) was born in Kingston, Jamaica, in 1805, the daughter of James Grant, a Scottish member of the British Army, and a Mrs. Grant (known as "The Doctress"), a black woman who practiced traditional African and Caribbean healing. Mary was proud of her heritage, writing (a bit provocatively), "I am a Creole, and have good Scots blood coursing through my veins ... I have a few shades of deeper brown upon my skin which shows me related—and I am proud of the relationship—to those poor mortals whom you once held enslaved, and whose bodies America still owns."

At a young age, Seacole became interested in her mother's work, and wanted to learn it for herself. As a child, she first practiced on a doll, and then was allowed to treat animals, before moving on to care for humans. Given her father's status in the army, she also witnessed the brutal wounds and afflictions of soldiers, which only made her more determined to develop medical skills.

In 1823, Seacole traveled to Britain to study medicine, and returned to her home two years later to continue her work and learning. In 1836, she married Edwin Horatio Hamilton Seacole, and the two settled into a home. Edwin's health was not good, so Mary attended to him as a nurse. He died in 1844, and her mother passed away not long after, losses that devastated her. But she continued with her mission, and when a cholera epidemic hit Jamaica in 1850, she was able to help treat patients and even cure some of them. She did so again in 1853, when malaria broke out on the island. And, once again, many of Mary's treatments proved successful.

Seacole returned to Britain in 1854, and, like Florence Nightingale, heard of the appalling medical conditions in the camps for the Crimean War. She applied to the British War Office to be sent to the region as a nurse, but the office refused her, a decision likely motivated to some degree by racism. But she wouldn't be discouraged. Seacole funded her own trip to Crimea and set up the "British Hotel" (a kind of store and convalescent hospital) near Balaclava. At the same time, Florence Nightingale was treating the sick and wounded in Scutari, which was much farther from the front lines than Seacole's setup. Seacole and Nightingale actually met at one point, and while Seacole reported that the meeting was pleasant, Nightingale didn't seem to want to associate with her because she offered alcoholic drinks to soldiers.

In addition to providing medical care and supplies, Seacole would travel to the battlefield (and sometimes came under fire, herself) to convey supplies and care to the injured soldiers. The troops became so fond of her that they dubbed her "Mother Seacole."

After the war, she returned to London, but had exhausted her money. Veterans of the war started a campaign to raise money for her, praising her work and her kindness in letters to newspapers and other publications. In 1857, a fund-raising concert gala was held in Seacole's honor, though she only received a small amount of money from it. But she also wrote her autobiography, *The Wonderful Adventures of Mrs Seacole in Many Lands*, which was a best seller. She then divided her time between London and Jamaica, still practicing as a "doctress," and eventually gaining royal patronage and employment (as a masseuse for one of Queen Victoria's daughters).

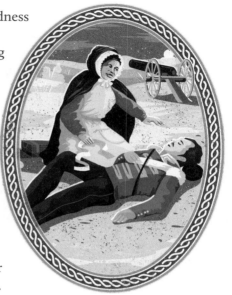

After her death in 1881, Seacole was largely forgotten, while Florence Nightingale became a legend. But interest in her life and work was revived beginning in the 1970s and '80s, and today, she is seen as a pioneering figure in British medical history, and was voted No. 1 in a poll celebrating 100 Great Black Britons in 2004.

Rivalry fact: Some modern supporters of Florence Nightingale believe that Seacole has been given too much credit, arguing that she was not a pioneer of nursing in the way that Nightingale was, and didn't come under enemy fire, as some have claimed. She was also not trained at an accredited medical institution, they argue, and so was not qualified. But others have hit back, noting that Seacole's skills in traditional medicine included better hygiene than some of the mainstream medical practices of the time, and stressing that her "traditional" treatments often worked.

ABDUL KARIM AND
QUEEN VICTORIA

In 1887, many celebrations were held to mark the queen's Golden Jubilee, which celebrated her fifty years on the throne. At one celebration in June of that year, she met the young Mohammed Abdul Karim (1863-1909), who had come from north central India as one of two young men to be trained as servants. Victoria took an instant liking to Karim, and soon was conversing with him about many topics. He helped her study the Urdu language (called Hindustani at the time), while she saw to it that his English skills improved.

Over the next year, Karim and the queen continued to deepen their friendship, and she came to call him "Munshi," meaning clerk, writer, or teacher. For his part, Karim continued to educate Victoria about India, its customs, and language. Perhaps one of his greatest achievements was introducing the queen to the joys of Indian food. While attending to her on the Isle of Wight (one of her favorite residences), Karim had a special dish prepared: chicken curry, served with dal and pilau rice. Victoria loved it so much that she had it added to her regular menu, and it became a lunchtime favorite of hers. She was very impressed by his talents and soon was bestowing gifts and favors on him. She made him her official Indian clerk, meaning that he no longer had to perform any of the tedious jobs a typical servant might be charged with.

Karim came to be a trusted advisor on Indian affairs, and she would often take his advice over that of the viceroys and governor in India, much to their displeasure. Seeing this unprecedented development, they could not help but wonder: Who was this young Muslim man that had such influence over the most powerful individual on Earth?

All of this was wonderful for Karim, but as you can imagine, many around him resented his rise in wealth, power, and influence, especially some of the royal family and their courtiers. One wished that Karim might die of the plague, while another hoped that he would end up in prison. But as long as Victoria favored him, there was little they could do about it. She knew about this hatred, and accused some of them of racism and jealousy (and she was no doubt right). She even signed some of her letters to Karim as "your loving mother," which would have spun heads around, if they'd known about it! Victoria arranged for Karim to bring his wife over from India, as well as his father, and it seemed as if he was in England to stay.

And stay he did, for the rest of her life. Victoria took pains to try to protect him after she was gone, knowing that he was resented, even hated, but there was little she could do in this regard. Though he was one of the chief mourners at her funeral in 1901 (an honor normally reserved only for family and very close friends), only a few hours later, her son (now King Edward VII) fired Karim from his position. He also ordered that any letters between Karim and his mother be destroyed, and Karim was soon deported back to India, where he lived until 1909 on land Victoria had given him.

The royal family was so mortified by Victoria's and Karim's connection that they tried to cover it over. And, for a time, they succeeded. But in the early 2000s, researcher Shrabani Basu asked Windsor Castle to view the queen's Urdu journal, the notebook she had used to learn the language. There, Basu found much more, including Urdu notes by Victoria about her friendship with Karim that had been unread for over 100 years. These entries revealed a lot about Karim's time in the queen's service. Not long after, a surviving member of Karim's family contacted Basu and revealed that the family still had his diaries. With this, she was able to piece together the story of their friendship and write the book *Victoria & Abdul*.

> **Mental health fact:** In 1897, the year of her Diamond Jubilee, the royal family and court were so alarmed by Karim's influence over Victoria (calling it "Munshimania"), that some considered trying to have her declared legally insane. Even her son (the future Edward VII) seemed

to be on board with the plan. Her own doctor, Sir James Reid, advised her that many in the upper circle considered her to be mentally unfit. She was, of course, outraged at the suggestion, and managed to fend off these ridiculous attacks and continue to reign.

THE ARTS AND CRAFTS MOVEMENT

Though it might sound like a children's project, the influential Arts and Crafts Movement began because a group of people were unhappy with Victorian society and the upheaval caused by the Industrial Revolution. As we've seen, throughout the nineteenth century, men and women left the countryside by the thousands to move into cities for factory work. But they often ended up in squalid slums with high crime and death rates, all while breathing unhealthy air from smoke stacks, and consuming terrible food and sketchy water. And industrial blight spilled ever farther out of cities, ruining the countryside and changing the landscape forever.

By the 1860s, this awful situation caused some people to look back to what they viewed as simpler times, and groups of them began to move away from the cities to create new rural communities that focused on traditional crafts as well as art, music, poetry, and more. Some wanted to bring back the idea of a "Merrie Olde England" and looked to the nation's past for inspiration, embracing the Tudor period, Shakespeare's plays, and the legends of King Arthur and Robin Hood, among other ideas. Some people were more forward-looking, and styles such as Art Nouveau also became linked with the Movement.

There were also political elements, with many believing the ruthlessness of Victorian England were unsustainable in the long run. Many people resented those few industrialists that grew wealthy off the backbreaking work of everyday laborers. The rise of unions and socialist thinking (sometimes coupled with religious justice movements) overlapped with Arts and Crafts devotees, with many A&C followers calling for a more egalitarian society that wasn't exploitative. Even the existence of the "British Empire" and its necessary colonial stance was viewed as a problem by many.

One of the Movement's main advocates was William Morris (1834-96), who was involved in just about everything creative: a poet (what he was best known for during his life), artist, textile designer, novelist, journalist, book designer, conservationist, political thinker, and socialist activist. He was a strong believer in traditional crafts and production methods, which of course, didn't sit well at all with the mass production and industrialization that was taking over the British economy. Morris even refused to enter any of his work into the Great Exhibition, because its glorifying of mechanization went against his ideas about what crafts should be. But he did not suffer from such a stance, instead attracting many followers and admirers, and his works are still well-regarded around the world today.

> **Arty and crafty fact:** The Arts and Crafts Movement was not only about Morris, of course, and it would live on for some time after him, into the 1920s. It would be fair to say that it never completely went away, and the William Morris Society, among many other groups, is now dedicated to keeping alive the works of those who saw a better way than the horrible industrial damage, exploitation, and ruin that was feared to be overtaking the country.

SIR ARTHUR CONAN DOYLE AND SHERLOCK HOLMES

S ir Arthur Ignatius Conan Doyle (1859-1930) was a writer, doctor, footballer, and amateur boxer, among many other things. He was also a prolific writer of historical fiction and even fantasy, with *The Lost World*—an early science fiction novel about the discovery of a lost land in the Amazon filled with dinosaurs—probably standing as his second-best-known work. But, of course, his most famous literary creation is his fictional detective, Sherlock Holmes. Doyle wrote four novels and fifty-six short stories about his ingenious sleuth, and Holmes, along with his good friend Dr. Watson, became one of those rare characters whose popularity never wanes.

Doyle was born in Edinburgh and lived there for the first nine years of his life. He was then sent off to boarding school, where some children bullied him and made him generally miserable. He cheered himself up by inventing stories and entertaining any students who would listen. Interestingly, Doyle came from a family of artists, who expected him to follow in his father's footsteps, but he chose to study medicine instead. It's a strange twist on the usual version of the story, where the offspring wants to study the arts, but the parents demand that he or she do something more "practical."

After traveling for a time, Doyle settled in Plymouth and began his medical career in earnest. But he also wanted to write, and struggled to balance the two professions.

That struggle came to a head in 1886, when he wrote the novel *A Study in Scarlet* in only three weeks! This book introduced the world to Sherlock Holmes, and was the first of many Holmesian tracts. Its success inspired Doyle to write more about his peerless detective, whose use of logic and deduction alongside his peculiar habits proved irresistible to readers. With the profits from his work, Doyle was eventually able to take up writing full-time.

Despite his medical training, Doyle had a keen interest in the paranormal and in the popular movement of Spiritualism, or the belief in mediums and attempts to contact the dead via séances. He even renounced his Catholic faith due to his devotion to the movement. He also championed the story of the Cottingley Fairies, a fantastic claim made in 1917 by two girls (cousins) that they had photographed actual fairies in their garden in Yorkshire, using their father's camera. While many people were skeptical, others, including some photo analysts, believed that these pictures were genuine, as did Doyle. The matter was never settled, until 1983, when the girls admitted that they had faked the photos ... all but one of them, that is. One cousin insisted that their last photo was genuine.

Could it be that Doyle was right, after all?

> Dead detective fact: Doyle's 1893 story, "The Final Problem," was meant to be the end of Sherlock Holmes. In this infamous account, Holmes and his archenemy, Moriarty, plunge to their deaths over the Reichenbach Falls in Switzerland. Doyle wanted to retire the character so that he could write more on Spiritualism. Except his fans weren't having it. Not at all. Angry letters and protests followed, and *The Strand Magazine*, which published Doyle's work, nearly went out of business due to all of the cancelled subscriptions! So, like it or not, Doyle brought Holmes back for his classic *The Hound of the Baskervilles* (set before "The Final Problem"), and again in the 1903 story "The Adventure of the Empty House," which explained how Holmes had not fallen to his death after all.

VICTORIA PASSES: THE END OF AN AGE

O ther than Queen Elizabeth I, no other British monarch is so associated with the time in which they reigned. The mere mention of the word "Victorian" instantly conjures up images of everything from *A Christmas Carol* and top hats to the Industrial Revolution, Sherlock Holmes, and a sooty London lit by gas lamps. During Victoria's years, Britain became the mightiest empire on Earth, ruling over almost one-fourth of the world. The nation had transformed swiftly from an agrarian society to an urban one, from premodern to the cutting edge of the modern world.

Victoria died on January 22, 1901, at the age of 81. She had been Britain's queen for almost sixty-four years, a lifetime for many. The last few years of her life were filled with tragedy: two of her children died, a grandchild also perished, and her best friend passed away. As 1901 began, the queen seemed terribly worn down, remarking: "Another year begun, I am feeling so weak and unwell, that I enter upon it sadly." She was also losing her sight and spent much of her time in a wheelchair. Still, her surviving children tried to ignore the warning signs, and the government was unprepared; there was literally no one alive who knew how to prepare a royal funeral, so long had it been since a monarch had died. And Victoria had requested a full-on military state funeral. She also requested to be buried not at Westminster Abbey, as was custom, but in the Royal Mausoleum at Frogmore, near Windsor Castle. The name "Frogmore" comes from the fact that the surrounding land is marshy and wet, and, presumably, full of frogs!

The planning of the funeral was a fiasco, since different groups wanted to take charge. The Earl Marshal (the officer who organised royal ceremonies and processions) and the Lord Chamberlain (who ran the royal household) argued over who was in charge, while the German Kaiser threatened to drag the Bishop of Winchester out into a courtyard and shoot him (don't worry, he didn't do it!).

On top of all of this, the British people were kept in the dark as much as possible during the queen's last days, and were only told she'd been ill when she had finally passed. The news shocked the country, as a large number of Brits had only ever known Victoria as their monarch.

Victoria's public funeral was held on February 2, 1901, her body was transported through London on its way to her final resting place. Again, a number of things went wrong. Enterprising individuals (i.e., con men) offered seats in their homes for "great views" of the parade, some charging thousands of pounds. After finally arriving at Windsor, several of the horses that were to bear the coffin broke away, causing it to nearly drop to the ground. By that time, the front of the procession had already set off, having no idea what was happening! And at the funeral service at St. George's Chapel, the clerics had arrived an hour early and had to stand around in the cold. But, finally, the queen was laid to rest. As all that chaos indicates, her passing had turned the country on its head.

Grave fact: In preparing for Victoria's burial, the royal undertaker came to London from the Isle of Wight, but he forgot to bring the coffin along with him!

EDWARD VII: KING AT LAST!

Prince Albert Edward had waited a very long time to become king. Growing up under Victoria's thumb, Albert had always been something of a rebel, but as a king-in-waiting, he wasn't able to be as riotous as he might have liked. His mother also seemed to view her son as an eternal child, referring to him with the pitiful moniker "poor Bertie," and keeping him at arm's length from helping her run the massive empire until 1898—nearly forty years after her right hand, Edward's father, Prince Albert, had passed away!

Naturally, when Edward's time came, he was eager to seize it.

He became king at the age of 59, following Victoria's death on January 22, 1901. But his official coronation was not until June 26 of 1902, which seems a rather long wait to formalize his reign! In any case, he was all ready to go, but a mere two days ahead of the big event, he was hit with an attack of appendicitis, and underwent a (still-risky) operation. That operation was a success, and he was sitting up in bed the following day smoking a cigar; just try that in a modern hospital! The coronation was postponed until August 9, and took place in spectacular fashion at Westminster Abbey.

The new king chose the name Edward, because he didn't want to use his father's name, even though that had been Victoria's desire. Instead, he became Edward VII, the latest in a long line of English kings with the name, which extends back to the late thirteenth century. Although, technically, there were three kings in Anglo-Saxon times that were also named Edward: Edward the Elder (c. 874-924), Edward the Martyr (962-978), and Edward the Confessor (1003-1066). And of course, there was Edward V, who was never crowned and may or may not have been murdered by Richard III. History is so confusing! So, Edward VII should technically be Edward X or XI, but it is what it is, and no one's going to revise it now.

In any case, the popular new king launched himself into his newfound role with enthusiasm. He was especially interested in foreign affairs and in securing British interests abroad, which didn't help a joke that was making the rounds at the time: some referred to Edward as the "uncle of Europe," because he was related to most of the other major European monarchs in one way or another. The German Kaiser Wilhelm II and the Russian Tsar Nicholas II were his nephews, and quite a few queens were his nieces. Other kings were cousins or second cousins, and one, King Haakon VII of Norway was his nephew *and* his son-in-law! Needless to say, the entire continent had become a dangerously confused tangle.

Edward had some progressive views, and consistently condemned racial prejudice, for example. But he was opposed to giving women the right to vote. And, as you might expect of a king, he still liked to live it up, and was said to have smoked something like twenty ciga- rettes and twelve cigars a day, which as you can imagine, ended up being his downfall. By 1910, Edward was very unwell, suffering from bronchitis. After several scares, he suffered more than one heart attack on May 6, but still refused to stop working until he lost con- sciousness. He was put to bed, and died within minutes, having not even reigned for ten years.

> Racy fact: On Edward's last night, his son George (soon to be King George V), told him that his favorite horse had won a race. Edward answered, "Yes, I have heard of it. I am very glad." These ended up being his final words.

ENGLISH MUSIC: A REBIRTH?

By the end of the nineteenth century, English music (what we would think of as "classical" music) was in a bit of a slump. At least some people thought so. Germany had been producing hotshot com- posers like Brahms and Wagner, and everyone was looking to them for the latest in musical excellence. In fact, these two composers were so popular that in England, music students often lined up on the side of one or the other, as they would for rival sports teams, only without the face paint and foam fingers.

The bigger issue is that many of these same young musicians felt like England had no voice of its own. Some people had even joked that England was "a land without music" and basically just copied what- ever the Germans and some other countries came up with. Part of this tuneless reality was due to the fact that the Victorians weren't really all that big on music. It was fine as an entertainment for parlors and parties, and for girls' education, but music wasn't a suitable career for men, not like, say, writing was. So, unlike the eighteenth century, when music was highly valued, English music didn't continue to advance in the early part of the nineteenth century, simply because far fewer folks wanted to actually be composers.

But that started to change in the 1880s, when a new crop of composers started writing music of real quality. But again, some of the younger generation felt that a lot of it was just copying what the Germans were doing. A few of these young composers, including Ralph Vaughan Williams (1872-1958) and Gustav Holst (1874-1934), started experimenting with the idea of bringing in melodies from English folk songs into their compositions. Composers in other countries had been doing this for quite a while, so why couldn't the English?

What Vaughan Williams and Holst unleashed with their approach was a wave of imitators who would travel the countryside, asking farmers and others if they knew any traditional songs and would they be willing to share them? Most were happy to, and so these composers collected hundreds, even thousands of folk songs, likely saving them from being lost forever. This process became a pursuit all its own for some of these aspiring composers, while others wanted to utilize these melodies and forms into their own compositions for orchestra, piano, violin, and other instruments.

The result was the birth of a new "English" sound during the Edwardian years, one that was fruitful enough to sustain itself for many years afterward. By the 1920s, the works of Vaughan Williams, Holst, and several others had set new standards for composing, though of course, not everyone was happy with it. Just as when the folk-inspired composers were young and wanted to break away from German ideas, a new generation of younger English composers wanted to break away from the pastoral influences that were now ubiquitous in English classical music. One composer even went so far as to say that one of Vaughan Williams' symphonies sounded like "a cow looking over a gate." Yes, this was a bit harsh (and also untrue), but it's enough to show that the cycle had started all over yet again.

> Composer credibility fact: Even after their music went out of fashion in the 1920s and '30s, the influence of these Edwardian folk-inspired composers helped to ignite a bigger interest in English music and make it a respectable field after decades of the Victorians saying music was not a proper profession.

THE SUFFRAGETTES AND THE RIGHT FOR WOMEN TO VOTE

The immense changes that came to Britain during the nineteenth century affected everyone's lives forever, and not always for the better. For every improvement there were new challenges and issues springing up to replace the ones that had been solved. And in some areas, it seemed like certain progressive issues had stagnated completely. Women's rights and the right for women to vote was one of these. Voting rights had been expanded between 1832 and 1884, when new laws were passed that guaranteed the right to vote for men of various classes and financial situations, but, each time, women were left out. Women were able to make some advances in having the right to vote in local elections, as well as gaining control over their property, but the big goal, universal suffrage (the right to vote for all) was still evasive.

Emmeline Pankhurst (1858-1928), an activist and advocate for women, grew increasingly frustrated by this lack of progress, which caused Pankhurst and some colleagues to found the Women's Social and

Political Union (WSPU) in 1903. Their motto was "Deeds not words," and they fully intended to put that idea into practice. Clearly, the time for being nice was over. Membership in the Union was limited to women only, and early on, they decided that simply negotiating and protesting peacefully were not enough. They were willing to resort to more extreme tactics, including violence, since they felt that they had been ignored for too long. Inspired by the WSPU's example, other voting rights organizations soon formed.

Civil disobedience was at the top of the list for WSPU actions, and members soon found themselves running afoul of the law. Locating their main office in London in 1906, the movement began to grow, and their newspaper, *Votes for Women*, had a circulation of at least 22,000 by 1909. The union itself had something like ninety branches around the country. Clearly, they were not going to be silent anymore!

With a headquarters in London, WSPU activists were close to the heart of the British government, and didn't hesitate to make politicians' lives miserable, frequently heckling them, disrupting meetings, and chaining themselves to buildings. Although many in the establishment thought that the group was nothing more than a collection of rabble-rousers and criminals, these activists gained a growing support for their cause. But politicians continued to ignore them, causing some WSPU members to target landmarks and works of art for vandalism, which led to arrests and imprisonment. Some of those women then went on hunger strikes to protest their incarceration. The government tried to force-feed them, and when this failed, a law was passed allowing for their release, but immediate rearrest once they were well enough to return to prison. Yes, it was ridiculous, and the Suffragettes called the policy the "Cat and Mouse Act."

In June 1908, the Suffragette movement converged on Hyde Park in London, with activists joining in from all around the country. An estimated 300,000 people showed up. And yet, despite this massive showing, the right to vote seemed as far off as ever.

When the First World War broke out, the WSPU and Suffragettes called a halt to their civil disobedience and many threw their support behind the war, though not all. The Women's Suffrage Federation, led by Sylvia Pankhurst (Emmeline's daughter) was a pacifist organization. Of course, the meat-grinder that was the war began killing off young men at an appalling rate, and there was soon a shortage of workers in factories to produce the needed materials for the war to continue. Women soon found themselves doing jobs that had traditionally been done by men. Since voting rights had so often been income- and property-based, many began to wonder: If women could do the same jobs as men, why couldn't they vote as well? After a lot of debate in the corridors of power, politicians finally hammered out a solution in 1918 and passed a law granting the right to vote to women over the age of 30—so long as they also met various other qualifications for property and education. More than eight million British women qualified, so it was a start, at least. Finally, in 1928, the Representation of the People Act was passed, giving all women over 21 the right to vote (regardless of race) and eliminating property-owning qualifications.

> **Bitter attack fact:** In an effort to paint the Suffragettes in a bad light, their enemies often said that they were "unnatural" and "unladylike." These women had failed to become mothers, which was the highest goal a woman could strive for, apparently. They were just angry old spinsters who were too "masculine" and went against the proper order of things. Of course, these attacks were all just sexist nonsense.

FAMILY SQUABBLES?
THE ROAD TO WAR

W orld War I was a horrific conflict that ended the so-called "Edwardian summer" of peace and prosperity. But the years leading up to it have raised some questions for historians. And one of the most interesting of these questions is: Was the Great War basically a big family feud? Queen Victoria had been called the "Grandmother of Europe," meaning that many of the royal families in Western Europe (and beyond) were related to the royal family that ruled the United Kingdom. Indeed, several of Victoria's and Albert's children married into other royal families. Victoria, who probably thought that these alliances would ensure peace in Europe, likely would have been shocked and horrified by what took place just over a decade after her death. Here is the tangled web fashioned by the queen's royal offspring:

Princess Victoria Adelaide Mary Louise: Married Friedrich Wilhelm of Prussia, and their oldest son became Kaiser Wilhelm II, the leader of Germany during World War I. Her daughter, Sophia, married Constantine, who became King of Greece, and Sophia became queen.

Prince Albert Edward: Became King Edward VII of England. His son, George V, was king of Britain during World War I.

Princess Alice Maude Mary: Her daughter, Alix, married Tsar Nicholas II of Russia (who was later overthrown and murdered by the Bolsheviks).

Prince Alfred Ernest Albert: Married the Grand Duchess Marie, daughter of Tsar Alexander II of Russia. Their daughter, Marie, married the Crown Prince of Romania, who later became King Ferdinand I, while Marie became queen.

Prince Arthur William Patrick: He became governor of Canada, and his daughter, Margaret, married Gustav Adolph, the crown prince of Sweden.

Princess Beatrice Mary Victoria: Married Prince Henry of Battenberg. Their daughter, Victoria Eugenie married Alfonso XIII, King of Spain.

How much influence did these relations have over world events? Historians have debated what role they might have played for more than a century, but, in truth, it probably wasn't all that much. In some countries, including Britain, the monarchy was more symbolic than having any actual power, while in others, such as Germany, they were very powerful and determined national policies. While it's true that there was friction between members of these royal families, the world-shaking events that took place in the early part of the twentieth century were much more complicated than their petty squabbles, influenced by colonial conflicts, territorial disputes, the build-up of military pride ... all the usual things that lead to war. Only this time, it was a war that would change the world forever.

> Face fact: The close ties between these royal houses was at time uncanny. King George V of Britain and Tsar Nicholas II of Russia looked very much alike, for example, so much so that many have remarked that they could have been brothers.

CHAPTER 8

TWO WORLD WARS
AND MORE

(1914–1945)

BRITAIN IN WORLD WAR I

The "Great War," as it was known for twenty years afterward, was a tragedy of almost unimaginable scale. Never before had there been such a terrible series of battles, filled with so much death, destruction, and misery. It changed European society and world history forever, and set the stage for an even worse conflict twenty years later. Between fifteen and twenty-two million people died and another twenty-one to twenty-three million people were injured, making it one of the bloodiest conflicts in human history. The war was typified by what occurred in the trenches of eastern France, where the British and French forces got bogged down on one side and the Germans and their allied forces were stuck on the other. Both sides would try to push a little bit farther forward each day, sometimes gaining just a small amount of territory before being beaten back. This terrible stalemate was little more than a slaughterhouse, with young men dying by the thousands, for little or no advantage either way.

Despite what you may have heard, this awful conflict wasn't really about in-fighting between the continent's royal families (see page 360); various developments during the late nineteenth century made Europe a ticking time bomb. It went off on June 28, 1914, when Archduke Franz Ferdinand of Austria, heir to the Austro-Hungarian throne, was assassinated in Sarajevo by a Serbian extremist, Gavrilo Princip. The Austrians and Hungarians blamed Serbia, and were able to convince Kaiser Wilhelm of Germany to take their side. But Russia, an ally of France and Great Britain, was also an ally of Serbia. Add in the reality that several of these countries had been building up their militaries in part for protection and in part to show off their general excellence, the atmosphere was suddenly ripe for war.

The whole thing was a powder keg, and when Austria declared war on Serbia, Russia was compelled to come to Serbia's defense. Like dominoes, the unprecedented sixty years of European peace disintegrated as alliances kicked in. Britain declared war on Germany on August 5,

1914, intending to defend France (imagine!) and stop Germany from becoming too powerful. Then the war spread from further east, as the fading Ottoman Empire in Turkey joined with Germany, perhaps in a last-ditch attempt to make itself relevant again.

In Britain, there was at first a great outburst of patriotism and general romantic feeling, with young men joining the army by the thousands for the chance to go off to war and win some sort of imagined glory. Many boasted with confidence that the war would be over by Christmas of that year. But as the reality set in, it was clear that this dreadful conflict, the first to use tanks and chemical weapons, wasn't going to end any time soon.

In the end, it lasted for four long and horrific years, years filled with hardship, misery, death, and uncertainty that would test people in all of the nations involved. Britain was already facing plenty of issues at home: its own crumbling empire, the demands from women for the right to vote, unrest in Ireland, and much more. As the conflict dragged on, it became more difficult for the government to continue to justify the fighting and to keep morale up, as supplies became ever scarcer and young people kept dying. But Britain, unfortunately, had no choice but to see it through.

> **Explosive fact:** The fighting and explosives in northern France were at times so intense that explosions could be heard across the English Channel, in southeast England.

FOUR WORLD WAR I BATTLES

The carnage of World War I still shocks those that read about it today. The sheer numbers of young men killed on battlefields over those four years also stunned people at the time, and changed attitudes forever about the "glory" of war and nationalistic duty. Many different battles were fought during the course of the conflict, but here are four of the most important.

The First Battle of Marne (September 1914): One of the early battles of the war, it was the first to used motorized transports, as well as radio messages. The Germans had hoped for a swift victory by neutralizing France before turning their attention to Russia, but it didn't work out that way. The French broke through the lines, driving Parisian taxis and buses to do so! The surprised Germans retreated. But soon, both sides would get dug in and barely budge, a tactic that would continue throughout the war.

Battle of Gallipoli (1915-16): This battle was a nearly year-long, drawn-out failure for the Allied Powers. It was an attempt to capture Constantinople (the crumbling Ottoman Empire was an ally of Germany), effectively removing Turkey from the war completely. But the British and the Australian and New Zealand Army Corps (ANZAC) underestimated the resolve of the Turkish troops, and had poor knowledge of the landscape. Still, the heroism of ANZAC troops in this battle is memorialized every year in Australia and New Zealand. One of the commanders of the Turkish forces, Mustafa Kemal Pasha, went on to be known as Atatürk, leader of post-Ottoman Turkey.

Battle of Jutland (May 31-June 1, 1916): This sea conflict, the main naval battle of World War I, is considered a turning point in the war. It took place off the coast of Jutland, Denmark's northwest landmass. A chaotic battle without a clear winner, Jutland saw the British lose more ships and crew than the Germans, but manage to maintain its shipping lanes, and they used this to their advantage when enforcing a blockade of Germany that eventually helped the Allied Powers win the war. Germany was never able again to challenge Britain for North Sea supremacy after this battle.

Battle of the Somme (July-November, 1916): This was the bloodiest battle of World War I, a dreadful conflict that raged for almost five months and cost the lives of 1.5 million. The battle was situated near the Somme River in northeast France, and was a joint effort between the British and French troops to win a decisive victory over Germany. Of course, that's not what happened. On the first day of fighting alone, there were more than 57,000 British casualties, and of those, nearly 20,000 were killed immediately. Over the course of the battle, the Allied Powers only succeeded in advancing about seven miles. Probably the one good thing that came of it was that they also developed new strategies that allowed them to advance more in future battles, bringing the whole horrid conflict to close sooner rather than later.

> **Transatlantic tragic fact:** The first American killed in World War I, Harry Butters, died in the Battle of the Somme on August 31, 1916. He was an American citizen with connections to Britain who enlisted to fight for the cause in 1914 (the United States would not formally enter the war until April 6, 1917). Butters had befriended his battalion commander Winston Churchill (yes, *that* Churchill!), who wrote of him after he died: "We realize his nobility in coming to the help of another country entirely of his own free will, and understand what a big heart he had."

THE END OF THE WAR

This gruesome, ghastly war finally came to an end on November 11, 1918. By this time, Germany realized its forces were exhausted and that it was facing an invasion. Its allies had already surrendered, so there was no other option but to give up. Germany's representatives signed an armistice with the Allies at just after 5:00 am in Supreme Commander Ferdinand Jean Marie Foch's private train near

Compiégne in France, though some fighting would continue for several hours afterward, until 11:00 am. The war had been dreadfully costly for both sides: nine million soldiers killed, another twenty-one million wounded, and at least five million civilians were dead. A war which many British thought would "be over by Christmas" in 1914 had dragged on for more than four terrible years. A whole generation of young men had essentially been wiped out in what many, as soon as it was over, saw as a completely pointless conflict that accomplished nothing other than leaving many nations and European culture much poorer.

The orchestra conductor Hugh Allen, for example, commenting on George Butterworth, a young composer who perished in the Battle of the Somme, said that he had died, "to pay a rotten debt to a bloody-minded lot of miscreants." The patriotism of "king-and-country," which had been proclaimed so loudly before the war, had obviously worn away. People were so appalled by the senseless slaughter that any shyness about voicing their opinions melted away, up to and including criticizing the monarchy and the government.

On the one-year anniversary of the ending of the war, at the request of King George V, a two-minute silence was observed, which continued in subsequent years. To this day, people also wear red poppy-shaped pins on November 11; red poppies are a symbol of remembrance, given how they sprang up in the former battlefields of northern France and Belgium. They are worn each year in memory of those who died in the war, and to support the Royal British Legion.

In the immediate aftermath of the war ending, though, people were also relieved and overjoyed, and they wanted to celebrate. The annual reverence for remembering the fallen on November 11 was often followed by "victory balls," celebrations of life and having survived the conflict. People dressed up in costumes and had a grand time at these events, though some leaders and religious officials felt that these parties were in poor taste. One vicar even called them "indecent" and said that all celebrations were "thoughtless and ill-conceived." But as these balls often raised money for charities and/or wounded soldiers, they were well intended and well received.

The peace was finalized in the 1919 Treaty of Versailles, but the treaty's terms were focused on punishing Germany for its role in the war. This led to severe economic problems in Germany and a lot of anger and resentment from the German people. It was the perfect climate for a new nationalist party powered by the modern innovation of fascism and a failed painter named Adolf Hitler to start making the case that he could restore Germany's greatness. And, increasingly in the 1920s, people started listening.

Sadly, the "war to end all wars" didn't actually end anything.

> **Unfortunate after the fact:** A German soldier, Lt. Tomas, was killed just after the 11:00 am deadline, by American troops who had not yet heard about the ceasefire.

THE INTERWAR PERIOD

The relief that came with the end of the war spilled over into everything and everywhere in Britain. There was celebration, of course, but also deep reflection on what had been lost. Many questioned what it had all been for, and the patriotic concept of supporting the British Empire no matter what took a huge blow. Many veterans tried to put the whole thing behind them; many more simply couldn't. A whole generation of young men had been lost, in what many people now saw as a completely pointless war. In 1919, no one could imagine that Britain would be dragged into an even bigger war only twenty years later.

Still, the decade started with a boom, and for some, it seemed that the good times had at long last returned. For those who were already wealthy, it was a time of parties and celebration, jazz clubs, and cocktail bars (Britain never prohibited alcohol like America had), and excesses of all kinds. Women celebrated being freed at last from Victorian fashions (especially the corset!), and started cutting their hair short and wearing more revealing dresses. The famed "flapper" look had arrived!

In entertainment, the BBC began radio broadcasts in 1922 (more about the "Beeb" in a bit), and movies became a popular diversion for members of every social class. International travel picked up, with airplanes now able to fly to the continent, though many people preferred to head to the seaside for vacations.

All of this hubbub made terrific fodder for a satirist, and author P. G. Wodehouse poked fun at the upper classes and the "Roaring Twenties" in his Jeeves and Wooster novels.

But for most of the population, there wasn't all that much fun to be had during this time, and still much work to do. The British Empire was crumbling, going the way of all empires eventually, and sizable economic problems were already on the horizon by the mid-1920s. Britain had overmined coal during the war and now had to import it. Unemployment started to rise, and once again, the striking contrast between the very wealthy and the rest of the people was obvious. A large general strike in 1926 only made these problems clearer. To make matters even worse, the stock markets crashed in 1929, plunging the world into the Great Depression for much of the 1930s. Only the wealthiest could ride it out in anything like comfort, while for many, it was a very difficult time, indeed.

And of course, in Germany, the Nazi party had been taking advantage of people's unhappiness and problems for several years, and a horrid little man by the name of Adolf Hitler was slowly building more power and influence, meaning Britain was, unthinkably, about to experience something even worse that the Great War.

> Fun fact: Roller coasters and crossword puzzles both appeared for the first time in Britain in the 1920s, though you probably wouldn't want to try both at the same time.

MI6/SIS

M16 (Military Intelligence, Section 6), now known as the Secret Intelligence Service (SIS), is the chief British intelligence service, mainly focused on overseas operations, akin to the CIA in the United States. The organization can trace its origins back to 1909, when Prime Minister Herbert Asquith, reacting to rumors that German spies were operating in Britain, ordered the Committee of Imperial Defence to investigate. While the rumors might have been exaggerated, the Committee decided that there was enough concern to establish an intelligence agency, the Secret Service Bureau, in July. It was initially divided into a Home and Foreign Section (the domestic organization would become MI5), under the direction of Mansfield Smith-Cumming, a Royal Navy officer with no intelligence training. He may have seemed an odd choice, but Cumming was enthusiastic about the job and took to it with great interest.

Over the next few years, the bureau set up several front addresses for security purposes, establishing a precedent that other intelligence agencies would follow. With the outbreak of World War I in 1914, the Foreign Section began to work closely with Military Intelligence. Throughout the war, the bureau worked with spies, turncoats and informants in Belgium and the Netherlands to obtain secrets about German plans, movements, and goals. In Belgium, a group known as La Dame Blanche (many of its spies were women) provided the bureau with much useful information. And this group was not exceptional: the bureau relied on women for a number of crucial tasks and occupations, alongside capable men who had been injured in the war and could not return to the front lines.

One of the main intelligence concerns for Britain after the war was the rise of the Soviet Union. Several agents were dispatched to Russia to report on the goings-on there, often at great risk. In 1923, Rear-Admiral Hugh Sinclair was appointed the organization's new chief; unlike Smith-Cumming, he had experience in intelligence work before coming on board. The agency continued to grow throughout the 1920s and '30s, and with the rise of Hitler, it found itself facing tremendous new challenges. Under a new directive in 1938 called Section D, plans were made to engage in sabotage of railways, electric lines, food supplies, and more, actions that would disrupt Germany's operations and infrastructure. These tasks became as important during World War II as gathering information. Also in 1938, the agency established itself at the stately home of Bletchley Park, to work on code-breaking, among other things. The mathematical genius Alan Turing (for more on him, see page 405) led the way in deciphering codes, and his work helped turn the tide of the war. Various intelligence networks, such as "Service Clarence" in Belgium and "Alliance" in occupied France were vital to passing on information about troop movements, the locations of key deployments, secret weapons, and more.

Up until 1943, training for SIS officers had been a bit sporadic and not well organized. But a serious effort began in that year to give officers better training to handle themselves in the field. By June 1944, the so-called Sussex plan successfully dropped agents behind enemy lines in France after D-Day, to provide necessary intelligence for Allied troops. In August, just two months after the invasion, there were more than thirty teams operating in German-occupied France.

After the war, the SIS focused on the advancement of the Soviet Union, and forged closer ties with the newly-created American CIA. Over the next several decades, the organization would continue to engage in espionage acts around the world, which it is still not allowed to talk about; nothing after 1949 can be revealed. This secrecy has led to many accusations that the bureau has abused its power and tried to undermine other nations' sovereignties, the same charges that have been brought against the CIA.

> Super-secret fact: It wasn't until 1994, with the passing of the Intelligence Services Act, that the government officially admitted that MI6/SIS even exists!

LAWRENCE OF ARABIA

Thomas Edward Lawrence (1888-1935), the dashing figure that most know from the epic 1962 film, *Lawrence of Arabia*, was a larger-than-life figure whose exploits in the Middle East remain legendary. But there is more to the man than a glittering Hollywood epic, of course. He was born in Wales and, as a child, showed an interest in old buildings and antiquities. By the age of 15, he was keeping an eye on building sites in Oxford, to ensure that if any objects were found, these would be delivered to the Ashmolean Museum. That must have made him really popular with local builders!

Lawrence studied at Oxford from 1907 to 1910, and while there, also completed a bicycle tour of France, where he collected photographs and other information about French castles, which would later be the subject of his dissertation. In 1909, he journeyed across Ottoman Syria for three months to study crusader castles. In 1910, he was offered a chance to work as an archeologist in Carchemish, a site in northern Syria, and eagerly accepted. Lawrence would go on to work on digs in Palestine and Egypt, as well.

When World War I began, Lawrence enlisted in the British Army and was posted to Cairo, working in intelligence. In 1916, he was sent to Hijaz (an area in modern Saudi Arabia) to work with the local tribes as a liaison, and it was here that Lawrence's legend was born. The British wanted to rally the Arabs to fight in a revolt against the occupying Ottomans, to further destabilize the faltering empire and tip the balance of the war. Lawrence, gifted in diplomacy, was a good choice for the job. He established a friendship with Faisal, a son of Sharif Hussein of Mecca, and was able to convince them that a revolt had merit. The Arabs began using guerrilla tactics (with British help) against the Ottoman forces, to great success. Lawrence didn't just manipulate his new friends; he had learned Arabic and famously adopted their clothing styles, which he wore proudly. He and Faisal led the Arab revolt out of Arabia and up into Syria, eventually marching with British troops into Damascus on October 1, 1918. The revolt was successful, and essentially drove the last stake into the heart of the legendary Ottoman Empire.

Lawrence wanted the Arabs to have their own independent state and advocated for them on several occasions, but unfortunately, Britain and France had already agreed to secretly carve up the region between them after the war (see page 377), leaving the Arabs rightfully feeling betrayed. After the war, Lawrence's reputation grew, but he was not always happy with the publicity. He worked as an advisor to Winston Churchill, and then joined the Royal Air Force (RAF) in 1922 under an assumed name, but he was discovered and thrown out! He was finally able to rejoin the RAF in 1925, and remained in service at various places in Britain and beyond until March 1935.

Only two months later, Lawrence was out riding his motorcycle in the countryside of Dorset near the south coast of England. A dip in the road meant that he was surprised by two boys on bicycles that appeared suddenly. He swerved to avoid them and was thrown over the motorcycle's handlebars. He died of his injuries six days later, on May 19; only 46 years old. The story of his life lives on, of course, not only from the famous film bearing his nickname, but also his 1926 memoir, *Seven Pillars of Wisdom*.

> **Safety fact:** One of the doctors that treated Lawrence after his accident, Hugh Cairns, was deeply upset by the matter and realized that adopting the use of motorcycle helmets would make a huge difference in terms of safety. It would take another thirty-two years, but thanks to Cairns's research, helmets eventually became mandatory for motorcyclists in Britain, a law that would save countless lives.

GERTRUDE BELL: JOURNEYS ACROSS THE MIDDLE EAST

Gertrude Margaret Lowthian Bell (1868-1926) is not as well-known as Lawrence of Arabia, but her accomplishments are no less impressive. An English writer, political officer, and archaeologist, Bell was born into a wealthy family in northern England and was well educated. She even attended Oxford University, and graduated having studied modern history, but she was not awarded a degree, since women were not treated even remotely fairly or equally at the time, and were not granted full membership at the university until

1920. Having left Oxford, Bell traveled in 1892 to meet with her uncle in Persia, who was serving as a diplomat there. On this trip, she fell in love with the Middle East, a region she would then devote much of her life to the study of.

For the next decade, she traveled widely, and developed a love for archaeology and languages. She eventually learned Arabic (which she thought was particularly difficult), Persian (Farsi), Turkish, French, Italian, and German. She also began writing and published a number of works, including travel books.

In 1899, Bell returned to the Middle East, visiting Syria and Palestine. In 1900, she was journeying from Jerusalem to Damascus and met the Druze, whose beliefs are an offshoot of Islam, but who incorporate teachings from many religions, including a belief in reincarnation, and do not consider themselves to be Muslims. She returned to Syria in 1905, and in 1907, published her travel book, *Syria: The Desert and the Sown*, which was a critical and commercial success. Bell traveled extensively across the Middle East between 1900 and 1912. When World War I began, she went to work briefly for British intelligence in Cairo, where she met T. E. Lawrence, and supported the idea of engaging the Arabs to dislodge the Ottomans.

Bell also became involved in the politics of the region and was sought out for her knowledge of the area and its peoples. She spent time in India and Iraq, and was even awarded the honor of Commander of the Order of the British Empire. After the war, she spent more time in Iraq, helping local leaders construct a stable infrastructure. She was the only woman present at the Conference in Cairo in 1921, which Winston Churchill convened to discuss the boundaries of the new Middle Eastern nations. While Bell was a British Empire loyalist, she also desired independence for the Arabs (with British input and advice), just as Lawrence did. Opposing this idea were some who wanted to impose direct British rule on the Arabs, as the empire had in India.

Bell supported the idea of Faisal—who had fought with Lawrence—becoming a leader of one of these independent nations. Faisal was briefly king of Syria in 1920, but was expelled by the French after several months. On August 23, 1921, he was declared king of the new nation of Iraq, which was made up of the former Ottoman *vilayets* (provinces) of Basra, Mosul, and Baghdad, and hoped to encourage a pan-Arab nationalism in the wake of becoming free of Ottoman rule.

Bell remained in Iraq as an advisor to the new king, and was instrumental in establishing the National Museum of Iraq. She was a strong advocate for the idea that antiquities belonged in the country where they were found, and shouldn't be taken away to museums in other nations. In 1922, Faisal named her director of antiquities, and in 1926, the museum formally opened.

Eventually, Bell died in Baghdad, due to an overdose of sleeping pills. It's not known if this overdose was accidental, or if the depression she exhibited in her final years pushed her over the edge.

> Mountaineering fact: Bell was also an avid mountain climber, who tackled some of the most difficult peaks in Europe, including Mont Blanc (the highest mountain in the Alps,) and the Matterhorn. She also did some climbing in the Rocky Mountains while on a trip to America in 1903.

THE SYKES-PICOT AGREEMENT AND THE MODERN MIDDLE EAST

In 1916, as it became apparent that the Ottoman Empire was in its final days, Britain and France signed a secret treaty, with the assent of Russia and Italy. It outlined how the lands once controlled by the Ottoman

Empire would be divided up and placed under the control of various other nations. Two diplomats, Mark Sykes (1879-1919) and Francois Georges-Picot (1870-1951), were the masterminds behind this pact.

The treaty gave Britain control over what is now southern Israel and Palestine, Jordan and southern Iraq, and various port cities. Britain would also have control over parts of Persia, which, along with Mesopotamia, would prove to be rich in oil. France gained control over southeast Turkey, Kurdistan, Lebanon, and Syria. Russia gained control of Constantinople and a part of Armenia, as well as the Dardanelles (the strait connecting the Black Sea to the Mediterranean), while Italy was given dominion over a part of Anatolia in central Turkey. It was agreed that much of the rest of Palestine, as well as Jerusalem would be under an international administration. None of the European nations "owned" these regions, of course, but they planned to install local administrators who would be loyal. It was a situation quite similar to what had existed under the Ottomans, actually, only now the people there would have to endure a European yoke.

This was all well and good for the signers of the agreement, since it gave them all sorts of extra territory to play with and exploit for resources. But, as you might expect, the people living in these Middle Eastern lands had absolutely no say in this agreement—in fact, they didn't even know about it. Those Arabs whom Lawrence had promised an independent nation in exchange for help in fighting the Turks during the war felt especially disappointed and betrayed.

So, if it was a secret agreement, how did the world find out about it? Well, when the Bolsheviks seized power, they denied any Russian claims to Ottoman territories. When they found a copy of the agreement in the Russian archives, they released it publicly. Lenin called it, "the agreement of the colonial thieves." In Britain, *The Manchester Guardian* printed the treaty on November 26, 1917, while the war was still raging. This story was hugely embarrassing to the Allied Powers, and forced them to rethink and forge a new plan.

In November 1917, the British government had also issued a public statement, the Balfour Declaration, that supported establishing a "national home for the Jewish people" in what was currently Palestine, but had, of course, once been Israel. Along with this, Britain and France devised new strategies to give the sense that they supported greater autonomy and self-rule in the region, while still also protecting their oil and strategic interests. At the Conference of San Remo in Italy in 1920, new agreements were drawn up, replacing the Sykes-Picot Agreement, and creating the states we now know as the Middle East. And again, while these new territories had more autonomy, there was not nearly enough input from the peoples of the region. The Kurds, for example, never got their own state, and politics and problems of the region are still influenced by the actions the British and French took over a hundred years ago.

Oily fact: In March,1908, geologist George Bernard Reynolds discovered oil in Persia, after several years of searching at the request of a wealthy Englishman, William Knox D'Arcy. The find was so important that D'arcy set up the Anglo-Persian Oil Company in 1909 to increase production. More reserves were soon discovered, and after that, it was only a matter of time before the region's oil riches would be coveted by the world's nations.

NANCY ASTOR: THE FIRST WOMAN TO SIT IN PARLIAMENT

Nancy Astor, later Viscountess Astor (1879-1964), took her oath in the House of Commons on December 1, 1919, a monumental day in British history: she was the first woman seated in Parliament. And yet, she wasn't even British, she was American! How did that happen?

Astor was born in Virginia to a large family. Her father, a former slave owner, made a fortune in the railroad business, meaning that Nancy enjoyed a very comfortable lifestyle and moved in extreme high society. She married Robert Gould Shaw II in 1897, a wealthy businessman and socialite, but their marriage didn't last and they parted ways in 1903. Afterward, Astor became convinced that Britain might be a better home for her, and she moved to London in 1905.

As a wealthy, educated American woman, she became one of the talks of the town, and soon caught the attention of Waldorf Astor, son of the Viscount Astor. The Astors themselves had come from America, so they had that in common. These two soon married and lived in the splendour of the British aristocratic lifestyle. Waldorf was interested in politics, seeing as his father sat in the House of Lords. Perhaps surprisingly, he was in favor of various reforms and measures to ensure greater social equality. Nancy herself became interested in political matters.

When Waldorf's father died in 1919, he gained the title of Viscount and was brought into the House of Lords, meaning that his Parliamentary seat in the House of Commons became vacant. Nancy, now Lady Astor, decided to run for the empty seat herself. The idea of a woman running wasn't as outlandish as it sounded. Another woman, Constance Markievicz, had already won an election to Parliament in 1918, but because she was Irish and a supporter of an independent Irish republic, she was not allowed to be seated. Lady Astor, running on her husband's reputation and her own charms, succeeded in winning the by-election. The Suffragettes were skeptical of her, feeling that she was simply wealthy and out-of-touch, but to her credit, she listened to them and adopted some of their ideas.

She would go on to serve in Parliament until 1945, which was a remarkable achievement, but her time in office was overshadowed by some terrible beliefs that forever stained her reputation. Lady Astor was deeply anti-Catholic, racist, and antisemitic. She initially saw Hitler's rise as the best response to both the Jews and communists, who she thought were secretly working with each other to rule the world. It was a popular conspiracy theory at the time that Hitler was quite eager to exploit. She continued to support Hitler throughout the 1930s, as the Nazis tightened their grip on power in Germany and began to threaten all-out war. She had tense standoffs, insults, and arguments with Jewish MPs, one of whom told her he wanted to hit her in the face. She was also a supporter of Prime Minister Neville Chamberlain's disastrous appeasement policies (see page 394 for more on this), and met with various Nazi officials during this time.

By the time the war broke out, Astor was forced to admit that she had made some "mistakes" in her assessment of Hitler, and eventually supported Britain's war efforts, though the Conservative party increasingly saw her as a liability. At the end of the war in 1945, both her family and colleagues told her not to run again, and she eventually made a bitter speech revealing that she'd been forced out. She never renounced her views, even as her husband became more liberal in his old age. She was proud that her father had owned slaves, and never let go of her Jewish conspiracy theories. While she was a ground-breaking individual who opened the door for many more women to become MPs, her outrageously offensive views mean that she really doesn't deserve praise for her political career.

Intense dislike fact: Lady Astor and Winston Churchill were sworn enemies. A famous quote says that during one exchange, she said to him, "If I were your wife I would put poison in your coffee!" Churchill replied, "And if I were your husband, I would drink it." This is a great story, but it seems that the joke existed long before these two argued with each other.

HOWARD CARTER AND
KING TUT'S TOMB

On November 26, 1922, Lord Carnarvon asked his friend and colleague, Howard Carter, "Can you see anything?" Carter replied, "Yes, wonderful things!"

After years of exploration, excavation, and frustration while working on digs in the Valley of Kings in Egypt, Carter and Carnarvon had made one of the greatest archaeological finds of the twentieth century: an intact burial chamber for an Egyptian pharaoh, that of Tutankhamun ("King Tut"), who had only reigned for a few years between 1333 BCE (becoming pharaoh when he was just nine years old) and 1323 BCE, when he died.

By any account, Tutankhamun was a minor pharaoh of little historical importance. After he died, he was embalmed and buried according to procedure, but it was done hastily and the tomb was sealed. Luckily for the modern world, it was, for the most part, forgotten by tomb robbers as well (though not completely), and Tut's tomb became by far the best-preserved Egyptian burial chamber. Because of this bit of fortune, this minor king has literally become the face of ancient Egypt.

Carter (1874-1939) was born in London, and from a young age showed an interest in all things Egyptian. He was also a gifted artist, and his skills eventually attracted the attention of Lady Amherst, who also had an interest in Egyptology. She arranged for Carter to go to Egypt and assist on a dig in 1891, where, among other duties, he made drawings of tomb decorations. He showed such promise and enthusiasm that in 1899 he was appointed as Inspector of Monuments for Upper Egypt, and was based in Luxor. After a row with some French tourists in 1905 (he took the side of the Egyptians), Carter resigned and drifted for a few years, before coming to the attention of George Herbert, Fifth Earl of Carnarvon, who hired him to oversee the excavation of some tombs at Thebes. This began a long working partnership, and by 1914, they had received permission to dig in the famed Valley of the Kings. Unfortunately, for them and the wider world, their work was soon interrupted by World War I.

Work resumed in 1917, but over the next five years, their efforts were disappointing. Carnarvon was ready to throw in the towel, but Carter convinced him to fund one more operation. Based on his studies, Carter was sure that the young pharaoh's tomb was near the area he was excavating. On November 4, a local water boy tripped on a stone that proved to be the top of a flight of stairs leading down to a doorway with cartouches on it (oval-shaped seals filled with hieroglyphs that are the sign of a pharaoh's tomb). Carter excitedly sent a telegram to Carnarvon in England, telling him what he'd found. Carnarvon and his daughter, Lady Evelyn Herbert, set out at once, arriving in Egypt on November 23. They were both present when Carter's hardworking crew of Egyptians opened the main door, cleared the hallway behind, and then made a small opening in the door of the tomb itself. Carter peered in, and, by the light of a candle, took in those "wonderful things."

Inside the tomb was a true treasure trove of items, untouched since young Tut's burial. Over the next few days, Egyptian officials arrived, and electric lighting was rigged up in the tomb. Everyone was in awe of what they beheld. There had never been a discovery like it: the gold (including the now world-famous death mask of Tut), the artifacts, the statues, and much more. It would take Carter almost ten years to catalog the nearly 5,400 items found inside. The tomb of Tutankhamun is by far the best and most detailed picture of ancient Egypt that the modern world has, a price-less look into the rites, beliefs, and practices of the time.

And yet, despite his work, Carter never received any honors from the British government (he was honoured with the Order of the Nile, bestowed on him by King Fuad I). He finished his work on the tomb in 1932, and then retired, dividing his time between London and Egypt for the rest of his life. Unfortunately, recent discoveries have shown that Carter stole some items from the tomb and kept them for himself, which definitely undermines his status as an archaeologist.

Cursed fact: Carnarvon died on March 19, 1923, only a few months after Carter opened the tomb. His death seems to have been caused by a mosquito bite, which was then infected by a razor blade cut. It led to blood poisoning and possibly pneumonia. Some began to whisper of a "mummy's curse," and no less than Arthur Conan Doyle suggested that Carnarvon had been killed by supernatural beings Tut's priests had summoned to guard the tomb. Carter dismissed it all as "rot", of course, but other tales circulated of people connected to the dig mysteriously dying, some real, some entirely made up. Carter ignored the hysteria, and lived for another sixteen years.

ALEISTER CROWLEY: THE MOST EVIL MAN IN THE WORLD?

D epending on who you talk to, Crowley (1875-1947) was either a great practitioner of ceremonial magic and a revolutionary thinker who revealed a whole new order of being, or he was a fraud, criminal, and con man. No matter where he went, his scandalous reputation preceded him, and he did nothing to play it down. Indeed, Crowley actively encouraged it, taking the idea of "there's no such thing as bad publicity" to heart.

Born into a devoutly Christian family in 1875, he at first conformed to their beliefs. But by his teenage years, Crowley questioned the entire religion and began to behave in ways intended to deliberately mock and go against its teachings, reveling in sex, drugs, and anti-Christian ideas. These newfound beliefs and behaviors would stay with Crowley for the rest of his life, and as such, he became extremely interested in the occult practices and various magical societies that were forming in England at the time.

After dabbling in various magical practices and joining certain established groups, Crowley produced his own system, Thelema, guided by a single commandment: "Do what thou wilt shall be the whole of the Law. Love is the law, love under will." While people have erroneously interpreted thus to mean "do whatever you want," Crowley intended it as a more complex philosophy than that. His ideology was defined in *The Book of the Law*, one of several texts that he claimed was dictated to him by an entity he called Aiwass. It incorporated ideas and workings from many different sources, including ancient Egyptian beliefs and the ritual magic that was popular at the time.

Some have labeled Crowley as a Satanist, in large part because he adopted the provocative names, "The Great Beast" and the "Beast 666," both of which were obviously taken from the *Book of Revelation*, and also because of his many scandals. But Thelema was a new religion for a new world, containing elements from numerous philosophical, magical, and occult traditions. However, it was rumored that his rituals and communities were places of appalling depravity, featuring drug-fueled orgies and possibly even human sacrifice. Newspapers had a field day when reporting his alleged scandals, and this reporting had a powerful effect: Crowley had established a commune, the Abbey of Thelema, on the island of Sicily, where he attracted a growing number of followers and devotees. But when the rumors of what happened there reached the ears of newly-in-power dictator Benito Mussolini, Crowley and his group were expelled from Italy in April 1923.

Crowley traveled widely after this expulsion, but eventually he ended up back in England, where he continued to devote himself to magical practices and to scandalize polite society. Crowley probably wasn't the absolute perverse monster some liked to claim, but even one of his admirers once called him an "appalling old reprobate," so there must have been some truth in the rumors that swirled around him.

> Tabloid fact: The tabloids were quick to label Crowley's funeral as a "black mass," which it wasn't, though such talk would certainly sell newspapers!

CHARLIE CHAPLIN

S ir Charles Spencer Chaplin Jr. (1889-1977), better known to the world as Charlie Chaplin, was an English comedic actor who is best known for his work during the silent film era.

Born into poverty in London, Chaplin's father was mostly absent and his mother was committed to an asylum when he was 14. But he had an interest in performing and began working in music halls as part of a children's dance troupe and later, as a stage comedian. This early interest in physical movement and comedy would eventually make him a star.

At the age of 19, Chaplin was discovered by Fred Karno, the British music hall impresario and slapstick specialist who is believed to have invented the classic custard pie-in-the-face gag. He took Chaplin to the United States in 1914, where Keystone Studios was impressed with the young man's talent. It was while working for Keystone that Chaplin created his famous "Tramp" persona, with the bowler hat, cane, and little mustache, the look that remains iconic in film culture. Chaplin advanced quickly and was soon directing his own films for various studios.

He had a string of silent movie hits in the 1920s, including *The Kid* (1921), *A Woman of Paris* (1923), *The Gold Rush* (1925), and *The Circus* (1928). Chaplin had a huge amount of control over these productions. He wrote, produced, directed, edited, starred in leading roles—he even composed the music for most of his movies!

When talking movies came along (and eventually pushed silent films out for good), he didn't want to act in them, and opted to continue working in silent films. His first talking film was *The Great Dictator* in 1940, a classic comedy drama that mocked Hitler. Chaplin had a similar mustache, of course, and played the lead roles, both the fascist dictator and a Jewish barber. The film strongly condemned Hitler, Mussolini, fascism, and antisemitism. For his first speaking role, Chaplin delivered a classic monologue at the end, where he urged the people of the world to rise up against fascism and dictators and work for peace. It is a moving and timely speech that still resonates. In 1997, the Library of Congress selected *The Great Dictator* to be included for preservation in the United States National Film Registry, a collection of films and clips that are, "culturally, historically, or aesthetically significant."

The British government at first decided that *The Great Dictator* would not be allowed to be shown in Britain, since the official government policy toward Hitler at the time was the disastrous experiment with appeasement. However, by the time the film was finished, war had broken out between Britain and Germany, and the government saw the film's value as anti-Hitler propaganda.

The Great Dictator continued to be popular over the years, but Chaplin's own popularity declined during the war and after, due in part to accusations that he was a communist, and his fathering of a child out of wedlock. The FBI wanted Chaplin removed from the United States, and set about smearing his name to achieve this end. People who had loved the Tramp character were now turning against him, and came to see him as a corrupting presence. There were even called for his films to be banned. After a series of court cases and hearings, Chaplin knew he would not be allowed to remain and relocated to Switzerland, where he continued making movies into the 1960s.

> Grave-robbing fact: Chaplin died on Christmas Day in 1977 and was buried at the Corsier-sur-Vevey cemetery, near Lake Geneva in Switzerland. On March 1, 1978, two men dug up his coffin and stole it, holding it for ransom to extort money from his very wealthy widow. Swiss police caught them in May, and Chaplin's body was returned to its resting place, but put inside a concrete vault.

THE BBC

The "Beeb" is a British institution, one that most Brits today couldn't even imagine living without. For the last century, it has been at the center of life for British news and entertainment.

The British Broadcasting Company began broadcasting daily on November 14, 1922, at 6:00 pm. Read by broadcaster Arthur Burrows, or "Uncle Arthur" to his devoted listeners, this initial broadcast included a report on a train robbery (still a thing in those days!), sports news, political news, and a weather report. Regular programming was to be a mixture of news, drama, radio, and talk, which is pretty much what it's been ever since.

In December 1922, engineer John Charles Walsham Reith was appointed as the general manger, after applying and then rethinking his application, successfully retrieving it from the mailbox, and revising it! While Reith felt he had the right credentials for the position, he admitted, "I hadn't the remotest idea as to what broadcasting was." Still, he did a pretty good job.

The company quickly thrived and by 1927, it was remade as the British Broadcasting Corporation, a non-commercial organization with a royal charter. Of course, what it chose to broadcast and censor was the topic of some controversy. The BBC's approach was to promote Britishness at the expense of foreign music and arts, and to try to keep its programming as highbrow as possible, while also being careful about overtly political broadcasts. So, it wasn't exactly a center for free speech. For several decades, it had very strict regulations about what could be broadcast, and how it would be presented.

Nevertheless, the BBC grew throughout the 1930s, by which time more than half of the homes in Britain had radios. In December 1932, King George V became the first British monarch to broadcast, allowing millions of listeners to hear his voice for the first time. During World War II, the BBC was a vital source of news, warnings of air raids, and much more, including entertainment meant to provide cheer and encouragement during the darkest hours of the Blitz.

With the beginning of regular television broadcasts in 1936 (there had been earlier experiments as early as 1929), the BBC eagerly moved into the new medium, even though televisions were a rarity in most homes until well after World War II. By 1948, the BBC moved into a regular television news broadcast, and in the same year, offered the first televised coverage of the Olympics. May 1950 saw the radio introduction of *The Archers*, the world's longest-running soap opera, and in 1953, coverage of Queen Elizabeth II's coronation was viewed by at least twenty million people across Europe.

The 1960s saw the introduction of color television and classic shows like *Doctor Who* and *Monty Python's Flying Circus*, and more classics followed in the next few decades, such as *EastEnders*, which debuted in 1985. In 1997, the BBC came to the internet, launching bbc.co.uk in December. Digital channels started the following year. Today, the BBC has local, regional, national, and world television channels and radio stations, and reaches tens of millions of viewers and listeners worldwide.

No news fact: On April 18, 1930, a BBC broadcaster announced, "Good evening, today is Good Friday. There is no news." This was followed by piano music. The original slow news day!

ALEXANDER FLEMING DISCOVERS PENICILLIN

Fleming (1881–1955) was a Scottish physician and researcher who would change the face of modern medicine and save millions of lives with his accidental discovery that a certain kind of mold spore can kill dangerous bacteria.

Fleming was born in Scotland, though much of his education came in England. In 1906, he completed his degree at St Mary's Medical School at London University. Initially, he was interested in going on to become a surgeon, but a curious twist of fate kept him at St Mary's, and thus destined for a career in research. Fleming was a fine marksman, and the captain of the rifle club at St Mary's was eager to keep him on the team, and so he convinced Fleming to stay on at the college!

During World War I, Fleming served in the Army Medical Corps, treating wounded soldiers. He noticed that many of his fellow soldiers died not from the wounds they received, but of the infections that set in, and there seemed to be nothing anyone could do about it. He used antiseptics during treatment, but these didn't always work, and in some cases, made things worse. Was there a substance that could neutralize bacterial growth?

After the war, he continued researching on this path, and in 1922, he discovered a substance called lysozyme, an enzyme with some antibacterial properties, though not enough to really stop harmful bacteria. But this discovery encouraged him to keep looking. In 1928, he was studying staphylococcal bacteria. One of the Petri dishes was uncovered and placed near an open window. It became contaminated with mold spores, which would normally ruin the experiment, but Fleming noticed that the staph bacteria near the mold was not growing; in fact, it was dying off.

He isolated the mold and learned that it was a part of the of the *Penicillium* genus. The mold itself wasn't killing the bacteria, but rather, a substance it produced, which Fleming deemed "mould juice," did the job. Further research confirmed that this substance, which he formally named penicillin, could kill an amazing number of what are known as Gram-positive bacteria, the dangerous kinds that cause all sorts of nasty infections, including scarlet fever, gonorrhea, pneumonia, meningitis, bubonic plague, and diphtheria. He published his findings in the *British Journal of Experimental Pathology* in 1929, but didn't go too much into the idea of penicillin being a potential cure-all. As a result, not many fellow scientists were interested. Further, Fleming wasn't sure how to manufacture "mould juice" in big enough amounts, or quickly enough for it to be practical.

In 1939, Howard Florey, Ernst Chain, and others at the Sir William Dunn School of Pathology at Oxford University delved further into the potential for penicillin as a life-saving drug. They worked out ways to grow the mold in large enough quantities to be useful. Their work coincided with the beginning of World War II, and ultimately, penicillin became a revolutionary treatment. During and after the war, work on manufacturing increased in Britain and the United States, and it would soon become a miracle drug used worldwide.

Fleming received numerous awards and honors, and later remarked: "When I woke up just after dawn on September 28, 1928, I certainly didn't plan to revolutionize all medicine by discovering the world's first antibiotic, or bacteria killer. But I suppose that was exactly what I did."

> **Artistic fact:** Fleming was interested in painting, and was a member of the Chelsea Art Club. In addition to watercolors, he also liked to paint with microbes, growing them to produce the different colors he needed! He enjoyed seeking out new strains of harmless bacteria to make use of the colors he could extract from them. While he was no great artist, his paintings were certainly original.

HITLER AND A NEW THREAT

One of the biggest mistakes that the winners of the Great War made was spending years trying to punish Germany for its role in the conflict. This policy wrecked Germany's economy, made it difficult for everyday people to get by, and made the German people as a whole increasingly angry and resentful. Of course, whenever there are troubled times, there are always those who try to take advantage of those problems and seize more power for themselves. And that's exactly what happened in Germany, with the rise of far right-wing thinking and extreme nationalism. It became easy to blame the country's woes on the allies, on minority populations, on neighboring countries, and others. And along with that blame came promises to return the nation to its former greatness. The Nazi party and Adolf Hitler set out to completely remake the German nation as they saw fit—unfortunately, their vision was that of a psychopath.

The Nazis didn't just arise overnight, of course; their many twisted and evil policies were the result of decades of other influences and philosophies that had been swirling around in Germany and elsewhere, and in the case of their antisemitism, centuries of persecution against the Jews. But even at the height of its power, the party was not nearly as popular as it claimed; people were often forced to go to Hitler's rallies to inflate attendance, for example.

But the Nazis were able to worm their way into power over a period of several years, and eventually, it was too late to do anything to get rid of them. The story of the rise of Nazi Germany is far too complex to tell here, but it became obvious to Britain and other nations as the 1930s progressed that this problem wasn't going away. A lot of people tried to convince themselves that if Hitler was just given what he wanted (at first, more territory for Germany), he would be satisfied. British Prime Minister Neville Chamberlain followed a policy of "appeasement," meaning that he tried to avoid another huge European war by simply allowing Hitler to take back lands in Czechoslovakia that were populated by Germans who Hitler claimed wanted to be under German rule. Chamberlain and French premier Edouard Daladier met with Hitler in September 1938, and agreed that Germany should take back this land. Czechoslovakia was never even consulted about it. Chamberlain returned to Britain, declaring to an assembled crowd: "I believe it is peace for our time."

Of course, it was no such thing, and soon Hitler's armies were on the march. Chamberlain, seeing that his policy had failed miserably, resigned in May 1940, to be replaced by Winston Churchill. Britain and Europe were about to be plunged into another terrible war that would tear the continent apart and reshape the world completely, once again.

> **Bluff calling fact:** Hitler had wanted to ignite a war with his move for Czechoslovakia, but Chamberlain and Daladier had forced him to accept a peaceful settlement for the time being. This only made Hitler angrier and more resentful, and guaranteed that he would strike out as soon as possible. Chamberlain thought he had achieved peace, but instead he set the stage for World War II.

EDWARD VIII ABDICATES THE THRONE TO MARRY WALLIS SIMPSON

The royal family had seen many monarchs come and go, and some of them brought more than a few controversies and scandals to their reigns. By comparison, the issues faced by Edward VIII might seem a bit unimportant, but at the time they were very serious. Edward was born in 1894, the son of George, Duke of York. George was the son of "Bertie," the Prince of Wales, who would go on to become King Edward VII, making this younger Edward Queen Victoria's great-grandson. So, he was directly in line for the throne, and it came to him when his father, King George V, died on January 20, 1936.

The problem was that the new Edward VIII wasn't cut out to be a king, and didn't even have all that much interest in it. He had served in World War I and discharged his royal duties, but he preferred tending to his garden and being with his friends. Still, fate thrust him into the spotlight when his father died. He might have been able to step up to the plate except for one big hurdle: he was desperately in love with an American socialite, Wallis Simpson, who was already married. This hadn't stopped them from beginning a love affair a few years earlier, even as the royal family looked upon the matter with horror. They despised "that woman," but assumed it would pass; it didn't.

After his father's death, Edward showed more interest in pursuing Simpson than in being king. Simpson's husband didn't seem to care, and was fine with divorcing her. The thing is, she'd already been divorced once before. Edward didn't care, but the Church of England certainly did. And since he was technically head of that church, he couldn't just go and have a civil ceremony without the church's participation. Desperate, Edward proposed that Simpson would take no royal titles if they married, but that wasn't accepted, either. Simpson did get her divorce in October 1936, but that didn't clear the path for her to marry Edward. The prime minister told him that there was no way the public or the church would accept his marriage to a twice-divorced "commoner" from America. It was either Wallis or the crown, and Edward made up his mind.

In his radio address to Britain on December 11, 1936, he said: "I have found it impossible to carry on the heavy burden of responsibility and to discharge the duties of king, as I would wish to do, without the help and support of the woman I love." He gave up his claim to the throne for love. He was never officially coronated and he married Wallis in France in June 1937. While technically known as the Duke and Duchess of Windsor, they had no real standing, and spent World War II in the Bahamas (with him acting as governor).

In later years, it seems that Simpson felt some resentment toward Edward, because so much anger had been focused on her, not only from the royal family, but also some in the British press and public. Some cynics even said that Edward didn't love her, and just married her as a way of getting out of having to become king, a burden he never wanted. But they stayed together until Edward died in 1972.

Twist of fate fact: Edward's insistence on giving up the crown paved the way for his younger brother, Albert, to inherit the throne. Upon doing so, he took the name George VI. It was George's daughter, Princess Elizabeth, who would ascend to the throne in 1952 as Queen Elizabeth II. She celebrated the seventieth year of her reign in June 2022, making her the longest-reigning monarch in British history. And it never would have happened without Edward's abdication.

THE BLITZ AND
THE BATTLE OF BRITAIN

After the Nazis completed their invasion of France in 1940, they began to eye Britain next. With only the narrow English Channel separating Britain from the continent, the threat loomed large. Germany was flying high on military victories, and given how easily France had fallen, Hitler thought that Britain would be willing to negotiate some kind of peace or surrender rather than deal with Germany's martial might.

The British, however, had no intention of surrendering, and were highly suspicious of entering into any peace deal coming from Germany. As a result, Britain had no interest in negotiating with Hitler, given how he had broken his promises so many times in the past. But Hitler was not going to be deterred. He wanted all of Europe under his control. And so, Germany started harassing and attacking Britain from the air, in preparation for a full-on invasion.

The Nazi government formulated what it called "Operation Sealion," its code name for invading Britain. It sought to use the Luftwaffe (the German air force) to destroy the British Royal Air Force, in order to

eliminate all resistance to its air attacks and demoralize the nation. And so began the Battle of Britain on July 10, 1940.

The Luftwaffe first targeted military and strategic sites along the south coast of Britain, such as airstrips and any spot where the RAF could launch its own planes. But Germany didn't count on such swift and furious resistance from the British, who were not about to have their country overrun by invaders—after all, no one had done it since William the Conqueror back in 1066! So, the Luftwaffe had to turn up the heat, hitting RAF airports farther afield, with the intent of grounding the Brits completely.

When this also failed to produce quick results, the Germans turned to bombing London. On August 24, the Luftwaffe bombed the East End. The next day, Britain retaliated by bombing Berlin. This only increased hostilities, as the Germans returned fire in a tit-for-tat exchange of bombings that trapped and killed innocent civilians on both sides. But the Brits strengthened their resolve and would not flinch despite the increasingly terrible bombings raining down on London. People hid in bomb shelters, sent their children away to the country for safety, and defiantly resisted the Blitz, as it became known.

As Germany became increasingly focused on terrorizing civilians, the RAF had time to regroup, repair damage done to its airstrips, and launch counterattacks. A little over two months after the beginning of Operation Sealion, on September 14, the Nazis realized that Britain would not be taken so easily, and put their plans to invade on hold. But the Blitz continued until May of 1941, and the suffering of Londoners went on.

Bombing fact: Up to 180,000 people took refuge in the London Underground tunnels every night during the worst of the Blitz, and this extensive network of tunnels deep underground no doubt saved countless lives.

WINSTON CHURCHILL

Churchill (1874-1965) is best known for his role in leading Britain through World War II, for standing up to Nazi Germany, and for his rousing speech delivered to the House of Commons in Parliament on June 4, 1940, which includes the famous section: "We shall fight in France, we shall fight on the seas and oceans, we shall fight with growing confidence and growing strength in the air, we shall defend our island, whatever the cost may be. We shall fight on the beaches, we shall fight on the landing grounds, we shall fight in the fields and in the streets, we shall fight in the hills; we shall never surrender."

But Churchill was already in his 60s by then. What had he done to reach that inflection point? He was born at Blenheim Palace in Oxfordshire into a wealthy, aristocratic family. His grandfather was the Duke of Marlborough and his mother came from American high society. But they were distant, and so young Winston was often rebellious and did poorly in school. Later, he would join the Royal Cavalry in 1895, and try to be transferred to dangerous places in the British Empire in order to make a name for himself. Churchill fought in Afghanistan, Sudan, and South Africa, narrowly escaping death in each spot.

In 1900, he was elected as a Conservative MP for the town of Oldham at the young age of 25, but given his political differences with the party, he defected to the Liberal Party in 1904. In truth, Churchill's positions were a mix of views held by each party. For instance, he supported unemployment insurance, but opposed strong labor unions and women's right to vote. His political career blossomed in the Edwardian years and beyond, and during World War I, he was the First Lord of the Admiralty (Minister for the Navy). But after a series of defeats, Churchill was demoted and then resigned, opting to join the Royal Scots Fusiliers and fight against the Germans at the Western Front. He returned after six months in the field and took up a place in government. After the war, he switched parties and joined

the Conservatives again. This flip-flopping earned him a bit of a reputation as someone not to be trusted.

In 1929, the Tories were defeated, and Churchill was out of government for the next eleven years. During this time, the so-called "wilderness years," he wrote extensively (newspaper articles and books) and gave speeches on a number of topics. Many people thought he was done with politics. But as Hitler grew in power, Churchill sounded the alarm, seeing the policy of appeasement as the disaster that it was. When the war began in September 1939, Neville Chamberlain appointed Churchill First Lord of the Admiralty, the post he'd held During World War I. After Chamberlain's resignation in May 1940, Churchill was chosen as prime minister, facing the weight and responsibility of protecting Britain from invasion and ruin. Within weeks, France surrendered and the British had to evacuate their 338,000 troops from Dunkirk on the north French coast. But Churchill's rousing speeches and firm intent to hold the line against invasion worked. The tide began to turn, culminating in D-Day and the Allied victory.

And yet, immediately after the war, in July 1945, the Conservatives lost the general election in a landslide to Labour, and Churchill found himself out of office once again. There were many reasons for the loss, including the usual dissatisfaction with any party in power for too long, a belief that post-war, a new vision was needed, and a further belief that Churchill had been the right man at the right time, but now needed to hand over the reins to someone else. In 1946, he made his famous speech about the dangers of the expanding Soviet Union, saying: "an iron curtain has descended across the Continent." Once again, he was in the wilderness, pointing out a serious danger that no one else took seriously. Churchill actually returned as prime minister in 1951, and sought to strengthen ties with the United States, as well as hold a summit meeting with the Soviets (which never happened). Despite some successes, he resigned in 1955, owing to health reasons. He had been unwell for some time, though he remained in government as an MP until 1964, and died the following year. He was given a state funeral, and will forever be remembered as the man who had guided Britain through its darkest hours.

> Smoky fact: Churchill absolutely loved cigars. He had a collection of thousands and would smoke eight to ten per day! Sometimes they were half-finished, but he still burned through an enormous number of them (pun intended). He also liked to start his day in bed reading the newspaper with a cigar and a glass of Scotch. Despite these unhealthy habits, he lived to be 90 years old!

FIELD MARSHAL MONTGOMERY

B ernard Law Montgomery, First Viscount Montgomery of Alamein (1887-1976) was better known by his (much easier to remember) nickname "Monty." He was one of the most capable and successful British military commanders of World War II, and his efforts helped turn the tide for the Allies in the early days when things were at their bleakest.

Montgomery had also fought in World War I, and was badly injured at the First Battle of Ypres (1914), when he was shot through the lung. A grave was even dug for him, but, always stubborn, he went on to make a full recovery. Clearly, Montgomery had resolve, but he had to wait until World War II to make his mark on history. Churchill appointed him as commander of the Eighth Army in the Western Desert of North Africa, where morale was low. Montgomery turned out to be just the man to rouse the troops. Soon, he and the army were squaring off against the very impressive German forces of General Erwin Rommel. Montgomery led his army to victory in the Second Battle of El Alamein in October and November 1942. This battle, fought in western Egypt, was a decisive victory for Britain and the Allies over the Axis forces of Germany and Italy, and signalled a turning point in the war.

Monty was then involved in planning and carrying out the Allied invasion of Sicily in 1943, which signaled the beginning of the end of Italy's involvement in the war, though there were disagreements with other generals, such as General George Patton of the United States, on how it should proceed. Some have suggested that Patton's arguments were caused more by jealousy than any issues with Montgomery's strategy. In any case, Monty was put in charge of the ground forces for the invasion of Normandy in June 1944, and again scored significant victories, though his plan for military action to the east of France (in the so-called Low Countries) failed. But he distinguished himself in the Battle of the Bulge, Hitler's last gambit to win the war. Troops under Monty's command advanced into Germany, and he accepted the surrender of the German forces in Northern Europe on May 4, 1945.

Later in life, Montgomery found himself embroiled in controversy, first for supporting South Africa's racist apartheid regime, and then for being against the legalization of homosexuality in Britain. His memoir, published in 1958, was full of criticisms for former colleagues, including Dwight D. Eisenhower, a distinguished World War II general himself, and by then president of the United States.

Monty was brilliant but difficult, and definitely full of himself. Once he was asked to name three great generals, and he answered, "The other two would be Alexander the Great and Napoleon." Churchill, as usual, summed the Monty experience up best, saying the great solider was "In defeat, unbeatable; in victory, unbearable."

Comedy fact: Montgomery might or might not have been the inspiration for one of the most famous comedy groups of all time, Monty Python (more on them later). In 1998, members of the group suggested that they got their name from his nickname as a way of gently mocking him, though later, Python member Eric Idle would say that the name came from a man at his local pub. Which is true? Well, why not both?

ALAN TURING AND THE CODE BREAKERS

Turing (1912-54) was a brilliant mathematician, computer scientist, and logician whose ground-breaking work has fortunately become more recognized in the last few decades—he's now seen as the father of modern computer science and the concept of Artificial Intelligence.

It's also fair to say that without him, Britain might well have lost the war to Nazi Germany, and yet his treatment by the government he served so well was nothing short of shameful.

After showing promise in chemistry and other sciences as a youth, Turing entered Cambridge University in 1931 to study mathematics, eventually being elected as a Fellow of King's College in 1935. One of his chief interests was probability theory; he also developed his so-called "Turing Machine," a prototype for the modern computer, during this time. He attended Princeton University for further study, but came back to Britain in 1938, just as the winds of war were beginning to stir. When war broke out, Turing went to work for the government at the Government Code and Cypher School at Bletchley Park, a Victorian Mansion southwest of Cambridge that became the center of British code-breaking efforts.

One of Turning's greatest successes came while taking on the cyphers generated by the German Enigma machine. This device generated codes for the deployment of submarines that patrolled the Atlantic and focused on sinking ships that were bringing supplies to Britain. But these codes had been unbreakable, giving the Germans a huge advantage, and bragging rights that they would never be broken. But Turing was able to crack the Enigma codes, allowing the Allies to determine submarine positions and take action to alter the courses of supply ships. Without this breakthrough, it's likely that the Allies wouldn't have been able to get sufficient supplies into Britain for the D-Day invasion.

Cracking Enigma was only one of Turing's many accomplishments, and he was appointed an officer of the Order of the British Empire (OBE) in 1946. But fate would soon take a cruel turn for him. Turing was a homosexual, and, in January 1952, he was found out. Homosexuality was still criminalized at the time, and Turing was stripped of his security clearances and forced to choose between imprisonment or chemical castration— injections of a drug which would reduce his sex drive. He chose the latter, an appalling and heart-breaking concession.

The ending of the story is even sadder. On June 8, 1954, Turing was found dead in his home, apparently the victim of cyanide poisoning. Next to him was a half-eaten apple. At first, the thought was that he had committed suicide by lacing the apple with cyanide, though it's possible that he accidentally inhaled cyanide from the electroplating machine in his spare room. While the official verdict was indeed suicide, Turing's mother believed that his death was accidental. In any case, the world of science and mathematics moved on, and Turing was largely forgotten.

That is, until a movement among British (and other) scientists to clear his name began in the 2000s. In 2009, then-Prime Minister Gordon Brown issued a statement after a petition for an official government apology. It said, in part: "While Turing was dealt with under the law of the time and we can't put the clock back, his treatment was of course utterly unfair and I am pleased to have the chance to say how deeply sorry I and we all are for what happened to him ... So on behalf of the British government, and all those who live freely thanks to Alan's work I am very proud to say: we're sorry, you deserved so much better."

Following this apology, his supporters launched a movement for a full pardon. After several debates in Parliament, the pardon was granted when Queen Elizabeth II signed it in 2014.

Pound fact: Turing has since been honored by having his image put on the back of the new £50 note, which was officially released on his birthday, June 23, in 2021. While it might be too little, too late, it is a fitting tribute to the man whose work helped the war turn in favor of the Allies.

THE WAR ON THE HOME FRONT

Thousands of people (especially children) were evacuated from London and other English cities during the war to protect them from bombing raids. This is, of course, the basis for C. S. Lewis's *The Lion, the Witch, and the Wardrobe*, where four siblings are sent away to live at a country manor house during the war, and discover a magical portal to an enchanted world. In real life, people had no such escapes, and living in the country didn't mean that they weren't affected by the war. Even in small towns and villages, residents worried about secret attacks, bombings, and spies infiltrating their communities. And, since these things really did happen, people were right to be concerned.

During this tense time it was common for locals to start training for what to do in case of emergencies such as bombings or fires, and how to help the wounded or defend their houses. Some homes took in evacuees from London, or even continental Europe. Those with large fields and gardens would offer to grow more food for both local residents and the displaced. German and Italian prisoners of war were made to work these fields in the absence of the British men who were away fighting.

Villages would set up night watches to scan the skies for enemy planes and sound the alarm if they were spotted. These night attacks were the greatest dangers that civilians, both in cities and beyond, had to face. If bombings commenced, many towns had plans for evacuation and even makeshift fire brigades to put out the flames. They would also provide gas masks in case of a gas attack.

While it was a terrifying time, it was also a time of incredible camaraderie and selflessness. People learned first aid and how to drive ambulances or other vehicles that could quickly spirit the wounded away from the chaos of a bombing attack. If certain homes in the village didn't have basements to shelter in during air raids, the locals would get together and dig new shelters. Some rural locations even planned for the worst; people dug ditches around their villages as a last line of defence should a German land invasion commence. Large country homes and estates were given over to be used by the military for housing, training, and as makeshift hospitals.

Something known as the Home Guard was even established for men who were not able to join the military. It allowed them to serve, train, and prepare in case of an invasion. It operated from 1940 to 1944 and was open to men aged 17 to 65 (and sometimes older).

Thousands of civilians signed up to serve at home. The number of volunteers who stepped up to help with the war effort was remarkable, in particular the number of women who contributed. By 1941, women were working as mechanics, engineers, fire engine drivers, and factory workers, among many other jobs that had been categorized as being exclusively for men. The Women's Land Army and the Women's Voluntary Service provided essential assistance to everyone and were crucial in helping Britain survive and resist German attacks. Ultimately, these massive efforts worked, and Britain was never invaded.

Royal volunteer fact: The future Queen Elizabeth II herself worked as a mechanic during the war.

D-DAY AND THE END OF THE WAR

C odenamed "Operation Overlord," D-Day was the largest military invasion ever planned, before or since ("Operation Neptune" referred to the invasion of the beaches itself). In the early hours of June 6, 1944, about 156,000 Allied troops crossed the English Channel (by water and air) to come ashore at five different beaches on the shores of Normandy in northern France: Utah and Omaha (where the Americans landed), and Gold, Juno, and Sword (where the British landed). Think of it like William the Conqueror's invasion, but in reverse, and much larger! Composed mainly of British, American, and Canadian forces, other nations, including France, Australia, Belgium, Greece, and Norway also provided troops. The goal was to begin the pushback against Nazi Germany and its occupation of France. By June 11, the Allies had landed over 326,000 troops. It would take almost a year to march to Germany, but D-Day was the beginning of the end of World War II in Europe.

Under the overall command of General Dwight D. Eisenhower, the plan was to surprise the Germans by landing in Normandy when Hitler was expecting an invasion farther east, near the mouth of the Seine River (he'd been fooled by agents posing as German sympathizers that this would be the location of the invasion, and had ordered his main army to establish position there). But Normandy was still not an easy target; it was lined with defensive walls, landmines, and concrete bunkers where gunmen were stationed.

The invasion came at a heavy cost in terms of life, but by the end of the first day, the Allies were securing the beaches, and would never be driven back. The Allies marched steadily through Normandy throughout the summer, even though the Germans had some advantages, such as better knowledge of the terrain. By August, the German forces were in retreat, and on August 25, Paris was liberated. After that, the march eastward slowed, but in December, a decisive battle near the Ardennes Forest in southern Belgium, known as the Battle of the Bulge, the Allies broke the German line once and for all. By the end of January 1945, the march to Berlin was all downhill—figuratively, at least.

At the same time, the Soviet army was closing in on Germany from the east, and Hitler knew it was over. Faced with destruction and inevitable defeat, he killed himself in a bunker in Berlin on April 30, 1945.

On May 8, Victory in Europe Day (V-E Day) was proclaimed, as celebrations broke out for the end of the war in Europe. While Japan continued the fight, for most of the British the conflict was over, and the long, painful process of healing could begin.

> Letter fact: The "D" in D-Day doesn't mean anything special, just "Day" (so, it's really "Day-Day"!). Since military operations can change starting points, this allows for the name to be used on any date. D-1 would be the day before, while D+1 would be the day after the event, and so on. In this case, June 11 would be D+5.

CHAPTER 9

MODERN BRITAIN

(1945-PRESENT)

AFTER THE WAR: WHAT NEXT?

I f World War I caused drastic changes in Britain, World War II was an even bigger jolt. This war altered societies and world civilization like no other, and Britain was no exception. In addition to India gaining its independence and the British Empire beginning to break apart, Britain itself went through some major social and cultural changes following the war. Here are just a few of the dramatic changes that transformed the country after the war ended.

The welfare state: As the war came to an end, people came to grips with the terrible toll it had taken. Sickness, and death abounded in wartime, and, as with World War I, many soldiers came back with injuries (physical and mental) that would never fully heal. There was a greater sense of needing to take better care of all of Britain's people, which led to the creation of both a national insurance program and the National Health Service (NHS). The insurance program guaranteed pensions, unemployment benefits, and more to help those in need, while the NHS provided for free health care for all British citizens. National health programs would eventually become a major part of several post-war European countries, and Britain's example would be adopted in many other nations around the world.

Nationalization: Clement Atlee's post-war Labour government was committed to reorganizing society into something more equitable, without the extremes of wealth and poverty that had plagued Britain for so many centuries. It was a noble goal for Labour, but one that was not always well thought out. Various industries were nationalized (about one-fifth of the economy), including the railways, aviation, coal, electricity, gas, and trucking. Some industries worked better under this model than others, becoming more efficient, while some seemed to get bogged down by bureaucracy. Conservatives condemned these changes, but they were often popular with everyday people.

Austerity and rationing: Britain was pretty badly banged up after the war. The nation was in bad economic shape from the financial outlay the war effort required, and had taken quite a bit of damage from the repeated bombings. Rebuilding the country was an absolute priority, and resources such as food had to continue to be rationed to make sure there was enough to go around. Obviously, this wasn't a popular policy, but most people reluctantly realized that it was going to be necessary for a while. Still, after a hard-won victory over Germany, many people were optimistic about the future, and the big changes that were sweeping the nation contributed to a sense that Britain could rebuild and become something better than it had been. The British "stiff upper lip," a commitment to enduring hardship, was put to the test even more in the years right after the war, and food rationing in particular contributed to Labour losing the general election in 1951.

Food fad fact: Despite food rationing, some new items became staples of the British diet during the war years and afterward. Among them were Spam (yes, the meat in a can, because it was easy to store and cheap to buy), Coca-Cola (an American import brought over by soldiers, which took Britain by storm), and instant coffee (even in a nation of tea drinkers!).

INDIAN INDEPENDENCE

India was the "crown jewel" of Britain's "possessions" during the Victorian era, but a growing desire for independence, both in India and in Britain, meant that India's freedom from British control was only a matter of time. Movements led by Mohandas (Mahatma) Gandhi and Jawaharlal Nehru continued to gain the support of the Indian people, and eventually, it was inevitable that India would again become an independent nation, though one still connected to Britain by trade and cultural bonds.

Unrest in India over colonization dates back to the Victorian era, but the movement for independence really gained momentum after the First World War. Gandhi, a devout Hindu, advocated for nonviolent resistance and peaceful protest, known as *Satyagraha*, (Sanskrit and Hindi for "holding onto truth"). He encouraged his followers (who would eventually number in the millions) to boycott British goods and refuse to pay taxes. At first, the British government was willing to make a handful of concessions in an attempt to appease the protestors, but these changes didn't go nearly far enough to satisfy Gandhi and his followers.

In 1942, as the Second World War raged, the desire for Indian independence gained even more prominence. The Indian National Congress supported the "Quit India Movement." Of course, the British weren't going to just leave their profitable colony that easily, and their response was to arrest thousands of protesters, including Gandhi himself.

While not all Indians supported Gandhi or his methods, they were united in their desire for freedom. Some petitioned the British directly for independence while others resorted to violent resistance, or supporting Britain's enemies during the war.

After the war, the move for independence became impossible to stop. Lord Louis Mountbatten, the Viceroy of India, knew that Britain had no choice but to assent to India's demands.

On July 18, 1947, the British government passed the Indian Independence Act, which was reluctantly accepted by the Congress. It created two different countries, India for Hindus, and Pakistan for Muslims, in an attempt to ease the tensions between the two religious groups. Pakistan was further divided into Pakistan and East Pakistan (which is now called Bangladesh). In the west, the regions of Punjab and Bengal were divided between the two countries. The creation of these two independent nations was called the Partition, and about fourteen million people were forced to migrate to new homes, a massive and chaotic relocation that wrought considerable damage—historians think that up to two million people died during the migration, which was the largest not caused by war or famine in history. Though these moves were meant to bring peace, riots and violence often broke out all along the new border and elsewhere, and tensions between the two countries continue to this day.

Politically, Mountbatten would continue as governor-general, but Nehru was appointed as India's first prime minister. In Pakistan, Muhammad Ali Jinnah became the new nation's governor-general and Liaquat Ali Khan was its first prime minster. The act also removed and repealed the title of "Emperor of India" that British monarchs had enjoyed since Prime Minister Disraeli's time.

British control of India officially came to an end on August 15, 1947, though by then, large numbers of Indian people were immigrating to Britain, bringing their unique cultures to enhance the nation. Indian curry, for example, is now seen as a quintessential British food, so popular has it become in the country!

Independence Day fact: India and Pakistan celebrate their independence on different days because Mountbatten attended Pakistan's celebration on August 14, and then traveled to Delhi for India's celebration on August 15.

THE BREAKUP OF
THE BRITISH EMPIRE

Britain's lack of resources after World War II meant that the country simply couldn't afford to hold onto its global empire anymore. London even contacted Washington, D.C. after the war to let President Harry Truman know that the British government didn't have the resources to help defend Greece and Turkey against possible aggression by the Soviet Union. Dean Acheson, Truman's secretary of state, said, "the British are finished," after reading the message. This, of course, opened the way for the United States to become dominant in world affairs.

Amazingly, at one time, tiny little Britain controlled fifty-seven colonies, territories, and protectorates around the world, ruling about 20 percent of the world's people and one-fourth of its land mass. Indeed, the "sun never set" on the British Empire, because it was always daytime in some colony. But the world had undergone massive changes, and this small island nation simply didn't have the sway that it once had. From the 1940s to the 1960s, more than twenty British territories and colonies became independent countries in one way or another. These included: India (partitioned to create Pakistan, a new Muslim-majority nation), Nigeria, Ghana, Israel/Palestine, Cyprus, Jamaica, and many others. Independence for other nations continued well into the 1980s, and when Britain returned Hong Kong to China on July 1, 1997, many, including Prince Charles, saw it as the true end of the British Empire.

Those that lived in these nations usually felt that independence was long overdue, as they saw the British Empire as little more than a colonizing presence, one that exploited their lands and showed no concern for the peoples that already lived in them. The exploitation of India and China (even though China was never under direct British rule) for wealth and profit were probably the most egregious examples of how ruthless British colonial practices could be, but there were no shortage of outrages around the world.

The Commonwealth, a collection of fifty-six former colonies, exists as a reminder of colonial days, though it is largely a symbolic and voluntary organization. There are now fifteen Commonwealth nations that continue to view the queen as the head of state, while being independent themselves. The largest of these are Canada, Australia, and New Zealand. One legacy of British rule is that English has become one of the most widely-spoken languages in the world, with something like 1.5 billion people using English as a first or second language. In addition, British engineering, architecture, and forms of government have all left their mark on the former colonies.

For many, though, the negatives of British rule far outweigh the positives, and they see the British as having destroyed their indigenous cultures and taken what they wanted with no consideration. While some older and more conservative Brits have lamented the loss of the colonies, most now see the dissolution as a good thing. No empire lasts forever, and the post-World War II world had no place for the Britain that had existed before.

Euro fact: When Britain joined the European Economic Community in 1973, it was another clear sign that the days of Empire were nearly over, as the EEC focused on partnership and trade within Europe as equals, with no nation dominating another. Britain's relationship with the continent has always been heated, and would only grow more so over time.

GEORGE ORWELL

ric Arthur Blair (1903-50) is much better known by his pen name "George Orwell." This nom de plume is so linked with his anti-totalitarian book *Nineteen Eighty-Four* that the very word "Orwellian" has entered the language as a synonym for the manipulations and crimes of authoritarian governments.

Born in Bengal, India, to an upper-class family (but one that had little money), Orwell was offered a place in England's prestigious Eton College, but after finishing his studies, he decided to return to Asia and become a police officer in Burma, living there from 1922 until 1927. He stayed in Britain for a short time after and then moved to Paris, before returning to Britain again in 1929. Orwell took up writing in earnest, penning novels, critical essays, political commentaries, and poetry. He had little success at first, and took a number of menial jobs to make a living. In his own words: "After my money came to an end I had several years of fairly severe poverty during which I was, among other things, a dishwasher, a private tutor and a teacher in cheap private schools."

Though he was essentially a democratic socialist, Orwell was also deeply critical of Stalin's communist regime (and the alleged intellectuals who supported it), as well as the infighting among those who opposed Franco's rising fascist regime in Spain. He joined a militia to fight against Franco during the Spanish Civil War, and was badly wounded in 1936.

His most celebrated works are his novels *Animal Farm* (1945) and *Nineteen Eighty-Four* (1949), both damning examinations of totalitarianism. *Animal Farm* mocks the Russian Revolution by telling a fable with animals and their societal struggles. The two pigs who struggle to lead the society are said to represent the two figures who battled to replace Lenin, Joseph Stalin and Leon Trotsky.

Nineteen Eighty-Four is a science fiction novel set in the future, where a dystopian society called Oceania is ruled by the enigmatic Big Brother. The main character, Winston Smith, lives in London, where he works for the Ministry of Truth. The Party has complete control over what citizens can do and think, and is even rewriting the language to create what it calls Newspeak. Even thinking about rebellion is illegal. Winston grows increasingly dissatisfied with his life and the world, and comes to believe that a high-ranking Party member named O'Brien is actually a member of the Brotherhood, a secret organization that wants to overthrow the Party.

Winston begins an affair with a woman named Julia, and the two are contacted by O'Brien, who meets with them and reveals that he is, indeed, a member of the Brotherhood, and wants them to join the resistance. He gives them Brotherhood literature. Winston and Julia are eventually arrested for possessing this material, and O'Brien reveals that he was a Party loyalist after all. Winston is tortured for months and eventually learns to feel nothing for Julia. He is released, and now loves Big Brother. Yes, it's as depressing as it sounds.

> Very wet fact: In addition to his health problems and injuries, Orwell once almost drowned. He was working on *Nineteen Eighty-Four* on the Scottish island of Jura, and in August 1947, attempted to sail in the dangerous Gulf of Corryvreckan with his nephew, Henry. There is a whirlpool in the water there, and at one point, it tore the motor off the boat. Orwell and his nephew attempted to row to shore, but the boat capsized and they were thrown overboard. Orwell managed to grab Henry and swim ashore, but being in the frigid water further damaged his already poor health. By December, Orwell was diagnosed with tuberculosis, and died of the disease in 1950.

GERALD GARDNER AND THE
REPEAL OF THE WITCHCRAFT LAW

Gardner (1884-1964) was the creator and initiator of the modern neo-pagan religion of Wicca, though he would claim that, at least in part, his ideas and practices came from a secret tradition that had survived in Britain since ancient times. In addition to birthing a modern religion, Gardner had the good fortune of living when Britain's Witchcraft Law of 1736 was repealed in 1951, just as he was really getting going.

Gardner's early life was unremarkable, being born into a well-to-do family in Lancashire. He spent much of his childhood in the Madeira archipelago off the coast of Portugal, the warm weather being seen as good for his asthma, in a way that cold, rainy Lancashire could never hope to be! As a young man, Gardner traveled widely and lived in Ceylon (Sri Lanka), Borneo, and Malaya, working for the British Civil Service and at other jobs. During this time, he developed an ongoing interest in magic, mysticism, esoteric ideas, and more. Upon returning to Britain in 1936, he and his wife Dorothea settled in Highcliffe on the south coast, between Bournemouth and the Isle of Wight.

In 1939, Gardner was introduced to a group called the New Forest Coven (New Forest is a national park near Highcliffe), a group of people practicing what they called traditional witchcraft, and was soon initiated into the group. He maintained that their spiritual beliefs were not novel, but from an ancient religion that had managed to survive into modern times.

In any case, Gardner stressed that witchcraft was never a form of Satanism, as portrayed by the Christian church, but rather centered on the worship of a Mother Goddess, or, in the case of what Wicca would become, a Goddess and a God. Gardner used the word *wica*, the Old English word for "witch," as the name for this new spiritual tradition, and he combined these pagan ideas with several practices that were currently in vogue in various magical and esoteric circles. He also met Aleister Crowley, and was influenced by "The Great Beast," writing several books about his new religion, including *High Magic's Aid* (1949), *Witchcraft Today* (1954), and *The Meaning of Witchcraft* (1959).

One problem Gardner faced was that the Witchcraft Act of 1736 was still in place. This was not a law against witchcraft, per se. It was an act that did away with the previous law's demands for the deaths of those accused of witchcraft, which had caused so much needless suffering in the seventeenth century. This new act redefined witchcraft practices as the stuff of charlatans and con artists, and set strict punishments for anyone claiming to have magical powers. It was an Enlightenment-era response to the superstition of the previous century. But it also meant that Gardner could face prosecution if authorities thought that he and his new religion were fraudulent. Happily for him, the repeal of the act in 1951 allowed him to continue developing and promoting his new spiritual path until his death in 1964.

> **Going their own (old) ways fact:** Though Gardner created Wicca, it wasn't long before various adherents began disagreeing about practices and breaking off to form their own sects (just as most religions do). Today, there might be up to 1.5 million Wiccans in the United States, and perhaps as many more worldwide. But given the secrecy of the religion (a measure often taken for the protection of its members), actual numbers are hard to calculate.

J. R. R. TOLKIEN

Tolkien (1892-1973) is without a doubt the most beloved fantasy author of all time. In his most famous books, *The Hobbit* and *The Lord of the Rings*, he created the wondrous world of Middle Earth, a fantastical land representing a kind of lost prehistory to our own world. The stories of its heroes, such as Bilbo, Frodo, Gandalf, and Aragorn, have enthralled generations of readers and spawned countless imitators. Indeed, the entire genre of epic fantasy can be said to be Tolkien's creation! But his motivation for writing these and other tales about Middle Earth was not to inspire legions of authors to follow in his footsteps.

Tolkien was an academic and a linguist, who adored languages (both living and dead) so much that he made up several of his own. Middle Earth was a place to put those languages, and he populated it with a whole cast of amazing characters and peoples, such as elves, dwarves, orcs, ents, and more. As a lover of myths, he wanted to create a new myth for Britain, to replace those from Anglo-Saxon times that didn't survive. In that, Tolkien succeeded beyond all expectations, as his books have a worldwide following.

Tolkien was born in South Africa, but his family relocated to England when he was 3, following his father's death. They settled in a village outside of Birmingham, whose surrounding countryside would become the inspiration for the Shire and other locations in his books. Tolkien was a bright young boy with a keen interest in languages, and began inventing his own as a teenager. By 1913, he was at Exeter College, Oxford, studying English language and literature. With the arrival of World War I, he enlisted (though his service was postponed until he finished his degree), knowing full well that he might not come back.

He was at the dreadful Battle of the Somme, and survived, but was then afflicted by a fever caused by lice and sent home in November

1916. He spent the rest of the war in various locations in England, and it was here that he first formulated some of the ideas for his masterpieces. In 1920, he obtained his first academic position, as Reader in English Language at the University of Leeds in Yorkshire. In 1925, he was at Oxford, as Rawlinson and Bosworth Professor of Anglo-Saxon at Pembroke College. He continued his work on Old English and language studies, as well as fleshing out his imaginary world, and writing a short little book called *The Hobbit* in the 1930s. By the end of the decade, he was sketching out a much larger project that he would work on for the next ten years, even as World War II raged. In 1945, he took up the position of Professor of English Language and Literature at Merton College, where he stayed until his retirement in 1959.

His magnum opus, *The Lord of the Rings*, was published in three volumes in 1954 and 1955 in Britain, and 1955 and 1956 in the US. Tolkien had wanted the story to be put out in one volume, but the publisher considered that too much of a financial risk. At one point, Tolkien worried that it might never be published at all. But the books soon proved to be massive hits, and began selling in large numbers, especially in the 1960s, when they became a counter-culture hit with youth on college campuses and elsewhere. Tolkien, as a fairly conservative Catholic, didn't know what to make of this, and despite the money that came from sales, he didn't like the idea of fame nearly as much. Instead, he wanted to continue with other projects, including finishing *The Silmarillion*, his great history of Middle Earth. He and his wife moved to Bournemouth on the south coast of England in 1968, but after she died in 1971, Tolkien returned to Oxford, where he died in 1973, *The Silmarillion* still unfinished. His son Christopher would finally finish the book and publish it in 1977.

Today, Tolkien is still arguably the most influential fantasy writer of all time, and his books have sold a combined total of over 600 million copies—quite a legacy, indeed!

Clapback fact: Tolkien's stories are strongly influenced by northern myths, and in the late 1930s, the Nazis were eager to use *The Hobbit* to promote their vile agenda. When a German publisher interested in doing a German language edition of the book wrote to Tolkien asking him if he could prove his "Aryan credentials," Tolkien wrote back that "Aryan" culture originated in India and parts of the Middle East. He added, "If I am to understand that you are enquiring whether I am of Jewish origin, I can only reply that I regret that I appear to have no ancestors of that gifted people." No doubt the publisher wasn't too happy with that response!

THE INKLINGS

B eginning in the 1930s and through to the late 1940s in Oxford, a remarkable group of men took shape. They were writers, scholars, university employees, and others, who would gather in small groups to discuss ideas, and more importantly, share their works-in-progress. Calling themselves the "Inklings," two of their number are among the most famous and beloved writers of the twentieth century: J. R. R. Tolkien and C. S. Lewis. The Inklings were not a formal club with rules, customs, and by-laws, but rather a gathering of colleagues and friends. Tolkien explained that the group name was a play on words. It was a group of "people with vague or half-formed ... ideas," and also, "those who dabble in ink."

The group had more formal meetings in C. S. Lewis' office at Magdalen College in Oxford on Thursday evenings, but they also met at various local pubs, most famously, at the Eagle and Child (affectionately known by the group as the "Bird and Baby"). This pub is still open, and on its walls are some photographs and other documents about the famous writers who used to gather in the one-time private parlor that is now open to the public. It's become something of a pilgrimage site for fans of Tolkien and Lewis.

At these meetings, the members would share the projects they were working on, read aloud portions of their work, and get feedback. But this wasn't a society just to make people feel good. Members had to be ready to accept criticism and suggestions for improvement. Another Inkling, Warren Lewis, said that criticism "for bad work—or even not-so-good work—was often brutally frank." Tolkien, of course, read from *The Lord of the Rings*, and he even dedicated the first edition of the book to the group. C. S. Lewis would read from many of his works (he wrote quite a bit more than just the *Narnia* books) and said of the group, "What I owe to them all is incalculable." Tolkien, for his part, doubted that he would have finished *The Lord of the Rings* without Lewis' support.

Group meetings fizzled out by the end of 1949, though the group didn't formally disband, they just stopped meeting. A new group of Inklings began meeting in 2006, not far from the Eagle and Child, to carry on the tradition of gathering with friends, fostering creative and community spirit, and critiquing each other's works—maybe not with such brutality, however!

> **Tragic coincidental fact:** C. S. Lewis died on November 22, 1963, the same day as President John F. Kennedy. Aldous Huxley (author of *Brave New World*) also died on the same day. As you might expect, news reports of both deaths in Britain were completely overshadowed by Kennedy's assassination.

QUEEN ELIZABETH II

Queen Elizabeth II is quite possibly the most famous woman in the world. She had the honor of being Britain's longest-reigning monarch, being Queen of the United Kingdom from 1952 until her death in September 2022. Shortly before her death, she celebrated the seventieth anniversary of her reign. The only other British monarchs who come close are:

- **Victoria (nineteenth and twentieth centuries):** 63 years

- **King George III (eighteenth and nineteenth centuries):** 59 years

- **James VI of Scotland / James I of England (sixteenth and seventeenth centuries:** 57 years combined on first the Scottish and then the English thrones

- **Henry III (thirteenth century):** 56 years

- **Edward III (fourteenth century):** 50 years

- **William I of Scotland (twelfth and thirteenth centuries):** just under 49 years

- **Llywelyn of Gwynedd (twelfth and thirteenth centuries):** 44-45 years

- **Elizabeth I (sixteenth and seventeenth centuries):** 44 years

Elizabeth II saw a remarkable number of changes during her reign and life, from serving on the home front in World War II to witnessing Britain's departure from the European Union. And while the British royals are only symbolic heads of state, the queen had a keen interest in politics and the governing of the country. The monarch still must give their "permission" for a newly elected Prime Minister to form his or her new government, for example.

Even into her 90s, the queen remained "on the job." British monarchs in general have not retired, but have seen the role as one that is life-long, ending only at death. Even mad King George III was still technically king during the last ten years of his life, when his son ruled as Prince Regent. And while there have long been calls to abolish the monarchy, Elizabeth was always popular in opinion polls, with about two-thirds of the British public saying that they want the monarchy to continue. The queen herself almost always ranked as the most popular member of the British royal family, and had approval ratings as high as 90 percent— not bad for someone who stayed at the top for seven decades!

And yet, she never did a formal press interview, and carefully managed her public image and who was allowed access to her. Still, Elizabeth's dignified manner and keeping of traditions, such as her annual Christmas day speech to the nation, endeared her to millions. As with those long-reigning monarchs who came before her, it will be difficult to imagine Britain and the world without her.

Travel fact: The queen didn't have a passport. During her life, the royal website stated: "As a British passport is issued in the name of Her Majesty, it is unnecessary for the Queen to possess one." Honestly, who would she have needed to show it to, anyway?

ROGER BANNISTER, THE "MIRACLE MILE," AND THE WORLD RECORD

Bannister (1929-2018) was an English neurologist, and Master of Pembroke College in Oxford. He wrote more than eighty papers about topics such as the autonomic nervous system and cardiovascular health. Oh, and one other thing. On May 6, 1954, he became the first documented man to run a mile in under 4 minutes, at the age of 25. He'd been pursuing this goal for a few years, after setting a British record in the 1,500 metres at the Helsinki Olympics (though he missed out on winning a medal). Two years later, at Iffley Road Track in Oxford, Bannister made history.

Bannister was born into a working-class family, but became interested in pursuing a career in medicine early on, while at the same time competing in various track and field events. He developed an interest in cross-country running, and shorter events, such as the 880-yard. He was selected as a possible participant in the 1948 Olympics, but decided not to compete, as he didn't feel he was ready. But inspired by what he saw in those Olympics, Bannister resolved to train hard enough to be ready for 1952. After his success at those Games, he nevertheless thought about giving up running completely, but decided that he would set himself a new goal: running a mile in under 4 minutes.

At Oxford on May 2, 1953, he ran a 4:03.6, which he would later say made him realize "that the four-minute mile was not out of reach." A month later, he finished the mile in 4:02. He was getting closer ...

The event where he would make history was an annual run between the Amateur Athletic Association (which Bannister represented) and Oxford University on May 6, 1954. It was a close race, but according to the BBC, "Just over 200 yards from the finish, Bannister took the lead with a final burst of energy. He sprinted to the line in record time and fell exhausted into the arms of a friend." When everyone realized what had happened, the crowd roared in approval and excitement. History had been made.

Bannister's duck under the mark was shockingly close; he ran the mile in 3:59.4—but the important thing was that he did it at all! He was destined not to hold the record for long, though. Just forty-six days later, Bannister's running rival, the Australian John Landy, broke the record in Turku, Finland, with a time of 3:57.9. In later years, a false story has circulated that at the time, most sports commentators thought that a mile in less than 4 minutes was impossible, but Bannister himself said that this wasn't true; there was no general feeling about this that either he or Landy had to fight against.

Since then, the record has been broken several times, and will no doubt continue to be so, as new generations of runners shave miliseconds off every track and field record every few years or so.

> **Miraculous fact:** An even greater fate awaited both Bannister and Landy in August of 1954, when they faced off against each other at the British Empire and Commonwealth Games at the Vancouver Exhibition. Landy led for most of the race, but Bannister overtook him on the last turn to win. The amazing thing was that both men finished the mile in under 4 minutes! The race was dubbed "The Miracle Mile," though Landy's record time from June wasn't bested by either runner.

CLAUDIA JONES AND THE NOTTING HILL CARNIVAL

Born Claudia Cumberbatch in Trinidad, Jones (1915-64) and her family moved to Harlem in New York in 1924. Growing up in poverty, Jones was 10 when her mother died, and she contracted tuberculosis at the age of 17. The disease damaged her lungs and she never fully recovered, spending several extended stints in hospitals during the remainder of her life. These early experiences made Jones acutely aware of the connections between poverty, disease, racism, and lack of opportunity, which led her to join the Young Communist League (YCL), after hearing about their defense of the Scottsboro boys, nine young African American men who were accused of raping two white women in Alabama. Despite no evidence that the crimes ever happened, the nine were railroaded by a racist system, convicted, and sentenced to death, though most of these sentences were overturned or commuted on appeal.

Jones became increasingly involved in activism and the YCL's ongoing work, which began to attract the attention of those in power, particularly those who were not thrilled with the idea of a Communist Party in the United States. With Senator Joseph McCarthy's investigation into American communists getting underway, Jones found herself in the crosshairs. Eventually arrested, she was sentenced to be deported back to Trinidad in 1950 (she had never become an American citizen). While waiting for this, she suffered a heart attack in 1951, and faced further trials for "un-American activities," based on her writings in activist journals.

When the governor of Trinidad refused to allow Jones to re-enter the country, fearing she would cause problems, Britain offered her asylum.

She relocated to London at the end of 1955, and immediately returned to her life's work, advocating for black citizens, improving social and living conditions, and promoting racial equality. In 1958, she founded and edited the *West Indian Gazette and Afro-Asian Caribbean News*, a major source of reporting for the growing Afro-Caribbean community in London. She later wrote that the newspaper was intended to raise "the awareness, socially and politically, of West Indians, Afro-Asians and their friends. Its editorial stand is for a united, independent West Indies, full economic, social and political equality and respect for human dignity for West Indians and Afro-Asians in Britain."

At the end of summer in 1958, following a series of race riots in Notting Hill, a neighborhood in north London, Jones met with prominent members and leaders of various black communities to discuss what could be done. One idea was to hold a carnival in celebration of these various cultures, and Jones secured permission to use St Pancras Town Hall for an indoor event that was held in January 1959, and televised by the BBC. Featuring a dance troupe and prominent jazz musicians, such as Cleo Laine, it was the first of a successful series of gatherings that, by the mid-1960s, morphed into a proper outdoor festival.

Jones' health problems finally caught up with her, and she died of another heart attack on Christmas Eve 1964. Though she was not a British citizen, she will forever be remembered as the "Mother of the Notting Hill Carnival."

Fun festival fact: The annual outdoor carnival, which now takes place in August, attracts about two-and-a-half-million visitors each year, making it one of the largest street festivals in the world.

1960s BRITISH POP CULTURE

"The Swinging Sixties" descended on Britain—London especially—during the middle of the decade. This was a new day and age defined by a new youth culture, with radical changes in fashion, social attitudes, entertainment, and much more ushered in within a period of just a few years. It was a great time for British youth to be alive, especially in light of the sacrifices made during the previous three decades, when depression and war severely affected life in the country. After so much giving up, there was finally a feeling of positivity in the air, and a new generation was ready to revel in it.

The popular model and actress Twiggy became an icon of the era, appearing on the covers of all the main fashion magazines (though she would later claim that she hated how she looked at the time). Women in the scene tended to be more visible and equal. TV shows like *The Avengers* (which ran from 1961-1969, and, no, it has nothing to do with Marvel's superheroes) and *The Prisoner* (1967) captured the stylish look and feel of the time, and are still beloved today.

The modern world had arrived, and the new "mod" subculture was there to revel in it. Originating in late 1950s London, "modernists" listened to the jazz of Miles Davis and Charlie Parker (among other genres of music, such as soul and R&B) and wore distinct fashions, often Italian-influenced. Scooters, such as the Italian Vespa, were the trendy way of getting around. As the Sixties progressed, various rock bands and other entertainers adopted the mod look, and the scene expanded beyond its original scope. Some bands such as The Who, The Kinks, and the Rolling Stones had large mod followings, and amphetamine use was common at mod shows, giving users the energy to dance the night away.

Mods were often in conflict with rockers, who wore leather jackets, rode motorcycles, and listened to classic rock 'n' roll music. Newspapers and politicians warned that the clash between the two groups would ultimately bring ruin to Britain. Of course, this never happened.

The mod subculture quickly spread beyond Britain and soon was all the rage in the United States, often as a look adopted by promising new bands. With the rise of the hippies and psychedelic music, mod at first blended with them, but was eventually overtaken by these newer movements, which themselves were absorbed not long after—as you can see, it was a time of radical and rapid change!

> Shagadelic fact: The popular *Austin Powers* films were a comedy revival of the look and feel of London's Swinging Sixties. Yeah, baby!

THE BRITISH INVASION, AT HOME AND ABROAD

B eginning in the 1960s, a new British invasion of America was about to take place. But this one wasn't led by generals commanding armies of redcoats. Instead, this was a cultural invasion, mostly in music, but also in film and fashion. Of course, the most famous and influential of these artists were the Beatles (more on these little-known chaps in the next entry), but dozens of other artists made a huge impact on American music and culture. While the heyday of this cultural invasion was the 1960s, British bands continued to be popular in the United States well into the 1970s and beyond, and in some cases enjoyed more success in America than in their home country.

Rock 'n' roll was an American invention born from the blues, of course, but the classic sound of the 1950s was waning in popularity, and fans were eager for something different. A whole new generation of British bands was starting to experiment with new sounds, still rock and blues-based, but with other elements (and this would only get more extreme as the decade progressed). Some bands were adding influences from American black musicians that were not popular in the United States, owing to societal racism, but once repackaged and presented by white British musicians, they found a new audience.

The sheer number of British bands that found a place in the American charts was astonishing, as they practically ruled the pop music world in the '60s and early '70s. The Rolling Stones, The Who, Kinks, Yardbirds, Animals, and many more were all essential in creating the 1960s "British" sound.

As the '60s turned into the '70s, heavy rock bands like Deep Purple, Black Sabbath, Motörhead, and Led Zeppelin led the charge to a brave new sound that thrilled listeners, and created the new genre of heavy metal.

Other bands were more experimental, bringing in the trippy new sounds of progressive rock, which grew out of the psychedelic rock genre, along with classical and jazz influences. Bands like King Crimson, Pink Floyd, Yes, Genesis (before they became pop sensations in the '80s), Jethro Tull (prog with a hefty dose of folk rock), and Emerson, Lake, and Palmer wowed the world with classically-trained musicians performing twenty-minute symphonic rock pieces about floating mountains, astral adventures, elves, and the like. These bands routinely sold out major venues, and grew so popular that for a time their influence seemed limitless—for instance: prog virtuoso keyboardist Rick Wakeman once staged a musical version of the King Arthur legends ... on ice!

New folk forms also found a place in the hearts of many, with groups such as Steeleye Span, Pentangle, the Incredible String Band, Fairport Convention, and Lindisfarne gave listeners a new spin on old favorites, while also creating their own new folk songs. I imagine Vaughan Williams and his folk-collecting friends (see page 355) would have approved?

By the mid-1970s, some rock fans wanted shorter and simpler songs that also reflected their displeasure with the state of the world. They craved music that was more aggressive and angry, and punk rock arrived to answer this call, with bands like the Sex Pistols, The Damned, the Buzzcocks, and The Clash all leading the charge.

> **British impact fact:** While American rock and pop music was also crucial throughout these years (Motown, for example), British artists dominated the charts. They gave the world an enormous amount of popular music of almost every style you can think of between the 1960s and 1980s, music that blew people away then and now, and still retains its immense popularity.

THE BEATLES AND BEATLEMANIA

Without a doubt, the Beatles changed the landscape of pop and rock music forever, to where it's hard to even imagine a world without their music. But they weren't so popular when they started, and had some trouble attracting any interest from record labels. The most famous "no thanks" they received came from the Decca label, who said that they didn't like the band's sound and that "groups of guitars" were on the way out, anyway (there are several versions of this quote, but it seems to be true!). This might be the biggest mistake in the history of the music industry!

The Beatles weren't always known as the Beatles, either. For a while in the early days, they were "Johnny and the Moondogs." They were also once called the "Quarrymen" and "The Silver Beetles." Music might have been quite different if we were listening to the song "Yesterday" by Johnny and the Moondogs!

America's interest in the Beatles started to grow at the end of 1963, when newspaper articles about the Fab Four began to appear. At the time, Americans were still in shock over the assassination of President John F. Kennedy in November, and the nation was desperate for some good news to cheer it up. The Beatles seemed like a great new band with a lot of potential appeal, and radio station WWDC (in Washington, D.C.) played their single, "I Want to Hold Your Hand." The response was overwhelming. Record stores in the area were inundated with requests for it, even though none had it in stock. Other radio stations picked up the single and got similar responses, so Capitol Records (the American distributor) decided to release the single three weeks early, on December 26. By January, the song was at the top of every hit list. Even news stalwart Walter Cronkite said, "The British Invasion this time goes by the code name Beatlemania."

Two days later, on February 9, the Beatles appeared on the Ed Sullivan show, and were seen by something like 45 percent of all television viewers in the country, or seventy-three million people! And a good number of them didn't even realize the importance of what they were watching.

While many parents objected to the mop-haired boys from Liverpool and their suggestive onstage gyrations, there was no denying their appeal to younger fans, a charm that wouldn't go away for the rest of the decade, even as the band went in wildly different directions and experimented with all of the new sounds that the 1960s allowed

for. By 1965, their "teeny bopper" era was over, and they committed themselves to writing more complex songs with deeper content, but this didn't dissuade fans from enjoying their music. Even after they stopped playing live in 1966, they would have numerous Number 1 hits until they broke up in 1970. In less than a decade, the Beatles changed popular music forever, a band that transcends everything that came before, and has followed.

Film name fact: The band's first movie, *A Hard Day's Night*, was originally going to be titled *Beatlemania*. It was difficult to film because the group was so popular that outdoor takes were hard to complete, given the number of fans that would show up at filming sites, hoping for a glimpse of the Fab Four. Beatlemania indeed!

ENGLAND WINS THE WORLD CUP

On July 30, 1966, at Wembley Stadium in London, in front of a crowd consisting of home fans and the queen herself, England beat West Germany, 4-2, in extra time to win the prized Jules Rimet Trophy, now known as the FIFA World Cup Trophy. Nearly 97,000 people were in attendance at the stadium, while something like 32.3 million viewers in Britain watched the match on television. It was a glorious victory for England, and one that they sadly have not repeated. So, one has to wonder, what allowed this particular group to succeed?

England, as hosts of the World Cup that year, fielded a team that was strong throughout the tournament, but not exceptional. They held their own, but as teams were eliminated along the way, most commentators thought that no one team looked dominant, and none of the favorites looked all that convincing. England beat Argentina 1-0 to win a place in the quarterfinals, but the game was not without controversy, as there were eruptions of violence. The same happened in the game of West Germany against Uruguay (which West Germany won 4-1), where Uruguay's captain was sent off for kicking a referee! In the semifinals, West Germany defeated Russia, while England sent Portugal packing. That set the stage for the final.

The British press was not overly confident in England's chances of victory, even though England had a strong history against Germany. In the match itself, the ugliness of some of the other games was set aside, and the players on both sides stepped up. England led 2-1 until a goal by the German team near the end of the game tied it up at 2-2, forcing the match into extra time. It could have gone either way, but England stepped up again and scored two additional goals (though one of these was controversial, since the ball may or may not have crossed the line into the goal), to cement their victory in front of the home crowd.

The German team was gracious in defeat and was welcomed back at home as heroes, unlike the Italians, who had returned home to boos and jeers! The England team was left to bask in the glory of something that no one had thought would be possible. They were honored by the queen and the nation rejoiced with them. England fans are still anxiously waiting for the men to do it again—but they did get to watch the women's team deliver a major victory in 2022 (see page 466).

> **Profane fact:** The Swiss referee Gottfried Dienst had observed the disgraceful behavior during some of the earlier matches, and banned the use of foul language in the final match, saying that he "knew all the German swear words and more English ones than many people think."

NORTHERN IRELAND: THE TROUBLES AND THE IRA

The Troubles (Irish: *Na Trioblóidí*) refers to a period between about 1968 and 1998, when a conflict raged in Northern Ireland between the Protestant Unionists (who wanted the region to remain a part of the United Kingdom) and the Catholic Nationalists, who wanted Northern Ireland to join the rest of the Irish Republic and be independent of British control. However, the conflict actually dates back centuries, because England and then Britain had been meddling in Irish affairs since the Middle Ages. Remember how medieval kings would style themselves as "Lord of Ireland"? And how English settlers moved in? And how Queen Elizabeth I and then Oliver Cromwell tried to quell Irish uprisings and crush the country's spirit under enforced foreign rule? By the seventeenth century, there were vast British holdings in Ulster, in northeast Ireland, and eventually, there were more British Protestants living in some areas than Irish Catholics. These Brits generally made no attempt to assimilate into Irish culture, and held strongly to their Protestant faith. In 1801, Britain passed the Act of Union, which formally incorporated Ireland into the United Kingdom of Great Britain and Ireland. But of course, this only spurred independence movements to spring up.

In 1916, the British army quelled an uprising in Dublin. In 1919, a formal war of independence began, when the Irish Republican Army (IRA) began carrying out guerrilla warfare against the occupying British troops. By 1921, the rebels had won significant victories, and it was apparent that Ireland would become independent—though not all of it. According to the terms of the Anglo-Irish Treaty of December 1921, Northern Ireland, with its large Protestant majority, was given the option of remaining under British administration, and it assented to this. The rest of Ireland became the Irish Free State, but was still a part of the British Empire. It only became completely independent in 1949.

For Catholics and Irish republicans in Northern Ireland, however, life could be a terrible struggle. They routinely complained of discrimination and being treated like second-class citizens in their own country, a land that they saw as still being occupied by a colonial power. Tensions grew and by the late 1960s, things were at a boiling point. Various groups of British loyalists held annual marches, often through Catholic areas (basically rubbing their noses in it), and in 1969, one such march led to rioting. It was enough for the British army to be sent in to try to restore order. This led to the growth of paramilitary groups on both sides, the IRA and the Provisional IRA on the Catholic side and the Ulster Defence Association (UDA) and Ulster Volunteer Force (UVF) on the Protestant side. The British army began to build "peace walls" to separate communities, but both groups began carrying out terrorist attacks on each other's communities.

The Loyalists focused their violence in Northern Ireland itself (and sometimes in Dublin), while the Provisional IRA began staging bombings in England. The 1970s through the 1990s would be a period of high tension, as there were always fears of a phone call warning of an imminent bombing somewhere. Despite the violence, negotiations for peace continued, and in 1993, Britain and Ireland signed the Downing Street Declaration, which stated that the troubles would have to be sorted out by the Irish themselves. The agreement was approved by the Provisional IRA's political party, Sinn Féin, and paramilitary groups on both sides agreed to a ceasefire in 1997. On April 10, 1998, the Good Friday Agreement was signed by all parties after months of negotiations. It created a plan for power-sharing going forward, and approved by voters in both the Republic of Ireland and Northern Ireland, bringing an end to The Troubles—for now.

Trauma fact: The effect of the decades of violence in Northern Ireland was particularly hard on young people, who showed stress responses similar to those in war zones all around the world. While the conflict has ended (again, for now), the lasting psychological damage might well continue for another generation or more.

MONTY PYTHON

The big social changes in the 1960s and '70s meant big changes in the entertainment industry. And perhaps the most enduring comic change of all came from the legendary *Monty Python's Flying Circus*. Though the show only ran for four seasons (called series in Britain) and a total of forty-five episodes, it changed comedy forever with its blend of surreal and bizarre humor, clever skits, brilliant acting, and memorable recurring characters.

Created by Graham Chapman, John Cleese, Michael Palin, Terry Gilliam, Eric Idle, and Terry Jones, *Flying Circus* was no ordinary skit show, but something entirely new, with bizarre routines often linked by the weird and whimsical animations of Terry Gilliam (the sole Yank in the bunch). Characters such as the Colonel, the Nude Organist, the "It's" Man, the Gumbys, the stomping Cupid's Foot (accompanied by a fart noise), and many more are now iconic and have been making millions laugh for more than fifty years.

The team would go on to create three original movies: *Monty Python and the Holy Grail* (1975), *Life of Brian* (1979), and *The Meaning of Life* (1983), of which *Holy Grail* is the most popular. The film's splendidly ridiculous retelling of the King Arthur legend is known for some of the most famous characters and scenes in comic film history, from the clacking coconuts that stand in for horse's hooves to the "loony" Black Knight, to Brave Sir Robin, to the Knights who say "Ni," and the deadly "no ordinary rabbit."

During the 1960s, back BP (Before Python), Jones and Palin attended Oxford, while Idle, Cleese, and Chapman were at Cambridge. But they set aside the chance to be mortal enemies at rival universities and even brought in a bloody American (Gilliam) to help them create their wacky new show that they would never completely escape. The group wanted to do something unlike anything else out there, and they managed to succeed beyond their wildest dreams.

The name *Monty Python's Flying Circus* doesn't really mean anything, by the way. The "Flying Circus" bit seems to have been thought up first, and Eric Idle may or may not have come up with the "Monty Python" bit. The story changes from time to time, as the tale of a nonsensical name for a nonsensical show should! The famous theme song (chosen by Gilliam) was John Philip Sousa's "The Liberty Bell," a military march from 1893. While it is still used in many "official" political and military events, it will forever conjure images of *Python*.

These six weirdos continued to work with each other on and off until the early 1980s, and then went their separate ways, doing occasional reunions, up to their (probably) final live shows in 2014. But their influence on British comedy and beyond is incalculable, to where their influence on comedy has been compared to the Beatles' influence on music.

> **Slightly controversial (though clearly joking) fact:** The second Python film, the religious satire *Life of Brian*, seems to have come about after Eric Idle, asked what the troupe's next movie would be after *Holy Grail*, joked, "Jesus Christ: Lust for Glory."

MARGARET THATCHER

Thatcher (1925-2013) was Britain's first female prime minister, and a very controversial one, to put it mildly! During her leadership between 1979 and 1990 (she was the longest-serving prime minister of the twentieth century), she won both admiration and scorn for her conservative policies. A Soviet army newspaper gave her the nickname "The Iron Lady," and she loved it. She was an ally of U.S. President Ronald Reagan, and both brought their specific brands of conservatism to their nations. Thatcher was able to diminish the power of trade unions, cut spending on various social programs, and oversee the privatization of certain industries, all in the name of fiscal responsibility. But after winning three elections, many of her policies became unpopular, and infighting in the Conservative Party brought an end to her time as prime minister.

Thatcher was born in Grantham and studied chemistry at Oxford, though she later switched professions and trained as a barrister. She was elected as an MP in 1959, and her political career took off from there; she was appointed as Secretary of State for Education and Science by Tory Prime Minister Edward Heath, during his time at the helm between 1970 and 1974. But Thatcher had bigger ambitions and defeated Heath in a leadership contest in 1975, becoming the leader of the Conservative Party. When the party won the General Election of 1979, she became Prime Minister.

She immediately introduced policies to try to combat inflation and what she saw as runaway government spending and interference. She advocated deregulation in the financial industry and angered unions with her unwavering stance against them. But her popularity waned as quickly as it had risen, until 1982, and the Falklands War (see page 451). With a British victory in the Falklands and an economy on the upswing, Thatcher's popularity shot back up, and she easily won the 1983 election.

During a coal miners' general strike by the National Union of Mineworkers (NUM) from 1984 to 1985, she used a number of strategies to break the strikers' resolve. Ultimately the strike was declared illegal because of balloting issues, and the NUM were forced to back down. Thatcher succeeded in not only weakening the NUM during her administration, but other trade unions, too. Her tough-as-nails stance carried her to a third election victory, but by the late '80s, cracks in her seeming invincible armor were starting to show. She gave her support to the Community Charge, a flat-rate tax (poll tax) on every adult, set by their local councils. It was implemented first in Scotland in 1989 and then in England and Wales in 1990. Right from the beginning, it was deeply unpopular all along the political spectrum, and contributed to Thatcher's waning influence. Thatcher also leaned toward the so-called "Eurosceptic" line of thinking that was opposed to closer ties with continental Europe. Finding herself increasingly at odds with her own party, its prominent members convinced her to resign in November 1990, to be replaced by John Major.

In the years after her resignation, Thatcher wrote books and remained active in political life, though a series of small strokes and other health problems plagued her for the last ten years of her life. She died on April 8, 2013, a divisive force to the last moment of her life.

> Actor fact: In the run-up to the 1979 election, one of Thatcher's advisors worried that she didn't sound "authoritative" enough. By chance, he happened to meet the great Shakespearean actor, Sir Laurence Olivier, on a train, who recommended his own voice coach. She learned from this coach how to sound calmer and more imposing, and would use these voice techniques to great effect throughout her years as prime minister.

THE WEDDING OF PRINCE CHARLES AND LADY DIANA SPENCER

It was the fairy tale wedding of the year, of the decade, and maybe of the century, if you believed the news coverage. On July 29, 1981, Prince Charles married Lady Diana Spencer at St Paul's Cathedral in London, with all the pomp and ceremony one would expect of such a momentous occasion. The British royal family was enjoying a wave of high popularity (from which they would plunge over the next decade), and the festivities were masterfully set up to take advantage of that fact, with the government even declaring the day a public holiday.

Up to two million people lined the streets of London to wish the newlyweds well, and at least twenty-eight million people in Britain watched the wedding on television. Worldwide, about 750 million tuned in to see the joyous event. Though the wedding itself took place at 11:00 am, the BBC was on it like a major sporting event, offering its own television coverage beginning early in the morning for those who couldn't get enough of the soon-to-be royal couple. Television and radio commentaries covered everything from the horse-drawn carriages that transported the royal family and the ceremony itself to the public mood on the streets and the history of the abbey—anything to fill the time and keep those eyeballs on the screen!

Over 3,500 guests were present at the actual ceremony, including members of various aristocratic families, heads of state, and church officials. In addition, over 4,000 police officers and more than 2,000 military personnel were on hand to provide security.

During the ceremony, there were a few hiccups and controversies. Diana got the order of Charles's names wrong; the correct order is Charles Philip Arthur George, in case you're wondering, and Diana said Philip too early. In addition, at the couple's request, Diana did not promise to "obey" Charles, which might seem a minor change and no big deal these days, but it was quite controversial at the time.

After the ceremony, the couple spent a few nights in Hampshire before embarking on a Mediterranean cruise. But despite their outward happy appearance, it was later revealed that there were problems and tensions almost right from the start. Charles still had a great affection for a former lover, Camilla Parker Bowles. Diana even found photographs of Camilla that had fallen out of Charles' diary, and she learned that he still wore cufflinks that Camilla had given him. While they presented to the world as a happy couple with a storybook love, Diana was increasingly unhappy with the restrictions of her royal role and her marriage, which she later termed being in a relationship with both Charles and Camilla. She also admitted to suffering from depression and other mental health issues during this period.

The royal couple formally separated in 1992, but continued with their royal duties. Diana in particular was active following the break, championing causes dedicated to caring for AIDS patients, as well as being an activist for those wounded by landmines, and worked to get landmines removed from former war zones. In August 1996, at the urging of the queen, they agreed to a divorce. Diana would remain Princess of Wales, but would relinquish any claim to the British throne. A year later, she would die in an automobile accident in Paris.

> Cake fact: In 2014, a slice of one of the cakes served at the wedding party sold in its original box at an auction for $1,375. No word on whether the buyer actually tried to eat it.

TABLOID NEWSPAPERS

There are bad newspapers, there are terrible newspapers, and then there's the British tabloids, which are almost legendary for their awfulness, filled with exaggerations if not outright lies, always seeking out celebrity and political scandals (and occasionally inventing them if they can't find the dirt they want), and dozens of other journalistic offenses. Many people condemn them for their irresponsibility, though even more can't wait to devour the next day's issue and get their fill of the strangely satisfying trash. It's thought that about twice as many copies of tabloids are sold each day in Britain compared to the more mainstream offerings. And while their influence has weakened a bit in recent years, tabloids remain an essential part of British culture.

The Daily Mail, which is still published, began in 1896 as a cheap newspaper that anyone could afford. It was known as a tabloid, because it was smaller than the so-called broadsheets, the "respectable" papers such as the *Times* and the *Guardian*. Even then, the outlet's focus was on scandals, murders, celebrity and royal news, titillation, and other topics deemed not suitable for the bigger papers, which focused on boring topics such as the economy, stocks, mainstream politics, and so on. In this way, the tabloids were not unlike the Victorian Penny Dreadfuls (see page 333), and could even be seen as an evolution of those publications. Other tabloids soon sprung up to meet the growing demand, and over the course of the twentieth century, several more waxed and waned with the times. *The Daily Mail*, *The Sun* (with its famous daily "Page Three" photo of a topless young woman), the *Daily Express*, and *The Mirror* (along with their Sunday versions) are Britain's top tabloids, though by no means the only ones. No matter which one you pick up, you can count on coarse language, terrible puns, plenty of innuendo, and crude humor.

While these publications are immensely popular, they are regularly criticized for vulgar content, unethical journalistic practices, outright racism, and creating a generally toxic culture. Opponents of tabloids charge that the papers have no concern for the lives of those they report on, and don't care if those lives are ruined in their pursuit of a scandalous story that might not even be true (and frequently isn't). They often focus on celebrity activities to stir up outrage while ignoring the consequences. Ultimately, they are nothing more than gossip rags, but they can still shape public opinion on important issues, like Brexit.

These problems are exacerbated by their readers, who sometimes seem like vultures, eager to feast on the carcasses of whatever lurid stories they can get their hands on. Some argue that there is a culture of resentment in Britain, that far too many people don't like those who are richer, happier, or more successful than they are. So, when a tabloid comes along and bullies these exalted people, such readers take delight in seeing them brought down a peg or two, thinking nothing of the lives that are potentially being ruined. Perhaps it makes such readers feel better in the short run, but is it good for the country as a whole? Many say no.

Tabloids aren't going away anytime soon, however, and will continue to be a thorn in the sides of celebrities and politicians, probably well into the next century.

Longevity fact: *The Daily Mail* is still owned by the same family, that of Lord Rothermere, that founded the paper in 1896. Not a family of high-minded, progressive reformers, it seems.

THE WAR IN THE FALKLANDS

In the spring of 1982, Britain and Argentina fought a war over a tiny archipelago of islands off the coast of Argentina, the Falklands. The Argentinian government claimed that it lawfully owned these, while the British, which had governed them since 1833, had a different view entirely. Was this Britain trying to preserve one of its last colonial outposts? Did the Argentinian government really have a valid claim to the islands? What was going on behind the scenes?

In 1690, British Captain John Strong set foot on these uninhabited islands, and by the eighteenth century, Britain tried to establish a settlement there, but it quickly abandoned the islands to Spain, which should have been the end of the story. But in 1820, Argentina, newly independent from Spain, claimed the islands for itself, stating that they were a part of the new nation by right of Spain's previous rule over them. Britain then decided that it wanted the Falklands after all, and in 1833 expelled the Argentinians and set the islands up as a British colony. There were attempts at compromises over the next 150 years, including a kind of joint governing, but none of these pacts really stuck.

By 1982, Argentina was under the rule of a military dictatorship that needed to distract people from the many problems at home. General

Leopoldo Galtieri found that something in the Falklands. On March 19, 1982, some Argentinian metal workers raised the Argentinian flag at an abandoned station on the island of South Georgia. Galtieri took this as his sign, and sent troops, who occupied the island on April 2, once again claiming the Falklands for Argentina.

In Britain, Margaret Thatcher, facing her own political struggles as prime minister, saw this as her opportunity, and committed to defending the islands against invasion. On April 5 she said, "We have to recover them [the Falklands] for the people on them are British ... and they still owe allegiance to the crown and want to be British." With strong popular support, she dispatched the Royal Navy to engage Argentinian forces. On May 2, the British submarine *Conqueror* sank an Argentinian cruiser, the *General Belgrano*, even though it was technically outside of the battle zone. More than 320 Argentinian crewmen died. Some condemned the attack as a war crime, while later assessments (including in Argentina) concluded that it was a legitimate act of war.

On May 21, British commandos made a landing on the islands and, after some heavy fighting, reclaimed them. By June 14, the war was over, and Britain had won. The war had wide British support and propelled Thatcher back into good standing with the public, allowing her to remain in power for the rest of the 1980s. In Argentina on the other hand, Galtieri and his party were removed, and a free election was held in 1983, seen by many as a victory for the democratic process.

Was the war one of the last gasps of British colonialism? Did Argentina have the right to invade the Falklands? So many years later, these remain complicated questions without simple answers.

Voting fact: The Falklanders have remained very supportive of being a British territory, even though they are independent in all ways except foreign policy and defense. When the most recent vote was held among the inhabitants to see if the Falklands should remain as a British over-seas territory, only three voted "No" among the 1,500 that were cast.

THE CHANNEL TUNNEL

O ne of the great engineering marvels of the later twentieth century, the Channel Tunnel (or "Chunnel," as it's sometimes called) linked Britain to Europe. Imagine being able to take a train from London to Paris, or simply drive onto a train car, go across to France, drive off again, and continue on your journey! Hopes of digging a tunnel from Britain to France dated back to the early nineteenth century and the beginning of the Industrial Revolution. The idea was suggested to Napoleon, and certainly would have made his plans to invade Britain a whole lot easier! An attempt to build a tunnel was even made in 1880, but abandoned. The engineering skills and technology involved meant that the Chunnel was only possible much more recently. In 1986, Britain and France signed a treaty allowing for the construction of the tunnel, since by then, neither country wanted to invade the other (as far as we know).

The idea of literally being connected to mainland Europe for the first time in over 8,000 years didn't sit too well with some Brits, but construction got underway in 1987 and over the next five years, work progressed at a steady pace, with tunnelling happening from both sides. Of course, you might be wondering, what if they'd dug in the wrong places and instead of connecting, they ended up missing each other? Obviously, this was pretty carefully planned out! On December 1, 1990, work-ers broke through and the two sides were at last connected! They exchanged British and French flags and toasted with Champagne at their incredible achievement.

The tunnel plunges down to a depth of about 150 feet under the sea bed, and there are actually three separate tunnels: one in each direction for trains, and a service tunnel. There are both passenger trains (leaving from London) and trains that carry cars, leaving from the south British coast. The tunnel stretches from Folkestone in England to Sangatte (near Calais) in France. The trip itself only takes about thirty-five minutes, not long really, but it's still the longest underwater tunnel in the world.

The Channel Tunnel opened to the public on May 6, 1994, and while the project was way over budget, took a year longer than planned to finish, and had several years of money problems, it eventually became a huge success, and is now considered a true engineering marvel. Some even call it one of the seven wonders of the modern world!

> Towering fact: The Channel Tunnel is just over thirty-one miles long (twenty-three of those are under water), or about 169 Eiffel Towers turned on their sides and laid out end to end!

ALAN MOORE AND NEIL GAIMAN

Moore and Gaiman are two of the more outstanding writers of speculative fiction in the late twentieth and early twenty-first centuries. Both made their name writing comic books (then also expanding to work on books and other more traditional writing), and both used that medium to transcend the genre and create works that are now seen as literature and art. And, of course, both are British!

Alan Moore's greatest claim to fame is his twelve-issue comic book series, *Watchmen*. This was no mere superhero tale, but a vast conception of a dystopian alternate earth. Set in 1985, it tells the story of a United States where costumed vigilantes have been outlawed, set against a backdrop of escalating nuclear tensions between the United States and the Soviet Union. Existentialist musings are worked into a murder mystery and geo-political commentary to produce a classic novel in comic form. No, seriously—*Time* includes the work on its list of the "100 Best Novels" written in the last 100 years.

Moore has written many other quality comics, including *V for Vendetta*, a story set in a futuristic, fascist Britain that many now see as an all-too-real possibility, as well as working on more typical characters, such as Batman and Swamp Thing, and creating new stories based on the mythos of American horror writer, H. P. Lovecraft.

Neil Gaiman has been called "literature's rock star." He made a name for himself in his *Sandman* comic, a rich and vast tapestry of storytelling and themes spread across seventy-five issues. It tells the story of Dream, also known as Morpheus, the "Sandman" of the title, and his attempt to rebuild his kingdom of dreams after being imprisoned by occultists for decades. The comic is a literary classic, and frequently also appears on "Best of" lists, right beside works of mainstream literature. It has recently been adapted for television by Netflix, with Gaiman closely involved in the critically acclaimed production.

A prolific writer, Gaiman has also produced books such as *Neverwhere* (originally a work for television), a story about the mysterious civilization that lives far beneath London, and *American Gods*, a book that follows the lives and travails of a series of gods from ancient pantheons, who now find themselves living mundane existences in contemporary America. Other notable Gaiman works include *Stardust*, a tale about a star that falls from the sky, written in fairy tale form, and *Coraline*, about a young girl who finds a mysterious "Other World" connected to her new home that is far more interesting than her own, but ultimately terrifying.

Both writers have taken a medium that was once considered mainly only appropriate for children and molded it into something much greater, proving that great art can take any form.

> Magic and religion facts: Looking quite like a wizard himself, Alan Moore is a self-proclaimed ceremonial magician and devotee of the Roman snake god Glycon, which he happily admits doesn't exist. He maintains that this is a safer bet than falling into a belief that one's deity is real and created the universe! In contrast, Neil Gaiman's father was an important figure in the Church of Scientology in the UK, though Gaiman has no connection with the organization at all.

TONY BLAIR

By 1997, the Tories had been in power for almost eighteen years, first under the leadership of Margaret Thatcher, and then under John Major. Almost two decades is a long time for any party to stay in power without seeming stale and out of ideas, and many people in Britain were craving a change. The Labour Party had not done so well in previous elections, but that was about to change thanks to Tony Blair. Blair, who had been an MP since 1983, was elected as party leader, which also made him Leader of the Opposition, the MP who sits on the opposite side of the Parliament chamber and offers counter arguments (these protestations are often met with a lot of snarky jeering) to the Prime Minister's own speeches.

Blair was unhappy with Labour continually getting left out in the cold, and saw what he thought were places in Labour's policies that needed updating. A good number of other MPs agreed with him, but some also resisted, as Blair wanted to move the party away from its more socialist outlook and toward a center-left position that kept some of Labour's traditional values, but also aligned it more with free-market ideas. It was in some ways similar to the shift that Bill Clinton had made with the Democrats in the United States (and which he used to defeat George H. W. Bush and become president in 1992. As you might imagine, Blair's reformation was met with both support and skepticism.

Making use of the phrase "New Labour," Blair removed the party's commitment to the nationalization of the economy, and embraced the free market and the European Union while still trying to advocate for socially progressive policies. It was a bit of a tightrope to walk, but he was successful in building a large coalition of supporters and voters. In the May 1997 general election, Blair's Labour defeated John Major's Conservatives by an astonishing number, winning power by the largest landslide in the party's history. The Tories were completely wiped out in Scotland and Wales (i.e., they had no MPs left in either country at all!). It was a humiliating defeat for the Conservatives, and a powerful mandate for Blair's new vision. He became the youngest prime minister since 1812, and he said that he wanted to bring in a new attitude, which he called "Cool Britannia." Yeah, that phrasing didn't age too well—seems a bit cringeworthy, eh!

Blair would go on to win two more general elections, in 2001 and 2005, before he resigned in 2007. He was leader of the UK for ten years, the longest run of any Labour Party leader, and made changes that would have a long-lasting effect, including the establishment of a Supreme Court, removing the majority of the hereditary peers from the House of Lords, allowing for the Welsh and Scottish to have devolved administration in their own parliaments (see page 460 for more on this), and helped negotiate the Good Friday Agreement in 1998, which put an end to much of the politically related violence in Northern Ireland. He also opened up the UK to more immigration (which many later objected to), and established a minimum wage, the Human Rights Act in 1998, and the Freedom of Information Act in 2000.

One of the bigger criticisms levelled at Blair was allowing Britain to be dragged into the invasion of Iraq and the military intervention in Afghanistan, policies that were condemned on both sides of the bench. The Iraq War was especially unpopular with the British public, as it seemed to never end, despite lacking all justification. Blair eventually resigned and was replaced by his less popular colleague, Gordon Brown, who went on to lose the next general election. The New Labour shine had been tarnished at last.

> Rock music fact: In the 1970s, Blair played guitar and sang in a band called "Ugly Rumours." He said that during the band's first gig in Oxford, the drum kit fell apart!

THE DEATH OF PRINCESS DIANA

On the morning of August 31, 1997, Brits woke up to shocking news: Princess Diana had been killed the night before in an automobile accident in a Paris tunnel. Diana was a beloved public figure in Britain, but also a controversial one, as her failed relationship with Prince Charles and problems with the British royal family were regular features in the UK tabloids. The news reported that Diana and her partner, Dodi Al-Fayed, were in a car that sped up to avoid being chased by the paparazzi. Henri Paul (head of security at the Ritz Hotel in Paris) was the driver of the car, but he had been drinking and lost control of the vehicle; it slammed into the tunnel wall, killing all three passengers. There was an immediate outpouring of grief from all over the world, but some people felt that the royal family were a bit too calm about it. Considering their displeasure with Diana, did some of them actually welcome this tragedy? Even worse, did they have a role in it?

Dodi's father, Mohamed Al-Fayed, soon declared that his son and Diana had been murdered. There were some details about the story that didn't seem to add up, and many began to question the official explanation. Here are some of the main conspiracy theories about that tragic night, and the events that led up to it:

Diana's death would make things easier for Prince Charles. Though they were already divorced in 1996, there were still legal issues, questions of titles, property, inheritance, etc. With Diana gone, Charles could marry again and not have to worry about any of it.

Diana was pregnant. Some believed that Diana was pregnant and Dodi was the father. The royal family would not have allowed an Egyptian Muslim man to father a child with a member of the royal family (divorced or not), so Diana was killed to avoid a huge scandal. But the autopsy showed no signs of her being pregnant at the time.

Diana was worried that she might be killed. This was actually true. In a letter from the mid-1990s held by her butler, Paul Burrell, she noted that she was afraid she might die as a result of her car being sabotaged. She'd had car troubles before and thought that someone might have been trying to make it unsafe. But an investigation of the crashed car found no signs of sabotage or previous damage.

Bright lights in the tunnel. Three different eyewitnesses claimed to have seen a bright light flash before the crash, which might have been set off on purpose to blind Paul, causing him to steer the car into the wall. But other witnesses in the tunnel made no mention of flashes, which, in any case, might have been paparazzi cameras.

An investigation, Operation Paget, was launched to examine all of these theories and more, but found no truth to any of them. The official explanation was that the deaths were a tragic accident, even if the paparazzi had contributed with their reckless behavior.

In any case, her death was a shock to the world. Newly elected Prime Minister Tony Blair, who looked visibly shaken, delivered a heartfelt address to the media after the accident, saying that he was "utterly devastated by the death of the Princess." Tributes from world leaders and celebrities poured in, and Diana's funeral at Westminster Abbey on September 6 brought out at least three million mourners in London. Clearly, she meant a lot to a very large number of people, who saw her as a champion for those who had no voice, and someone who was taken from the world far too soon.

> Worldwide watchers fact: Over thirty-one million watched Diana's funeral in Britain, and the estimate for the worldwide viewing number was about 2.5 billion. Whatever her troubles and controversies, Diana clearly affected many people.

DEVOLVED PARLIAMENTS

Y ou might have heard about the "devolution of parliaments" in Britain, which can be confusing, since for so long there has been just one Parliament in London. And that's the whole thing about it: devolution gives some of the powers of Britain's London-based Parliament to regional governments. It's not something that came about easily, even if many wanted it for a good long while. So, if some of the powers of Parliament are "devolved," where do they go? Well, to the other members of the United Kingdom: Scotland, Wales, and Northern Ireland. Since each of these nations was once a separate country, many who live in them have felt that they deserve to have their own governments back, even if they continue to live under British rule. Here is a quick look at the complicated history between England and each of these countries:

Northern Ireland: This one is the most controversial and the biggest headache of all. British involvement in Ireland has been ugly, messy, and very problematic for centuries, owing to English kings wanting to subdue the "uncivilized" Irish and bring them under the rule of England. Medieval English kings were already calling themselves Lords of Ireland, among their many other titles, for a long time. As we've seen, after Ireland became independent in the early twentieth century, a part of it, Northern Ireland, remained under British control. This divide set up decades of dissent, and open violence began in the 1960s. Various peace agreements have been made, and the government (the Assembly) has been convened, dissolved, and re-convened several times.

Scotland: Ever since the 1706 Acts of Union brought Scotland under the control of the Parliament in Westminster, many Scots have been agitating to have their own parliament restored, if not for full independence. Arguments for and against raged back and forth until 1997, when the Scots voted to have their parliament restored and set up in Edinburgh. It has the power to make all sorts of decisions for Scotland, but not to decide on issues such as national defense and diplomacy. The Scots held another vote in 2013, this time for independence, and while it lost, it was reasonably close: 55.3 percent for "No" to 44.7 percent for "Yes." Scottish nationalists have insisted that they will have another vote for independence, since Scotland overall voted in favor of remaining in the European Union and rejected "Brexit" (see page 469).

Wales: Wales has always had a testy relationship with England, going all the way back to the Anglo-Saxons referring to the Britons as "foreigners." As with Ireland, England tried to subdue and control Wales for centuries, not always successfully. King Edward 1 built a series of huge castles in Wales to show off his power, but eventually, the Welsh had the last laugh (for a while) when the Tudors took the throne. By the nineteenth century, several Welsh groups were advocating for more autonomy and independence, being resentful at the suppression of Welsh culture and language. As with Scotland, a 1997 vote gave Wales its own parliament (it was a narrow victory), and the contry now has its own National Assembly, or *Senedd Cymru* in Welsh.

> **More devolving fact:** Other regions are starting to look at devolving power, as well, with support for greater independence in Cornwall, Yorkshire, Northern England, and even all of England itself. Will the United Kingdom be able to survive all of these challenges? Will we see the return of Wessex, Mercia, Northumbria, and more? Stay tuned.

HARRY POTTER AND J. K. ROWLING

The story of the Boy who Lived has resonated with countless people around the world, enthralling generations of readers for the last twenty-five years. Almost everyone knows the story of how young Harry, living in a closet under the stairs, learns that he is a wizard and is invited to attend Hogwarts, the School of Witchcraft and Wizardry. There he makes friends who will prove to be lifelong allies, Hermione Granger and Ron Weasley, and together they have many adventures, discovering that a mysterious enemy, a dark wizard known as Voldemort, is planning to return and conquer the world.

The books grow increasingly long and more mature in tone as the series progresses, ending in a dramatic climax at Hogwarts between the wizards on the side of good and Voldemort and his minions, a battle that will decide the fate of the world.

The books have sold an astronomical number of copies (over half a *billion* copies sold, and counting), and with blockbuster films being made of each book, a series of new spinoff movies, a stage play, theme parks, and other related materials, Harry Potter's world has made a huge impact on our own.

All of this is the brainchild of author J. K. Rowling, who began the stories humbly enough, after an idea came to her at a train station in 1990. Over the next several years, she labored on the books, at one point even living on public assistance; she was later destined to become the world's first billionaire author. While she was able to obtain a literary agent, the first twelve publishers who reviewed the first book rejected it. It so happened that the daughter of the head of Bloomsbury Publishing read the first chapter and liked it, and she wanted to keep going. So Bloomsbury decided to take a chance on the book, and the series paid off in ways they never could have imagined. Within a few years, Harry Potter books were selling in the millions, often within the first few weeks of publication.

While related Potter products continue to be produced and con-sumed, opinions about Rowling and her works have cooled in recent years. The *Fantastic Beasts* prequel films have not had the same kind of box office or critical success (the COVID-19 pandemic notwith-standing) as the originals, and Rowling herself has become embroiled in a bitter controversy over remarks about transgender rights that has left many fans feeling angered, hurt, and even betrayed. Critical reviews of her "adult" literary novels have not been overly positive, and increasingly unfavorable re-reads of the original books are now appearing. Some readers now question the portrayals of the house elves (who are basically slaves) and express concern about potential antisemitic imagery (the long-nosed goblin bankers). Many feel that the magic has faded. While Rowling's empire probably won't be disappearing anytime soon, it is safe to say that the shine has been tarnished, and a reevaluation of her life and works is already underway.

> Scholastic fact: When Scholastic Books acquired the American rights to the first book, *Harry Potter and the Philosopher's Stone*, they renamed it *Harry Potter and the Sorcerer's Stone* (in consultation with Rowling), because they felt that the word "philosopher" would not appeal to American readers. The Philosopher's Stone is a substance from medieval alchemy that can turn regular metals like copper or tin into precious metals like gold. It has nothing at all to do with philosophy. Confusing, right? Perhaps Scholastic was right to steer clear of that title.

PRINCE HARRY AND MEGHAN MARKLE STEP BACK FROM THE ROYAL FAMILY

On January 8, 2020, Prince Harry and his wife, Meghan Markle, the Duke and Duchess of Sussex, used Instagram to announce: "We intend to step back as 'senior' members of the Royal Family and work to become financially independent, while continuing to fully support Her Majesty The Queen." They also decided to divide their time between Britain and North America. Their decision was dubbed "Megxit" by *The Sun* (in imitation of "Brexit," see page 469), and caused quite the sensation on both sides of the Atlantic. This was not the first time that royal family members stepped away from their roles, of course. Diana relinquished any claim to the throne after divorcing Prince Charles, and Edward VIII abdicated to marry Wallis Simpson before he was even crowned. But what happened to make these two young people decide that they'd had enough? The short answer was: the British press. The long answer was: many things.

From the start of their relationship, Harry and Meghan were the subject of intense press scrutiny and potential violations of privacy, both of which are very common when famous people have to deal with the British tabloids. The couple also took legal action against various tabloids, including *The Sun*, the *Daily Mirror*, and the *Mail on Sunday*, alleging that the *Mail* published one of her private letters illegally, and that the other papers had been involved in phone hacking to try to find out more about them. Further, they accused the press of racism (Meghan has a black mother and considers herself to be multiracial).

Support for the couple was mixed—some loved them, while others were unimpressed. It was obvious from the start that Meghan struggled somewhat to fit into the rigid protocols and traditions required of her new station, and this became more of an issue after the couple's marriage on May 19, 2018. The British family is, theoretically, politically neutral, but Meghan was quite vocal in support for progressive causes (to be fair, she always had been). The press began to criticize her for some of her behaviors, and some of these criticism seemed tinged with racism.

News articles said that Harry and Meghan didn't consult with the royal family before making the announcement, and reports described those family members as being "hurt" and "disappointed." Meanwhile, the duke and duchess did insist that they had broached the subject with the family before going public.

Over a year later, on March 7, 2021, the couple appeared on the CBS network in an interview with Oprah Winfrey to tell their side of the story. The duchess again alleged that she had faced racism, not only from the press but from within the royal family itself, while also talking about how trapped she felt and how difficult it had been to receive proper mental health treatment when she was distressed. There were questions about what security they would receive going forward, and who would pay for it. There were discussions of gossip and accusations about feuds. The duke said that having seen what had happened to his mother, Princess Diana, he didn't want the same things to happen to his wife.

In the end, it was their word against the family's, and people are still debating whose version is the truth. But the couple made good on their promise and now live outside Britain, only occasionally going back for official visits and functions.

> **Popularity fact:** After the interview with Oprah, Brits were less than impressed with the couple, while more Americans warmed up to them. Polls were all over the place on the matter, but in general only about one-third of Brits had sympathy for the pair, while about two-thirds of Americans did. Seems like the Americans are still rebelling against the institution of the British monarchy in some way!

THE LIONESSES BRING HOME A FOOTBALL CHAMPIONSHIP

On July 31, 2022, England's professional women's soccer/football team, the Lionesses, secured a 2-1 victory over Germany in the UEFA European Women's Championship. Under the direction of coach Sarina Wiegman, this was England's first major football title since the men's team won the World Cup in 1966 (see page 439), and support for the team reached a fever pitch. Over 87,000 fans packed London's Wembley Stadium for the final match, and about 17.4 million more watched the match on television. Obviously, these ladies had captured the country's imagination.

A few years before, had anyone proposed that a women's team would pull in those kinds of ratings, no one would have believed them. But

the entire championship was the most-watched women's football series in history. It was a full-on triumph not just for women's sports, but for sports in general, as the women did what the English men have failed to do for more than fifty years: win a major, multinational championship.

Strange as it might sound, women's professional football is both a pretty recent phenomenon in Britain, and one with a history of popularity. In 1920, women's football was very big in the country (over 50,000 people watched a women's game in Liverpool around this time), often even more popular than men's soccer. This didn't sit well with certain people (aka men), and the Football Association, in their infinite foolishness, decided the game was "not fitted for females" and banned women's elite leagues. Yeah, they were jerks. Unfortunately, that ban would stay in place for half a century, and it has only been since 2018 that the Women's Super League (formerly the Women's Premier League) has been fully professional.

With this championship win, women are having the last laugh. Usually, they are relegated to much smaller salaries, no big corporate endorsements, and general obscurity, but with the recent surge in popularity, that might all be about to change. Though it has a long way to go before equalling the status of the men's Premier League, the Women's Super League is starting to pull in amazing players and great coaches, much more sponsorship, and its matches are televised more often. And with England's national side (team) having won such a great victory, it's almost guaranteed that the WSL will enjoy higher ratings and much more visibility going forward. The future of women's European football is looking up, and the English women's win will be a huge boost for the sport going forward. As for the Lionesses, might the Women's World Cup be in their sights?

> Big hit fact: When it was announced that England's women's team would play the American women's team at Wembley in October 2022, there was a website crash because so many fans wanted to buy tickets. One of the queues was 45,000 people long! So take *that*, you 1920s sexist male football jerks!

BREXIT

One of the most controversial topics in Britain in recent years has been Brexit, with countless arguments for and against it. Short for "British Exit," it refers, of course, to the highly controversial action of Britain withdrawing from the European Union (EU). Britain has had an uneasy relationship with its continental neighbors all the way back to 1066. But Britain's membership in the EU tied it closer to Europe than ever before. Britain had been a member of the European Economic Community (EEC) since 1973, with the EU being the more recent version of the organization. For many, this membership offered great advantages, including freedom of movement, employment, and much more. But some felt that these close ties were eroding Britain's sovereignty, allowing too many people to immigrate to Britain from other European nations, and damaging the economy.

Things came to a head in 2016, when then-Prime Minister David Cameron allowed for a referendum (a public vote) on whether Britain should stay in the EU or leave it. "Leavers" and "Remainers" squared off against each other, often in heated arguments, each claiming that a win for the other side would be disastrous. The vote took place on June 23, and after fierce campaigning, and numerous accusations of lying and misrepresenting the issues, Leave beat Remain by a narrow vote of 52 percent to 48 percent (about 17.4 million votes to 16.1 million). But there were immediate problems: as only about half of the country had voted, that meant that only about one-quarter of all voters had voted to leave, which could hardly be considered a "majority." Also, the vote was supposed to be advisory, meaning that it had no force of law, but would simply be taken into consideration by the government.

The Conservative government had many MPs who were eager to push Brexit through, and began that process without paying much attention to these and other issues. This led to even more argument and fierce debate. But in the end, the Leave side won out and Britain officially exited the EU on January 31, 2020, losing all of its privileges as a member state. This very complicated move has caused all sorts of problems for Britain and its economy in recent years, and realized very few benefits—just as many Remainers predicted. Brexit supporters argue that it will take time for everything to settle down, but some have admitted it could take decades to stabilize, which is hardly a good argument for their case. Many Remainers feel that Leavers lied about the benefits of leaving to get quick votes, and polls have shown that a significant number of people who voted to leave would change their vote if they could vote again. A large number of people, both in Britain and in Europe, hope they get that chance.

One last fact: Brexit is just the latest in the ongoing story of Britain's sometimes-uncertain place in Europe and the world. From the Celts to the Romans, from the Anglo-Saxons and Vikings to the Normans, from the Tudors and Stuarts to the Victorians and the Blitz, this island's people have often trod through uncertain times. No one quite knows what will happen as Britain tries to go it alone again in the world. As always, we'll just have to wait and see how it all turns out.

QUEEN ELIZABETH II PASSES AWAY

Just as this book was being finished, Queen Elizabeth II passed away on September 8, 2022, at Balmoral Castle in Scotland. She reigned for over seventy years, an astonishing length of time by any measure. Hers is the longest reign of all British monarchs, and is the world's longest recorded reign for any female head of state. The years of 1952 to 2022 witnessed some of the most dramatic transitions in human history, and Elizabeth's reign encompassed a truly mindboggling set of changes in Britain and the world.

Most Brits have never known any other monarch except for her, and her passing truly marked the end of an age, a second "Elizabethan Era," at least for England. The queen's death was a cause of sorrow for many, ambivalence for others, and even outright anger for some. In addition to the expected tributes from world leaders, editorialists, and the general public, the days after her death saw a flood of harsh criticisms about the queen and the British monarchy in general: of it being an outdated institution, a symbol of colonialism, that the queen tried to hold onto Britain's remaining colonies and advocated for them not to become independent, and a host of other charges. On the other hand, Elizabeth was immensely popular, and many pointed out her genuine sense of wanting to do good in the world.

Historians and political science experts will be sorting out these views for decades. No doubt, many new biographies will appear in the coming years, taking different sides in their assessment of her life and reign. Right now, all that is clear is that Elizabeth's story is not yet fully written.

But her time and her reign are at an end. Her son, Prince Charles, is now King Charles III, the first monarch to bear that name since the seventeenth century. Some people had speculated that he might take the name George VII, but he was and remains Charles. Rather like Victoria's son, Edward VII, Charles has inherited the throne as an older man and will have a far shorter reign of his own. His oldest son, William, is now Prince of Wales and heir to the throne.

Whether people like it or not, the British monarchy will remain a symbol of this island nation for many years to come.

INDEX

473

ABOUT THE AUTHOR

TIM RAYBORN has a significant amount of British ancestry, which may or may not have qualified him to write this book. A life-long lover of all things British, he has written a huge number of books (about forty at present!) and magazine articles (more than thirty!), especially in subjects such as music, the arts, general knowledge, the strange and bizarre, fantasy fiction, and history of all kinds.

He is planning to write more books, whether anyone wants him to or not. He lived in England for several years (it was that whole "love of all things British") and studied at the University of Leeds for his PhD, which means he likes to pretend that he knows what he's talking about.

He's also an almost-famous musician who plays many unusual instruments from all over the world that most people have never heard of and usually can't pronounce. He has appeared on more than forty recordings, and his musical wanderings and tours have taken him across the US, all over Europe, to Canada and Australia, and to such romantic locations as Umbrian medieval towns, Marrakech, Vienna, Renaissance chateaux, medieval churches, and high school gymnasiums.

He currently lives in Washington State with many books, recordings, and instruments. He's pretty enthusiastic about good wines, Scottish whisky, and cooking excellent food.

www.timrayborn.com

ABOUT CIDER MILL PRESS BOOK PUBLISHERS

Good ideas ripen with time. From seed to harvest,
Cider Mill Press brings fine reading, information, and
entertainment together between the covers of its creatively
crafted books. Our Cider Mill bears fruit twice a year,
publishing a new crop of titles each spring and fall.

"Where Good Books Are Ready for Press"
501 Nelson Place
Nashville, Tennessee 37214

cidermillpress.com

The **Middle Ages**, see page 83